SOCIAL MARKETING IN THE 21st CENTURY

Dedication

For Jean Manning, my inspiration and intellectual touchstone, and for the late Gerald Gaull, a mentor in the world of food and nutrition

SOCIAL MARKETING IN THE 21st CENTURY

Alan R. Andreasen
Georgetown University

SAGE Publications
Thousand Oaks ▪ London ▪ New Delhi

For information:

Sage Publications, Inc.
2455 Teller Road
Thousand Oaks, California 91320
E-mail: order@sagepub.com

Sage Publications Ltd.
1 Oliver's Yard
55 City Road
London EC1Y 1SP
United Kingdom

Sage Publications India Pvt. Ltd.
B-42, Panchsheel Enclave
Post Box 4109
New Delhi 110 017 India

Printed in the United States of America.

This book is printed on acid-free paper.

Library of Congress Cataloging-in-Publication Data

Andreasen, Alan R., 1934–
Social marketing in the 21st century / Alan R. Andreasen.
    p. cm.
Includes bibliographical references and index.
ISBN 1-4129-1633-X (cloth) — ISBN 1-4129-1634-8 (pbk.)
    1. Social marketing. I. Title.
HF5414.A527 2006
361′.0068′8—dc22   2005022466

05 06 07 08 09   10 9 8 7 6 5 4 3 2 1

Acquiring Editor:	Al Bruckner
Editorial Assistant:	MaryAnn Vail
Project Editor:	Diane S. Foster
Typesetter:	C&M Digitals (P) Ltd.
Copy Editor:	Catherine M. Chilton
Proofreader:	Scott Oney
Indexer:	Molly Hall
Cover Designer:	Janet Foulger

Contents

Preface

Social marketing has been around a surprisingly long time; its origins are in the 1960s. It had only modest growth in the next two and one half decades but blossomed in the 1990s as it focused more carefully on behavior and gained acceptance and support from heavyweight institutions such as the Centers for Disease Control and Prevention. However, today, it is in danger of being pigeonholed as a *downstream approach*. Most observers and many practitioners see social marketing as an approach to influencing people with "bad behaviors"—smoking, neglecting prenatal care, not recycling. However, this narrow view hugely underestimates social marketing's real potential. Social marketing is simply about influencing the behavior of target audiences. There are many more target audiences who need to act besides "problem people" if we are to solve major social problems.

Take drunk driving. For a society to achieve fewer drunk driving fatalities, many people have to do many things. Of course, potential drunk drivers have to refrain from drinking and driving. However, police also need to increase enforcement. TV news directors have to carry stories about fatalities and enforcement efforts. School boards need to add curricular materials on drinking and driving. Beer and liquor distributors need to speak to tavern owners and high school students about the problem—and alcohol packagers need to pay them to do this. Bartenders need to stop serving potential drunk drivers and arrange for alternative transportation for them. Community leaders, such as ministers, rabbis, union bosses, and politicians, need to speak out to change community norms. Taxi company executives have to offer free rides home. Friends need to encourage potential drunk drivers not to imbibe or at least not to drink and drive. Foundation program officers need to fund intervention programs. Legislators need to pass laws fining establishments that permit—or even encourage—excessive drinking by drivers and laws offering incentives to transportation firms that offer free rides.

All of these are instances in which target audiences have to do something to make a social problem go away. That is precisely where social marketing is potentially most valuable; it is what social marketing is all about. *We are the behavior-influencing people!* Some may argue that expanding social marketing's domain to these new applications would be overstepping its bounds. Influencing the media is the "proper" domain of communications specialists. Influencing religious leaders is the province of experts in community mobilization. Legislators are best approached by lobbyists and political scientists.

I do not deny that these other paradigms have much to offer, and in the pages to follow I borrow from all of them. However, I am making three points. First, social marketing has a very powerful set of concepts and tools that can approach a very wide range of instances of behavioral influence, in a unique way. Second, because we draw extensively from the private sector, which has a long history of bringing about mammoth social changes—some wonderful (PCs, Polartec, Jiffy Lube) and some not so wonderful (fill in the blank!)—we have the benefit of a constantly innovative knowledge base. Third, relying on social marketing concepts and tools means that change agents can rely primarily on a *single* approach to social change. They need not become deeply involved in learning community mobilization skills or political theory or hire consultants with such capabilities. Social marketing can serve as the change agent's basic platform and can carry a good deal of the intellectual and practical burden.

In an earlier book, *Marketing Social Change,* I focused on influencing the behavior of downstream targets: those who are exhibiting or might exhibit problem behaviors. I have come to believe that this is too narrow a perspective. In the past, social marketing has been maligned as "merely communications" or as advertising or as selling social products, such as condoms and insecticide-treated bed nets for malaria, at below-market prices. It must not suffer new misunderstandings about its range of applicability as we move through the 21st century.

The goal of this book, then, is to reposition social marketing as an approach to social change that reaches both upstream and downstream, so that foundations, government agencies, and various nonprofits will use it in an ever-widening range of applications. The book will outline potential roles, restate fundamental principles, and then suggest how social marketing might be applied to a sample of nontraditional (for social marketing) challenges. To accomplish the latter, I will rely on my own particular set of social marketing frameworks (as outlined in the earlier book) and show how they might be applied to influence such diverse audiences as legislators, community leaders, media executives, corporate managers, and health professionals.

I intend for the reader to see that social marketing offers an extremely robust set of concepts and tools that are "intellectually portable" across contexts. One can apply a relatively small set of simple frameworks to any target audience and set of behaviors one wishes to influence. (Indeed, one could argue that the principles can be used by the reader just as readily to get a date, achieve a pay raise at work, or induce his or her children to clean up their rooms.)

Objectives and Target Audience

By this point, my objectives and assumptions here should be transparent. I believe that social marketing has great potential to drive social change and has a very wide range of uses, both upstream and downstream. We have barely touched the upstream potential. I am hopeful that this book will spur wider and deeper usage of social marketing—for more problems, at more points in the process, by more people, by more types of organizations, and with greater impact.

I invite a wide target audience to consider these propositions, including social marketing scholars, students, and practitioners who are looking to understand social marketing's broader potential and how its concepts and tools might be applied to their own issues. An important secondary audience comprises those executives, managers, foundation officers, and other gatekeepers and program specialists who might use social marketing approaches if only they better understood the field's potential and relevance to their work.

Structure of the Book

The book is divided into three parts plus a concluding chapter. The first section comprises two chapters that frame the context in which social marketing concepts and tools may be applied. It begins by asking, in chapter 1: Where do social problems come from? What brings some issues onto the radar screen, and why are some issues addressed by a society? The second chapter recognizes that not all social problems make it to the front burner, or are even addressed, at any point in time. It looks at how issues rise on three types of agendas: the media agenda, the public agenda, and the political agenda.

The second section considers social problems and the role of social marketing. Chapter 3 asks: How are social problems structured so that alternative and complementary solutions may be applied? How do social change agents view the current "hot topic" of childhood obesity (a problem that I return to at various points in later chapters)? Chapter 4 offers a brief historical perspective on social marketing and describes the set of relatively straightforward concepts and tools that I use in my own consulting and teaching. Chapter 5 completes the section by considering how priorities for social change are set and how social marketing can help in this process.

The third section takes the reader into four domains where social marketing has not traditionally been used to show how the frameworks introduced in chapter 4 have very broad applicability in upstream settings. Chapter 6 focuses on the specific behavioral challenges of influencing communities. Chapter 7 considers lawmakers and regulators. Chapter 8 asks how one applies social marketing to the challenge of recruiting potential business allies; chapter 9 focuses on ways to influence media and health-care professionals.

The final chapter returns to the central objective of the book—repositioning social marketing for the 21st century—proposing challenges for individuals and organizations who wish to build the field's intellectual capital to make this happen. The chapter (and the book) ends by considering some of the ethical issues that those thinking of using social marketing in these new ways ought to keep in mind as they move forward.

What This Book Is Not

This book does not purport to be exhaustive in the application areas it considers. It is not a comprehensive treatment of the nature of social problems and the agenda-setting process. Although it focuses on one specific social problem—childhood obesity—it is neither exhaustive in its consideration of all of this problem's nuances and challenges, nor does it expand on how other social problems might differ. The chapters on various upstream social applications are necessarily cursory, and the examples are hypothetical, for the most part. The objective is simply to show how social marketing *might* be used, not to present specific examples of applications. Part of the reason for this is that such applications are very hard to come upon.

On the other hand, an extensive bibliography is provided for those seeking to delve more deeply into the topics presented. Indeed, I will consider this publication a considerable success if others are motivated to deepen and expand on the topics I have considered here. Social marketing has so much more to offer. I will be delighted if the future finds others joining the crusade to reposition and broaden social marketing's application to the critical social problems that affect our world.

Acknowledgments

A book that is at once speculative and prescriptive has its provenance in years of work trying to apply social marketing concepts and tools while at the same time broadening and deepening those same concepts and tools. For this reason, the present volume is the outgrowth of interactions with a wide array of thinkers and practitioners—too many to list here—over the course of many years. Over many years—too many to list here.

I have had much assistance in preparing material for various chapters and creating the set of references. Of particular help was Andy Furrow of the McDonough School of Business at Georgetown University. Editors at Sage Publications, especially Catherine Chilton, performed exceptional service in improving and simplifying both the language and the structure of the book.

Finally, any author has personal support from many people. I have particularly benefited over the years from the encouragement of Paul Bloom, Gerard Hastings, Philip Kotler, William Novelli, Michael Rothschild, and Bill Smith. However, the most profound support—both emotional and intellectual—has come, as always, from my wife, Jean Manning. Jean has given matchless inspiration for all my work and has been a very frequent source of new frameworks, new wrinkles on old frameworks, and innumerable improvements in the way I articulate what I think I have to say. It need hardly be said that, without her, this book would have been very different and, indeed, might not have seen the light of day at all.

PART I

Introduction

1

Social Change, Social Problems, and 21st Century Social Marketing

In 1980, 51,091 people were killed in traffic accidents. Of those accidents, 55% involved alcohol. This was tragic, but it was only one of many social problems about which those in the 1980s worried. However, one of the people killed was Cari, the teenage daughter of a California woman, Candace Lightner. The man who killed her had been released two days before on bail for a hit-and-run drunk driving crash that followed two previous drunk driving and one "reckless accident" convictions. Lightner and friends with similar concerns decided to do something about it. They founded MADD—Mothers Against Drunk Drivers (later changed to "Driving").

It was an idea that caught fire. By 1981, there were 11 chapters, and 70 in 1982, most of them started by victims eager to do something about the system that had caused their pain. In 1983, NBC produced a TV movie about Candace Lightner, and 122 more chapters opened. By this point, 84% of the population had heard about the organization and its mission.

By 1990, MADD had 402 chapters and affiliates in Australia, New Zealand, England, and Canada. A Gallup survey showed that Americans listed drunk driving as the greatest highway safety problem. MADD's greatest accomplishments include the passage of thousands of stricter drunk driving laws around the United States and a federal regulation requiring states to increase the legal age for drinking to 21 or lose funding. MADD is equally well known for the *promotion of the concept of the "designated driver." The impact of MADD's efforts—along with those of many other supporters and partners—is seen in the statistics. By 1990, alcohol-related fatalities had declined by 20% and composed 51% of all highway deaths. By 2001, alcohol-fueled deaths had fallen 23% from their 1990 levels and composed only 41% of all deaths (Mothers Against Drunk Driving, n.d.).*

Social Problems and Behavioral Influence

Societies are never perfect. Many are dramatically imperfect. Problems such as hunger, poverty, crime, and disease are found everywhere but especially in less developed parts of the world. In developed countries, we have these same afflictions, but we add to them modern, compelling problems and annoyances such as road rage, cell phone abuse, child pornography, and drunk driving.

Societies are also constantly seeking change—seeking ways to overcome problems both grand and trivial and to make the lives of individuals and their environment significantly (or at least somewhat) better. They seek change through grassroots mobilization efforts such as MADD. They rely on major organizations such as the United Nations Children's Fund (UNICEF), the U.S. Agency for International Development (USAID), or the Ford Foundation to address problems such as high birthrates in struggling Asian, African, and Latin American economies or finding missing children in the United States. They work through nonprofits or corporations such as Avon to tackle breast cancer. They ask their legislators to pass laws and regulations requiring better product labeling or prohibiting smoking in public places.

They also worry about *preventing* change! There are many problematic situations in which the goal is to prevent people from taking up behaviors—what I will call here *conscious inaction*. Society does not want men to exploit women, parents to abuse children, teens to smoke or use illicit drugs, businesspeople to adopt unethical practices, journalists to slant their reports, ballplayers to take steroids, or legislators to vote cuts in funds for favored programs. The celibate, at-risk, poor Nigerian or Thai girl needs to be encouraged to postpone sex until marriage. The inner city adolescent in Bucharest needs help in not ever taking up smoking or drugs. The poverty-stricken man living in New Delhi who is down on his luck needs assistance so he will not take up crime to improve his family's economic circumstances.

These important social challenges are the domain of this book. It is a book about influencing socially important behaviors and how to make them happen. For 35 years, I have been involved in programs to influence the actions of individuals who need to change their ways or not take up new antisocial behaviors such as smoking or bullying or drug use. The broad label for that work is "social marketing." Over the years of working on a very wide range of social problems, I have come to believe that what I and my fellow social marketers do is both underappreciated and underused. This book seeks to change that perception—and, one hopes, broaden the application of what I believe is a very powerful set of concepts and tools.

I will claim here that social marketing has a broader and more powerful role to play in social change. The reason for such bravado is simple: Social change requires individuals to act. For social change to happen, someone—or many "someones"—must bring the issue to our attention. Someone has to assemble possible solutions and evaluate them. Someone has to decide on the best courses of action. Someone—presumably many someones, in many kinds of arrangements—must mount efforts big and small to make change happen or to *prevent* change from happening. Finally, someone has to keep track of how things are going, what modifications and redirections are necessary, and whether more or less effort is necessary.

In all of these cases, people need to be motivated and empowered to make a difference. That is, *greater social welfare comes about only through individual behaviors.* Of course, many social movements involve crowds and community organization. Even there, however, leaders must decide to act and followers need to get on board. How does one get people to act or get people not to act? One can hope that there will be individuals such as Candace Lightner who will be motivated by events in their own lives and become dedicated to making things happen—or, in the case of drinking and driving, make sure things *do not* happen. If we are to bring about massive social changes such as reducing poverty, providing shelter for every poor person, or reducing the impact of growing levels of obesity or child abuse, however, a lot of people have to act in a lot of different ways or make irrevocable commitments *not* to act. For this to happen, there are roles for gatekeepers in the media, legislators, corporate executives, community activists, and television and movie scriptwriters—and on and on.

Thus the fundamental question here is, How do we go about influencing these kinds of behaviors?

THE POWER OF MARKETING

There is, of course, a wide range of techniques and approaches to influencing behavior under labels such as education, law enforcement, community mobilization, political lobbying, and personal persuasion. This book, however, makes the case that social marketing provides, in many ways, a more flexible and robust array of concepts and tools that can be used at many levels and in many corners of the social influence process. This is for two principal reasons. First, social marketing can be applied wherever one has a target audience and a behavior one wants to influence. Second, its conceptual underpinnings are drawn from what is clearly one of the most impactful and constantly evolving forces for social change in the world: *commercial marketing*. Over the last 100+ years, commercial marketers have developed a rich array of proven powerful concepts and tools that have induced American office workers to choose McDonalds over Burger King, the Japanese government to choose Airbus over Boeing, European teenagers to choose cargo pants over chinos, and readers everywhere to buy books and CDs online without ever seeing or touching a product or meeting a salesperson.

A leading marketing expert described the commercial sector's potential for affecting drug abuse this way:

> We are an industry credited with—or sometimes blamed for—selling America fast food, soft drinks, cars, and jeans. But better than that, we've done a lot of changing of opinions and beliefs in people. We need to take those brains and energy that have sold so much to the world and convince people that drug use is not chic, not acceptable, and is plain stupid. The public is used to hearing us holler "BUY!" Now we can tell them not to buy. Unselling may be tougher than selling. (Backer & Rogers, 1993, p. 13)

Commercial marketing is not without its criticisms—many of which I have made over the years (Andreasen, 1975; see also Johansson, 2004; Ritzer, 2004). In the late 1960s, when Philip Kotler and his colleagues at Northwestern University first ventured into the social and nonprofit world, critics argued that marketing has no place outside its traditional domain in the economic marketplace (Luck, 1969). Others said that marketing had "an identity crisis" (Bartels, 1974). Fortunately, their views did not prevail, and over the last 40 years, marketing has been introduced into more and more "strange" environments. Social marketing has accumulated a significant track record and a considerable storehouse of knowledge about how to market social behaviors well.

SOCIAL MARKETING IN THE 21ST CENTURY

My 1995 book, *Marketing Social Change,* represented my first attempt to set down what I believed to be this accumulated wisdom about good social marketing practice at the time. I sought to give the field a distinct structure, set of concepts and tools that I hoped would be useful in a wide range of applications. However, those applications—and my own thought processes—were largely focused on what are called "downstream applications," focusing specifically on the target audiences who are exhibiting, or might exhibit, problem social behaviors. The emphasis was on how to get men with high blood pressure to take their pills and cut down on their salt intake; how to get teens to give up or not start smoking; and how to get mothers in developing countries to get their kids immunized.

In the last 10 years, I (and many others in the field) have come to realize that a downstream focus is both too narrow and too limiting for social marketing's vast potential. Larry Wallack (1990) was already arguing that social marketers were too focused on downstream behaviors (of victims) and that society really needed to fix the structures and processes *upstream* that caused the problems in the first place. Marvin Goldberg, in 1995, asked: "Are we fiddling while Rome burns?" Were we too worried about influencing smokers or would-be smokers, when perhaps we should be paying much more attention to influencing the behavior of the tobacco industry that is creating smokers in the first place?

Then, in 2002, Gerard Hastings, head of the Institute for Social Marketing at Stirling University in Scotland, and Rob Donovan, coauthor of a major textbook in the field, sent out a call to action in *Social Marketing Quarterly*:

> We now call collectively for social marketing to embrace a broader perspective that encompasses not just individual behavior, but also the social and physical determinants of that behavior. . . . [T]his broadening still involves behavior change, but among those who make policy and legislative decisions on behalf of groups, corporations, and governments, as well as individual citizens. (Hastings & Donovan, 2002, p. 4)

The potential for a broadened role for social marketing is being recognized by other scholars. In a recent review of public communication campaigns, Coffman (2002) makes a distinction between efforts to affect individual behavior and public communications campaigns designed to promote the *public will* for change. She concludes, "evaluations of campaigns that use social marketing techniques (most individual behavior change campaigns) provide lessons for evaluating public will campaigns" (p. 10). In her view, too many public information campaigns simply provide information and do not pay enough attention to turning this awareness into action through what she calls "public will." I argue that this, too, is a role for social marketing.

The consensus, then, is that we need a new view of what social marketing is all about—a view of social marketing for the 21st century. That is what this book is designed to offer.

The issue now before us is not just whether we should consider upstream interventions but *how to do so*. In the pages to follow, I wish to show how social marketing concepts and tools can be brought to influence media gatekeepers, legislators, community activists, corporate executives, and virtually anyone else who can or should play a role in bringing about improved social welfare. I will argue that, with the proper adjustments, social marketing concepts and tools can apply in all of these cases and perhaps prove superior to many alternatives. I will illustrate this by adapting my own approach to social marketing strategy to a wide range of new domains. Most of these domains have their own special kit bags of concepts and tools: political science approaches, media advocacy, lobbying, public relations, and so on. I argue that, although these other approaches have much merit in their own domains, the approach that I am advocating here at least has the advantage that *it is portable across applications*. One needs only to learn how social marketers would approach the media or legislators or business executives to possess a set of viable approaches for meeting a wide range of upstream challenges. The chapters to follow will provide illustrations of this 21st century social marketing approach in a range of contexts—not just downstream.

The Case for a Wider Role

As I have said, a significant majority of social marketing interventions designed to bring about social change in the past has focused on what in the private sector would be called "final consumers," those who are causing the social problem by carrying out undesirable behaviors. These and other social problems also require preventive approaches aimed at individuals who *might* exhibit problem behaviors. Experience shows, however, that in most of these domains, the entire burden of social change cannot and should not be placed on these downstream targets. It is very often the case that structural and policy change at the broadest level will have to take place if long-term solutions are to be achieved. School policy has to be changed if kids are to exercise more, and streetlights have to be provided by city bureaucrats if kids are to walk to and from schools or use playgrounds. For many kinds of social change, community norms and social priorities will need to change to bring the issue higher on the public and political agendas. This means that, for many campaigns, the focus of social improvement at some point needs to be on the community—perhaps the society as a whole—and not the "problem individual." Also, of course, individual, structural, and community changes will probably not happen unless funding and private or public organizational resources are put behind such efforts.

Despite the seeming diversity of all of these challenges, they have one thing in common: For social improvement to take place, *someone has to take action*.

- People are healthier and societies more attractive when mothers take their children to be immunized, when HIV-positive men begin to use condoms, and when middle class householders recycle. Many such changes have important economic benefits.

- Structural conditions (external conditions that allow individuals to help themselves to better physical and economic circumstances) get better when city fathers approve and finance new recycling centers, doctors and hospitals provide prevention programs so pregnant women will have healthy babies, and ministers in African countries initiate programs to empower women to start small businesses.
- Norms are changed when journalists write articles, TV or radio scriptwriters introduce characters modeling desirable behaviors, religious leaders speak from their pulpits, advocates write letters and visit their legislators, and opinion leaders speak out to their followers.
- Communities get better when leaders urge others to join them to create "a movement," existing groups agree to take on a new challenge and marshal allies, politicians decide to speak out and assume leadership roles, community media report on the issues and steps taken, and corporations mount programs for their staff to get involved. (Community mobilization can, of course, also lead to unfortunate outcomes, as when radical ideologies foster discrimination and even violence.)
- Programs get mounted and organizations created when a foundation executive writes a check, an entrepreneur assembles talented people and motivates them, corporate leaders invest real or in-kind support and give time off to employee volunteers, strategists and implementers attend courses to get better at what they do, colleges change curricula and provide classes to equip the next generation of change agents, and scholars write articles and books and conduct studies to help others discover and share best practices.
- Prevention takes place when laws get on the books because legislative staffs write them, legislators pass them, and law officers publicize and enforce them.
- Finally, social change becomes lasting when a target audience's doctor, spouse, rabbi, or teenager commends the people on their good behavior, politicians and group leaders are reelected for supporting change programs, the media gains awards and bigger audiences for exposing social deficits, and foundation program officers, educators, and consultants circulate and teach award-winning best practices.

Of course, the actions of a few isolated individuals will not by themselves bring about significant and broad social change. For programs to go to scale, there must be important changes in the public agenda, partnerships must be formed, significant resources need to be brought to bear, and programs need to be institutionalized and made lasting. For example, significant progress was finally made on the smoking front in the 1980s and 1990s when a leading health-care funder, the Robert Wood Johnson Foundation, made the issue a major priority and when a coalition of state attorneys general got involved. The HIV/AIDS challenge achieved much greater attention when the Centers for Disease Control and Prevention (CDC) gave special attention to it in the 1990s. Now, both the Robert Wood Johnson Foundation and the CDC have turned their attention to the latest major public health crisis—the growing problem of obesity.

Creating change is often not enough. Sometimes, emphasis needs to be put on *continuing* desirable behavior. This means that foundation program officers need to resist the temptation to pursue new, sexier topics—especially when existing programs have met with early success and year-to-year gains are slowing down. Politicians need to stick with an issue when other topics come on the horizon and public interest has perhaps moved elsewhere.

In all of these situations and for all of these reasons, social change ultimately boils down to *influencing* individual behavior—sometimes getting someone to start something, someone else to stop, and still others to just keep doing what they are already doing. This is precisely the domain of 21st century social marketing.

WHY MARKETING?

If social change means influencing individual behaviors, then there is clearly a role for marketing to play. Over the past 30 years, I and a number of other authors have argued in books, articles, and assemblies that social marketing is an extremely powerful set of concepts and tools for bringing about changes in individual behavior (e.g., Andreasen, 1995). The commercial sector frameworks that get us buying hula hoops or Viagra, patronizing day spas, and adopting cell phones that take photos can change lives, and not just in economic ways.

Marketing does not come without "baggage," of course. Although there is an imposing array of marketing success stories that would seem to offer *prima facie* evidence for the power of the approach, many critics find the assertion that social marketing is a good thing to be vaguely offensive. Private sector marketing has brought the world a range of social changes that many people find distasteful or downright injurious. Critics point to worldwide campaigns based on trivial incentives or global branding efforts that seem to induce poor families in developing countries to overspend on brand name necessities (Johansson, 2004; Ritzer, 2004). They charge marketing with making unsafe products (Nader, 1965) and distorting and trivializing values in wealthier countries by emphasizing the need for wearing the *right* clothing labels, driving the *right* car, drinking the *right* beer, and otherwise becoming the latest version of "cool" (Burke, 1996). They are horrified at the intrusion of brands and advertising into our schools (Petersen, 1990).

Marketing, it is charged, can encourage outright antisocial behavior through the promotion of "gangsta rap" and $125 Air Jordan sneakers that are literally "to die for." Critics cite infant formula campaigns that induce mothers of poor children to waste money and forego the disease protection benefits afforded by breast milk (Jordan, 2004). They point to campaigns using skinny models that prompted a rash of anorexia, bulimia, and deaths among teenaged girls in developed countries. The tobacco industry has created a worldwide smoking "epidemic" that kills millions each year, and the food marketing industry emphasizes high-fat products and "super-sizing" to a world population growing more and more obese (Critser, 2003).

Distasteful as these tactics and initiatives may be, they do attest to the power of marketing. The challenge here is to find ways to *use that power for social good beyond the marketplace*—for influences that clearly improve individual lives, communities, and entire countries or regions of the world. All marketers are successful when they influence individuals. Private sector top management and stockholders are ecstatic when more people choose their company's brands or shop at their stores, patronize their fast food chains, fly their airlines, stay in their hotels, and spend more money in their gift shops. However, marketing power can also be used to influence men in Bangladesh to let their daughters attend high school. It can induce teens to wear seatbelts and mothers to put their babies to rest on their backs to prevent sudden infant death syndrome (SIDS). Marketing promotions and distribution strategies have achieved remarkable effects with high blood pressure in the United States and accelerated family planning successes all around the world (Harvey, 1999).

In one sense, social marketing has a major advantage over private sector marketing in achieving public support. In the private sector, marketing's ultimate goal is to make a corporation bigger and more profitable and stockholders happier. In the social sector, although an indirect goal sometimes makes an organization or program grow, the ultimate goal is to improve the lives of individuals or the society of which they are a part. Social marketing is about making the world a better place for everyone—not just for investors or foundation executives. Also, as I argue throughout this book, the same basic principles that can induce a 12-year-old in Bangkok or Leningrad to get a Big Mac and a caregiver in Indonesia to start using oral rehydration solutions for diarrhea can also be used to influence politicians, media figures, community activists, law officers and judges, foundation officials, and other individuals whose actions are needed to bring about widespread, long-lasting, positive social change.

Outline of the Book

As I hope I have made clear, the goal of this book is to take social marketing to the "next level" of influence and impact. To do so, we must ask: Does one need to change or adapt traditional methods of social marketing that are now well developed when they are to be applied in nontraditional areas, such as influencing legislators, foundation officers, TV news directors, or members of street gangs? Do we need new concepts and tools, new kinds of education and training, new research, or new measures of success to permit effective diffusion of social marketing into these new contexts?

These are some of the questions that we shall address in this book. Fortunately, the answers are reassuring. Careful analysis makes clear that the basic concepts and frameworks that have been used to influence "final consumers" are highly flexible and adaptable. However, each application in these "new" domains has its own peculiarities, norms, and customs that must be accommodated to allow social marketing to attain its full potential for helping.

To appreciate what these roles might be, we need both vertical and horizontal perspectives. We need vertical perspectives to understand where social problems come from, how they arise on various social agendas, and how they are addressed. A horizontal perspective then is needed to consider the range of players who need to act and the kinds of changes that have to happen for the social change process to move forward. This chapter begins at the beginning by considering the roots of social problems and how they are discovered. Concrete evidence that something is wrong is almost always the starting point for eventual efforts at social change. However, social problems do not get addressed— let alone resolved—unless they rise on the public agenda to the point where one or more segments of society attempts to address them. Chapter 2 will consider this problem of agenda setting and the roles various parties play in advancing social issues, using as a framework a set of eight stages through which most social issues move. These stages are

1. Inattention

2. Discovery

3. Climbing the agenda

4. Outlining the choices

5. Choosing courses of action

6. Launching initial interventions

7. Reassessing and redirecting

8. Success, failure, or neglect

Chapter 1 addresses the first two of these stages and chapter 2 the third stage. Chapter 3 looks at how one might sort out the issues and outline the various courses of action. Here, to give concreteness to the discussion, I focus on the very hot current topic of childhood obesity as a complex case in point. I then use it as a touchpoint for discussion at several points in succeeding chapters.

Chapter 4 begins to address the fifth stage in the process by considering courses of action involving social marketing. The recent history of the approach is reviewed and key frameworks and conceptual models are introduced. A variety of ways are recognized in which frameworks and conceptual models are brought to bear. However, for simplicity's sake, I emphasize my own approach to social influence problems, which I use in the new domains, discussed in later chapters, where I argue social marketing should belong.

Chapter 5 specifically addresses the problem of choosing among various promising courses of action by considering how such choices might optimally be made. Commercial sector concepts are introduced here from the realm of new product introduction. It turns out that heretofore unexplored private sector concepts of *response functions* and *transition matrices* are potentially useful frameworks for understanding the likely effects of interventions among which planners must choose.

In chapters 6 through 9, I turn to a horizontal view of the possible application of social marketing concepts and tools to various kinds of upstream influence problems. Chapter 6 looks at social problems in which community action is critical if change at the individual level is to happen. This will necessarily cause us to look at questions about the nature of communities and how one activates social movements. Chapter 7 discusses the challenge of bringing about structural solutions by considering how social marketing ideas might be used to influence legislators and regulators. Chapter 8 considers the challenge of recruiting business allies. Chapter 9 reflects on the role of the media and the health-care community, both of which have important supportive roles to play in social change. In each of these chapters, I pay particular attention to the problem of childhood obesity.

The last chapter returns to the implications of the central argument. If social marketing has an important role to play in the 21st century at other steps in the social change process and with other types of target audiences, how does one go about making *this* change happen? That is, how might we use our own concepts to market social marketing?

In the Beginning: Where Do Social Problems Come From?

Social problems seem always to have been of concern to every society everywhere in the world. Poverty, starvation, disease, and discrimination have been present for centuries in both the simplest and the most evolved societies. What is not constant is the relative importance of these problems as societies change and as seemingly intractable challenges find competition from new, emerging frustrations and concerns. Changes in prevalence can bring about such shifts, as with the emergence of AIDS in the 1980s and the virtual elimination of problems such as polio and smallpox worldwide in the last three decades.

Unique events can cause an issue to gain or lose prominence, as evidenced by the World Trade Center disaster and its effect on worldwide concerns about terrorism. Human stories can also have a big impact, as when Rock Hudson and later Magic Johnson said they had AIDS, or when Betty Ford told the world she had breast cancer.

An issue also becomes "hot" because an organization or a politician wants to make it hot. Issues also get "tired." Urban pollution was considered a crisis 10 years ago but has faded in popularity as a cause in recent years—despite considerable evidence that the problem is still with us. The prominence of problems also varies regionally. Global warming and genetically altered crops are social problems high on the radar screen in Europe but of lesser concern in the United States. Issues may also mutate and change in focus. For many years, employment discrimination spotlighted the negative treatment of racial minorities. Then, in the 1980s and 1990s, women challenged the "glass ceiling." Now, working seniors are a major concern as the worldwide population ages dramatically.

The way we address social problems can affect their prominence and how we think about them. For example, legislative solutions are ultimately needed for urban growth issues. On the other hand, a combination of legislation, community action, and social marketing (in its old sense) is needed to address problems of environmental pollution and degradation. Ten years ago, the prevailing sentiment was that drug abuse needed to be addressed by law enforcement efforts to restrict supply and punish dealers and users. Lately, sentiment is rising for social and behavioral interventions with first-time felons, to get them into treatment programs rather than put them in jail where they may well develop a lifelong habit and learn to be really good criminals. We once thought that education and shame would "cure" smokers, but now we think first of imposing no-smoking regulations in public places and raising cigarette taxes.

Clearly, social problems have both dynamic and structural characteristics, as well as both concrete and perceptual dimensions—they are partly real and partly what we think they are. They vary in the importance and urgency we each think they deserve. What explains this process? The obvious place to start would be with the facts.

THE "DISCOVERY" OF SOCIAL PROBLEMS

In this book, I focus on how social marketing can help drive social change through initiatives that address social problems. Thus a logical place to start is learning to understand where social problems come from, how they grow and diminish in importance for a given society, and how decisions are made to address them. This will be our concern for the remainder of this chapter and the next.

First, we need a definition of a "society" for which a social problem exists. A textbook definition of *society* is simply "people who interact within some territory guided by culture" (Macionis, 2002, p. 2). A society can be as narrow as a group of members in a neighborhood bridge club or as broad as the member states of the United Nations.

Next, what denotes a *social problem*? Macionis (2002) defines it as "a condition that undermines the well-being of some or all members of a society and that is usually a matter of public controversy" (p. 4). A social problem can be relatively minor—such as the bridge club's displeasure over an ugly, neglected vacant lot in the members' neighborhood—to unquestionably major challenges, such as those outlined in the United Nations' Universal Declaration of Human Rights: "barbarous acts [of genocide, infanticide, violence against women] which have outraged the conscience of mankind" (Office of the High Commissioner for Human Rights, 2003).

Social problems in one "society" may be low on the radar screen elsewhere. The bridge club members may not care at all about poverty or hunger (perhaps because they don't see or haven't experienced them) but worry a great deal about road rage or unemployment. On the other hand, for the nonprofit Share Our Strength, road rage pales in comparison to the abject poverty, hunger, and homelessness its members encounter in every major city.

Having data is usually helpful but may not be enough. A given set of concrete facts may be defined as a social problem by one group and not another. Take minimum wage laws. Employers in a developing country may believe that the absence of such laws is not a social problem—indeed, that this allows companies to be more competitive and provide more jobs for the unemployed. On the other hand, to a union leader, the absence of such a law means denying workers a "living wage" and creating sweatshops. Quantitative statistics may look bad to some groups and not to others. Religious groups may find the 50% divorce rate in the United States and high rates of premarital cohabitation to be serious social problems. Social liberals may see these same figures as evidence that individuals now have more relationship options and increased individual freedom.

Social problems emerge on the public radar screen in many ways. Among the more common sources are the following.

Statistical Surveillance. We live in a century inundated with statistics that track both the reality around us and what we think about this reality. Most governments in the developed world and many international agencies conduct regular censuses that can spot potential problems. A minor trend may suddenly worsen—for example, the number of citizens without health coverage may increase dramatically, or the gap in income between rich and poor may grow to embarrassing levels. Detailed analyses of surveillance data can yield insights into undiscovered impacts on unique populations; consider the recent highlighting of high obesity rates in African American women in the United States.

Special One-Time Quantitative Studies. Many problems emerge because an organization or a government agency undertakes a specific study. This can be a special interest group, such as AARP, or a university that considers conducting such studies a major social role. Government agencies routinely conduct special studies, and a growing number of "think tanks" such as the Brookings Institution, the RAND Corporation, and the American Enterprise Institute carry out studies in their domains of interest. These special studies can comprise formal surveys, reanalysis of available data, or, more recently, polls on the Internet. For example, scholars at Johns Hopkins University reviewed studies of women in 50 countries and found that from 10% to 50% of women in these countries reported being physically abused by a male partner at some time in their lives (Heise, Ellsberg, & Gottemoller, 1999). Such studies provide powerful ammunition for efforts by organizations like the United Nations or the International Federation of University Women to support efforts to increase women's social power worldwide.

Special Nonquantitative Studies. Systematic conversations or careful observation can often reveal problems that need addressing. Newspaper reporters or doctoral students can often discover a pervasive systemic problem with dramatic impacts simply by talking with a range of victims and their families or by carrying out focus groups or simple surveys. These anecdotal data are often combined with quantitative studies. In one such example, Gerbner, Gross, Morgan, and Signorelli (1980) used a number of methodologies to track the influence of violence in television entertainment content on violent behavior. They concluded that heavy television viewers were more likely to be accepting of violence as a solution to social problems than those who watched less.

Individual Insight or Argumentation. Sometimes a social problem is below the radar screen because of the way we think about it. The situation can change when perceptive and articulate scholars, social critics, or journalists look at a situation and, by rethinking and reframing it, bring it vividly to our attention. Feminist legal scholars in the 1980s and 1990s highlighted the fact that a great many statutes and regulations are written from a male perspective. Catherine MacKinnon concluded that the absence of antipornography laws in many countries permits pornography to be purchased and viewed privately as a free speech right. She argues, however, that the content of pornography demeans women and is produced primarily to satisfy the dominance needs of male members of society. The absence of gender-neutral laws, therefore, perpetuates inequalities we claim to abhor (Mackinnon, 1987).

A Vivid Event. Sometimes, some event is so shattering as to reposition specific problems or bring to the fore whole new classes of problems. The series of explosions of gas tanks in Ford Pintos in the 1970s resulting from rear-end collisions raised the issue of auto safety dramatically (Davidson & Goodpaster, 1983). In a much more profound way, the attacks on America on September 11, 2001, and the later anthrax scares raised all sorts of concerns for public safety that had been neglected in previous decades. Until the anthrax attacks, few in the United States thought that the mail could be a source of personal danger and that greater protections were needed.

Personal Tragedy. Sometimes, the simple, dramatic story of an individual or a family can have a powerful effect. The tragedy of Ryan White, a boy who contracted AIDS during an operation and was subsequently ostracized at school, turned out to be a propelling force behind efforts to rethink how we treat people with AIDS (White & Cunningham, 1991). This heart-wrenching story led to the passage of the Ryan White CARE Act (CARE = comprehensive AIDS resource emergency) on August 18, 1990, a federal program designed to improve the quality and availability of care for persons with HIV/AIDS and their families. The disappearance of a child from foster care in the District of Columbia 3 years ago called for a pervasive overhaul of the city's foster care system (Higham & Horwitz, 2001). Finally, the shocking stories of Catholic youngsters abused by priests in the 1970s and 1980s initiated cataclysmic changes in church hierarchy and governance. The issues became so traumatic that the pope himself had to intercede (O'Malley, 2002).

Uncovered Evidence. Sometimes a social problem is kept under cover by individuals or organizations that do not wish to call attention to it. Investigative reporting or a brave whistleblower can bring such a critical social problem to light. The U.S. Air Force Academy for many years ignored instances of sexual harassment and assault of female cadets. A vivid story by one cadet initially brought attention to this issue. A subsequent formal study by Pentagon officials then revealed that the academy had covered up the extent of the problem and their neglect of it (Aguilera, Migoya, & Sherry, 2003). Major reforms quickly followed.

Pseudoevents. Sometimes issues pop up on the radar screen because activists or aggrieved parties stage some sort of event or protest that gets wide coverage. These are what Daniel Boorstin called "pseudo-events" (Boorstin, 1992). In Europe, a commonly engineered social event designed to bring attention to a social issue is the traffic blockade. High fuel taxes were a serious problem for truckers and farmers in the United Kingdom in 2000. Haulers believed that the taxes imposed on British fuel were so high that they put the haulers at a disadvantage in competing with French trucking companies. A group of truckers established a blockade of the United Kingdom's oil distribution centers and refineries in September 2000, which quickly brought the UK to a standstill, with petrol stations running out of gas quickly. This meant that food deliveries were disrupted and commuters were unable to get in to work. Panic buying of food and general chaos ensued, putting great pressure on the Blair government to reconsider its tax policy on petrol in subsequent budgets (*Blair Stakes Credibility*, 2000).

MOVING UP THE AGENDA

Even when a social problem is widely recognized, progress in addressing it may not be forthcoming because there is no agreement on solutions. Take the problem of drug abuse. Many groups oppose punishing drug users as "blaming the victim," discriminating against minorities, creating overcrowded courts and prisons, and potentially increasing the social stockpile of hardened criminals. These groups favor more drug treatment programs. Opponents see drug treatment for convicted drug users as coddling evil people, rewarding instead of punishing criminal behavior, and turning a blind eye to what the illegal drug industry is doing to neighborhoods and to future generations.

Social problems like these also ebb and flow as the culture changes. In the United States in 1900, women could not vote, were rarely found in the workforce unless they were very young or widowed, and were expected to defer to their husbands or other males in authority on every "important" decision. Today, we would see this as a very inferior position. However, at the time, U.S. society (with a number of notable exceptions) did not think that *women's rights* was a major social problem. Yet today, despite dramatic changes in voting laws and gender discrimination in the workplace, the (restricted) integration of women into the military, and many other improvements in women's status, women's rights is now a vibrant, top-of-the-agenda issue. Many argue that there are still not enough women in corporate boardrooms or running TV networks. Women are still not found in great numbers at the highest levels of government, have unequal representation in the courts, and still cannot fly fighter planes. Still, the reality is that, since 1900, their objective status has dramatically improved.

HISTORICAL TRENDS

Social problems very often ebb and flow in importance, depending on two broad sets of factors: sweeping long-term trends and shorter term, more immediate events, studies, and crises. Changes in the dominance of political parties and their priorities can affect our perception of important social problems. The rise and fall of advocacy groups and dramatic events that occur and draw public sympathy, media investigations, calls for action, and so forth all can affect what issues are "hot." However, if one wishes to make long-term systemic change, it is very important to understand the sweep of broader social changes that can also have profound impacts on today's social problems.

The recent United Nations *2001 Report on the World Social Situation* (United Nations Economic and Social Development, 2001) provides such a broad look. Among the broad social changes this 2001 report cited are the following:

- There has been a dramatic worldwide decline in birthrates, with positive impacts on family life and the role of women and negative impacts on such issues as social security funding. The number of children born to each woman of childbearing age has decreased since 1960, from 6 to 3 in developing countries and from 2.7 to 1.6 in more developed countries. As a consequence, some European countries will soon see a decline in their populations. A dramatic result is that fewer people will have close living relatives to provide support for them when social problems arise, thereby putting a significant strain on government services.

- The rapid development of global commerce and less government intervention in the marketplace has led to significant economic growth in many parts of the world—but this growth has had different impacts across and within countries. Countries that rely on natural resources, that have low education levels, and that have heavy urban concentrations have suffered compared with other countries where these conditions are less dominant. Within the former countries, workers in the formal sector of the economy are better off and those in the informal sector are worse off. Because the informal sector more often comprises family enterprises, the resultant business setbacks will lead to social problems that these families and their few relatives cannot address themselves.

- Freer markets make it easier for criminals to globalize, move drugs across borders, and surreptitiously launder criminal profits. Money laundering is made even easier by the growth of electronic commerce and the Internet.

- Increased poverty in certain population groups within countries has led to a worldwide increase in prostitution and child trafficking. Hopelessness in these poor populations has given rise to substance abuse involving cheap, consciousness-warping commercial solvents and glues.

- Globalization has helped social change organizations in developed countries to understand and focus more closely on problems in developing countries, to the latter's considerable benefit. One dramatic example is the growing awareness of worker exploitation and the use of child labor in the developing world, which has led to a shift in policies and behavior by major worldwide brands such as Nike and Wal-Mart. However, globalization has also spread health problems from one part of the world to other parts. A good example is tobacco, the use of which is declining in the West but growing dramatically in the emerging nations of Asia and Africa. Environmental pollution is becoming rampant in the developing world as these countries take over more production from the developed economies under laxer laws. Tourism, business travel, and the migration of jobs around the world have all dramatically affected the spread of influenza, HIV/AIDS, and malaria.

- Globalization and economic growth has increased urban densities and caused increased migration from rural areas to the cities. Overcrowding and inadequate housing, sanitation, and water supply are the result. Health risks then escalate, along with unemployment and family dysfunction. There is also evidence that growing income disparities have driven up the cost of basic housing, once affordable to the poor and near poor.

- The rise of the information sector has put tremendous pressure on educational systems. Employers want trained workers, especially workers with knowledge skills as opposed to physical prowess. Again, some countries and some population groups are better positioned to take advantage of this trend; others may be left behind. The burgeoning information sector has also increased opportunities for doing evil for pornographers, pedophiles, and sexual predators of all types.

- Countries seeking rapid market growth have often created business-friendly changes in taxation that encourage enterprise and trade but reduce governments' ability to address the social problems of ordinary families.

- The AIDS epidemic is eliminating male heads of household in many countries, especially in Africa. This has forced more women into the workplace, which leaves their children less well tended, as child care can less often be borne by their increasingly fewer relatives. This will affect children's health but will also reduce what the UN report refers to as "inter-generational learning, an important means to transfer life skills from the old to the young" (United Nations Economic and Social Development, 2001).

- On the plus side, despite many of the negative influences outlined here, there have been significant improvements in health and education levels worldwide. As a consequence, people are living longer. The average age of the world's population rose from 47 years in 1950 to 65 years in 2000. The negative impact of this change is that the diseases of the elderly, such as various cancers, have become much more prevalent. In earlier times, people simply died before certain cancers could become problematic.

- Armed conflicts are now more often within countries than between countries. This has led to governments or warlords conscripting children, using food for patronage or punishment, and being unable to control civil crime. The UN report describes the long-term costs of such internal violence as "extensive emotional and psychological stress; mental illness; sense of insecurity, especially for women and children; displacement and exile; and lost educational opportunities" (United Nations Economic and Social Development, 2001). Of course, many conflicts significantly increase ethnic and religious tension and discrimination—a situation dramatically portrayed today in Africa, the Middle East, and Afghanistan.

Organizations such as the United Nations have played major roles in the attempt to keep track of these problems and to keep the world's attention focused on them. From time to time, they have sought to refocus the attention of politicians, the media, and the general public on the most prevalent and most serious social issues. One major effort in this regard is the United Nations' Millennium Project, which identifies areas where significant social change is needed and sets out concrete goals to achieve it. The project focuses on 18 major targets for 2015, as indicated in Table 1.1.

PROBLEMS OF INTERPRETATION: THE CASE OF INCOME INEQUALITY

Statistics are just a starting point. A given set of conditions only becomes a social problem to be addressed because some group thinks it is worth addressing. A set of objective facts may seem to offer prima facie evidence that a problem exists and imply a set of objectives for change. However, having an objective basis for defining a social problem requires that one agree not only to the facts but also to definitions and to some standards that would allow one to say "there is a problem here." It is not surprising that these standards are not always cut-and-dried. Statistics can be interpreted many ways.

Take, for example, income inequality. In most economies, it is taken as a sign of existing or potential social problems if there is too great a gap in income and wealth between the rich and the poor, which also means there is likely to be greater poverty, crime, social unrest, and violence. A large inequality is the sign of an undesirable society—possibly a very corrupt one. Great inequality would seem to merit a high place in a ranking of social problems. First,

Table 1.1   United Nations Millennium Targets in Brief

Target 1	Halve, between 1990 and 2015, the proportion of people whose income is less than $1/day
Target 2	Halve, between 1990 and 2015, the proportion of people who suffer from hunger
Target 3	Ensure that, by 2015, children everywhere, boys and girls alike, will be able to complete a full course of primary schooling
Target 4	Eliminate gender disparity in primary and secondary education, preferably by 2005, and to all levels of education no later than 2015
Target 5	Reduce by two thirds, between 1990 and 2015, the under-5 mortality rate
Target 6	Reduce by three quarters, between 1990 and 2015, the maternal mortality ratio
Target 7	Have halted by 2015 and begun to reverse the spread of HIV/AIDS
Target 8	Have halted by 2015 and begun to reverse the incidence of malaria and other major diseases
Target 9	Integrate the principles of sustainable development into country policies and programs and reverse the loss of environmental resources
Target 10	Halve by 2015 the proportion of people without sustainable access to safe drinking water and sanitation
Target 11	Have achieved by 2020 a significant improvement in the lives of at least 100 million slum dwellers
Target 12	Develop further an open, rule-based, predictable, nondiscriminatory trading and financial system (includes a commitment to good governance, development, and poverty reduction both nationally and internationally)
Target 13	Address the special needs of the least developed countries (includes tariff and quota-free access for least-developed countries' exports, enhanced program of debt relief for HIPCs and cancellation of official bilateral debt, and more generous ODA for countries committed to poverty reduction)
Target 14	Address the special needs of landlocked countries and small island developing states (through the Programme of Action for the Sustainable Development of Small Island Developing States and the outcome of the 22nd special session of the UN General Assembly)
Target 15	Deal comprehensively with the debt problems of developing countries through national and international measures to make debt sustainable in the long term
Target 16	In cooperation with developing countries, develop and implement strategies for decent and productive work for youth
Target 17	In cooperation with pharmaceutical companies, provide access to affordable essential drugs in developing countries
Target 18	In cooperation with the private sector, make available the benefits of new technologies, especially in the information and communication fields

NOTE: HIPC indicates heavily indebted poor country; ODA, official development assistance.

however, can we agree on what the data say? For example, do we have an economic inequality problem in the United States today? Is income inequality getting better or worse? How does it compare with other parts of the world— are we overemphasizing it? Here is what Lawrence Harrison, writing in the *Christian Science Monitor* in early 2003, thought:

> Brazil's President Luiz Inácio da Silva—"Lula," as he is widely known—has made Brazil's gaping gulf between its few rich and many poor a focus of his new administration.
>
> The United States should do the same. While not as vast as Brazil's, the gap between the rich and the poor in the US is too wide—the widest among all the rich democracies.
>
> According to World Bank data, the poorest 10 percent of Brazil's population receives just 1 percent of the country's total income, while the richest 10 percent receives almost half. In the US, the poorest 10 percent receives 1.8 percent of total income, while the richest 10 percent gets almost a third.
>
> In no other rich democracy does the poorest 10 percent receive less than 2 percent of the total. (The average for rich countries is 2.9 percent.)
>
> Don't leap to the conclusion that this extreme inequity in US income distribution reflects the policies of the Bush administration. The data are for a Clinton boom year—1997.
>
> In fact, Census Bureau data show a steady erosion of income inequity [sic] since the 1970s

As suggested by Harrison, a common definition of income inequality is to compare the income of the top of the income distribution to the same-sized segment at the bottom. Harrison compares the top and bottom 10% and says things are really bad. A more common—and less dramatic—comparison is the ratio between the top fifth and the bottom fifth. The relevant data for the last 30 years in the United States as measured by the U.S. Census Bureau (2005) are shown in Table 1.2.

Do we have a problem? The data would suggest at least that there is a *growing* problem—the ratio has become 17% *worse* in the last 30 years. As Harrison argues, those at the bottom of the distribution would seem to be much worse off today than they were 30 years ago. Consider two other pieces of information, however. First, consider the mean incomes for households in the bottom and top fifth of the population *in constant 2001 dollars* for 1970 and 2000, as shown in Table 1.3 (U.S. Census Bureau, 2004).

Now we might reach a different conclusion. These data indicate that, although the ratio has worsened, the absolute income level of the lowest 20% of the population in current dollars *has increased* over the 30-year period. Although it is true that the incomes of the top earners have risen more in current dollars (66.2%), the mean income for the lowest 20% has gone up more than a quarter (26.8%).

These data are for household income, so we need also to look at household size. In 1970, the average household had 3.14 people in it. In 2000, there were

Table 1.2   Income Inequity

Year	Inequality Ratio
1970	.394
1975	.397
1980	.403
1985	.419
1990	.428
1995	.450
2000	.462

SOURCE: U.S. Census Bureau (2005).

Table 1.3   Mean Household Incomes in Constant 2001 Dollars

Year	Bottom Fifth	Top Fifth
1970	$8,010	$85,607
2000	$10,157	$142,269

SOURCE: U.S. Census Bureau (2004).

only 2.62 members per household. Thus one could say that the average income *per family member* in the lowest 20% of the population had *increased* 52%.

Many readers and social arbiters would look at these data and conclude that the incomes of the bottom 20% of the population have dramatically grown in terms of real spending power—although they have fallen further behind the top 20th percentile. Does this mean we have a social problem? Recall that social problems have both factual and subjective dimensions. Individuals and groups from the liberal end of the political spectrum would argue that, although the absolute incomes per family member of the poorest segment have grown 52%, the top 20% has seen a 99% growth (controlling for the same average family size changes). They would conclude that economic growth is unfairly benefiting the well-off and leaving the poorest segment further and further behind. They would also argue that something ought to be done about this!

Should the comparison be with the past? An alternative might be to compare the present income distribution in the United States to that of other countries. Certainly Harrison would argue that we are not as badly off as Brazil.

To make these comparisons, it is useful to introduce another commonly used statistic for this purpose called the "Gini coefficient." The Gini coefficient is considered a more comprehensive measure of a country's income equality or inequality because it considers *all* of the incomes in a country, not just the top and bottom percentages, and compares their distribution to a hypothetical condition in which everyone earned the same amount—that is, zero income inequality, or a Gini coefficient of 0. The higher the Gini coefficient, the higher the inequality. Going by a World Bank definition (Deininger & Squire, n.d.), the Gini coefficient for the United States was 37.94 in 1991.[1] This is certainly dramatically higher than the ideal and much worse than the industrialized countries shown in Table 1.4.

On the other hand, there are many countries where the Gini coefficient is much worse than that of the United States and where there is significantly more justification for calling this a major social problem (see Table 1.5; Deininger & Squire, n.d.).

Ultimately, the question of whether any of these data suggest a serious social problem depends on how the objective data are framed. This is where social change agents typically play their role. Liberals see vast income inequality and urge action. Conservatives admit to the inequality but point to the fact that the objective conditions of the lowest segment have improved *and* the wealthy have benefited from economic growth, which, in future years, will

Table 1.4   Gini Coefficients for Six Countries

Country	Gini Coefficient
Spain	25.91 (1989)
Finland	26.11 (1991)
Belgium	26.92 (1992)
Canada	27.65 (1991)
Taiwan	30.78 (1993)
Indonesia	31.69 (1993)

SOURCE: Deininger and Squire (n.d.).

Table 1.5   Eight Countries With Very Serious Income Inequity

Country	Gini Coefficient
Philippines	45.00 (1991)
Costa Rica	46.07 (1989)
Mexico	50.31 (1992)
Thailand	51.50 (1992)
Mali	54.00 (1994)
Chile	56.49 (1994)
Brazil	59.60 (1989)
South Africa	62.30 (1993)

SOURCE: Deininger and Squire (n.d.).

support the kinds of social improvements that wealth can bring—better shopping malls, road systems, universities—which will provide improvements in the quality of life of those at the bottom.

Of course, whether any action will be forthcoming on this issue will also depend on what other problems there are on the societal radar screen and whether there are socially palatable solutions people are willing to entertain. Relative importance also depends on who is pushing for change. If it is the party in power, it is one thing. If it is someone like Ralph Nader, it is another.

CONDITIONS OR CAUSES?

Even where there is agreement on the data, the data themselves typically do not point to causes. Outcomes tell you where something might be bad or at least problematic, but they do not tell you where to go for solutions. Does one tackle income inequality by changing tax codes, funding more job training, or promoting greater charitable giving? Descriptive data are not very helpful in suggesting solutions, although they help pinpoint areas for further investigation. It is essential to understand causes.

One area where policymakers have looked beyond outcome data to identify causes is public health—a domain in which a great many social marketing interventions have been introduced in the last 30 years. The U.S. National Institutes of Health and the Centers for Disease Control and Prevention (CDC) have

Table 1.6   Top 10 Causes of Death in the United States (1900 and 1997)

Condition	1900 (%)	1997 (%)
Heart disease	6.2	31.4
Cancer	3.7	23.3
Stroke	6.2	6.9
Pulmonary disease		4.7
Injury	4.2	4.1
Pneumonia and influenza	11.8	3.7
Diabetes		2.7
Suicide		1.3
Kidney disease		1.1
Liver disease	5.2	1.1
Tuberculosis	11.3	
Diarrhea	8.3	
Senility	2.9	
Diphtheria	2.3	

SOURCE: Centers for Disease Control and Prevention (2000).

undertaken several sets of priority-setting exercises around the existence and causes of health problems as the basis for setting public health goals each decade. The most recent version of this exercise is known as *Healthy People 2010*.

The investigators begin by looking at causes of death, both current and past. Outcome data make clear that the top 10 causes of death have shifted dramatically since 1900, as shown in Table 1.6.

The data show that we have been very successful in reducing the fatal effects of infectious diseases. The major problem today is chronic diseases of various kinds, particularly those associated with an older population in which such diseases can take their toll.

As suggested earlier, however, these data are not very helpful because they report outcomes and not causes. If the current negative outcomes are to be

Table 1.7   Health Indicators for *Healthy People 2010*

Indicator	*Group*	*Measure*	*2000*	*2010 Goal*
Exercise	Adolescents	Exercise 20 min. 3 times/week	65%	85%
	Adults	Exercise 20 min. 3 times/week	15%	30%
Overweight	Under 20	Are overweight or obese	11%	5%
	20 or older	Are overweight or obese	23%	15%
Smoking	Adolescents	Smoke once in 30 days	35%	16%
	Adults	Smoke once in 30 days or not more than 100 days in a lifetime	24%	12%
Substance abuse	Adolescents	No drugs or alcohol in 30 days	79%	89%
	Adults	Binge drinking in 30 days	17%	6%
		Drug use in 30 days	6%	2%
Responsible sex	Adolescents	No sex or use condoms	85%	95%
	Single women 18-44	Use condoms	23%	50%
Mental health	18 or older	Depressives get treatment	23%	50%
Injury, violence	All	Vehicle deaths/100,000	15.6	9.2
		Homicides/100,000	6.5	3.0
Environmental quality	All	Are exposed to poor ozone	43%	0
		Are exposed to secondhand smoke	65%	45%
Immunization	65+	No influenza in 12 months	64%	90%
		No pneumococcal infection ever	46%	90%
	19-35 months	Get DTP, polio, etc, shots	73%	80%
Health care access	Under 65	Have health coverage	83%	100%
	All	Have primary care	87%	96%
	Pregnant females	Get prenatal care first 3 months	83%	90%

SOURCE: Centers for Disease Control and Prevention (2000).

NOTE: DTP indicates diphtheria, tetanus, and pertussis.

addressed, one would need to trace them to their sources. To this end, the CDC has developed a set of "Leading Health Indicators" that identify key causal factors and establish goals for each of these "social problem areas" for the year 2010 (CDC, 2000). The indicators and goals are listed in Table 1.7.

The United Nations has undertaken a similar exercise with respect to the global social problems set forth in its Millennium Goals (United Nations General Assembly, 2000; see also Jones et al., 2003; Sachs, 2005; Sahn & Stifel, 2003).

Setting Priorities

The logical next questions, then, are these: Which one or more of some set of problem conditions will take top priority, and which will get addressed? Notice that I said "*will* get addressed," not "*should* get addressed." Whether or not a given set of objective facts or a clear set of causative factors leads to social action depends on the social priorities of a given society. The bridge club may want environmental quality to have higher priority than health issues, whereas the mayor of Cleveland says that his constituents want high priority given to substance abuse. How these various views and preferences get sorted out and how solutions are pursued is the process of *agenda setting*, the topic of the next chapter.

Note

1. Other calculations of the Gini coefficient give it a range of 0 to 1.

2

Creating and
Framing the Agenda

Words can make a difference when you are trying to get the public to pay attention to a problem. For years, the Republican Party tried to get the public—and politicians—to do something about the "estate tax." This was a tax to be paid from an estate when it was passed on to heirs. The Republicans argued that this constituted double taxation on people's earnings and was unfair on its face. However, the public seemed to associate the word estate with wealthy people and apparently felt that the wealthy had too much money anyway, and maybe they got it from coupon clipping, not real work.

Republican consultant Frank Luntz proposed a simple solution: Call it a "death tax." This simple word change did much to increase public sympathy. Luntz found in his polls that, although a narrow majority would repeal an inheritance or estate tax, an overwhelming majority would repeal a death tax. Presumably, it seemed really unfair to penalize people for dying ("Interview: Frank Luntz," 2004).

Social marketers, of course, do not typically play a role in the creation of baseline objective data that can identify important social problems. At later stages, they may suggest data collection strategies that will help *advance* particular behavior influence strategies. However, they can help move issues *up* the social agenda. To appreciate the potential for social marketing to have such an upstream impact, it is important to understand how issues go from being objective data to becoming social *problems* and then being subject to intervention efforts by a society. This process is called *agenda setting,* or agenda building (Berkowitz & Adams, 1990). Just how do social issues obtain prominence and gain attention, and where does social marketing fit? In the past, social marketing has primarily been used to try out solutions to social problems. However, different behavior influence challenges appear at different stages and involve different target audiences. Therefore social marketers have much to contribute at earlier points in the process. This means we must learn how to apply our kit bag of concepts and tools to different unique target audiences with different specific behavioral objectives.

First, we need a better understanding of the agenda-setting process.

The Three Agendas

Three types of agendas dictate how any society addresses social problems (Soroka, 2002). First, there is the *public agenda.* This comprises the general public's perceptions of what is important and is typically reflected in polls by organizations such as Gallup and the Pew Charitable Trust and in the positions taken by important interest groups and influential leaders. In the 21st century, the public agenda can also be seen in chatrooms or "blogs" (Web logs), employing what McNutt and Boland (1999) call "cyber advocacy." Second, there is the *media agenda*—what the newspapers are writing about, the television networks covering, and the talk shows emphasizing. Finally, there is the *policy agenda,* heavily influenced by political perspectives; views of political leaders; positions taken by political parties; and input from consultants, lobbyists, think tanks, and government bureaucrats.

The three agendas obviously interact. Lang and Lang (1983) call this "a collective process in which the media, government, and the citizenry reciprocally influence one another" (p. 59). Lobbyists seeking to influence the public policy agenda often try to first influence the media and public agenda by going on television or writing op-ed pieces for major newspapers urging people to pay more attention to the problem or advocating a particular solution. On these occasions, the media play a gatekeeper role in controlling the access of specific groups and spokespeople to channels that will broadcast their positions to other agenda setters.

Of course, the media are not necessarily passive. Newspapers and investigative TV shows such as *60 Minutes* or *Dateline NBC* often bring social problems to the fore by both providing factual information and portraying real victims with real consequences. Also, newspaper columnists and editorial page writers regularly take positions and call on legislators or the public to rise up and take action about something they believe to be important.

However, it should be clear that the media do not necessarily influence the public's priorities. Bernard Cohen noted in the early 1960s that the print media

> may not be successful much of the time in telling people what to think, but it is stunningly successful in telling its readers what to think *about*. And it follows from this that the world looks different to different people, depending not only on their personal interests but also on the map that is drawn for them by the writers, editors, and publishers of the papers they read. (Cohen, 1963, p. 13, emphasis in original)

The media can also play a critical role in what Wallack and others call "framing the issue" (Wallack, Dorfman, Jernigan, & Themba, 1993). For example, in the early stages of the HIV/AIDS epidemic, the media portrayed AIDS in the United States as affecting a relatively narrow set of specific, high-risk groups. Only later did it acknowledge that AIDS was a general problem potentially affecting everyone. Today the media—and other leaders—differ in how they have portrayed the AIDS epidemic internationally. Some see it as a tragic human problem, especially for those countries such as South Africa and Zimbabwe, where infection rates are especially high. Others recognize the human dimension but frame the issue as a matter of global political stability and therefore an issue of foreign relations. Former Secretary of State Colin Powell was particularly vocal through the media in urging Americans to see the worldwide AIDS problem as potentially destabilizing and therefore a possible cause of serious domestic consequences for the United States. As he said in a September 2003 speech at the United Nations:

> AIDS has left 15 million orphans, and unless we stem the tide, that number will swell to 25 million by the end of this decade. The vast majority of these children are likely to live without emotional support, without the barest of physical necessities, and without any prospects for the future.
>
> Unless we act effectively, these precious children are likely to perish in the same cycle of disease, destitution, despair and death that took the lives of their parents. The appalling statistics do not begin to describe the magnitude of the destruction wrought by AIDS. AIDS is more devastating than any terrorist attack, any conflict or any weapon of mass destruction. It kills indiscriminately, and without mercy.
>
> As cruel as any tyrant, the virus can crush the human spirit. It is an insidious and relentless foe. AIDS shatters families, tears the fabric of societies, and undermines governments. AIDS can destroy countries and destabilize entire regions.

The interaction between the public agenda and the policy agenda can also vary by issue. Polls reflecting the public agenda can have important influences on the political agenda because they signal legislators about what their constituents seem to want—and what they do not want. Despite politicians' protestations that they *never* make judgments based on the latest opinion poll, it is often clear that they do. Politicians want to be reelected, they want to be seen as leaders, and they want to get in front of powerful causes. By sensing the public agenda, they can advance a fourth agenda—their own.

There are other ways in which the public and political agendas interact. Advocacy organizations with large memberships, such as the National Rifle Association (NRA) or AARP, lobby politicians, claiming they are merely conveying what their members want. Sometimes the public makes its wishes known more directly, and legislators realize that they must hurry to get out in front of the parade. In 2003, the U.S. Federal Trade Commission established a national "do-not-call" registry in an effort to reduce the number of intrusive telemarketing calls citizens were experiencing. The telemarketing industry mounted legal challenges to the Federal Trade Commission's (FTC's) authority to create such a list, and a judge ruled on September 23, 2003, that the FTC did lack proper authority. Still, 50 million Americans had already signed up for the registry—which would explain why the House and Senate passed legislation the very next day giving the FTC the necessary authority, and President Bush signed it into law the following Monday, September 29 (*Mainstream Marketing v. FTC*, 2003).

The political agenda also often follows the public agenda because of politicians' needs for campaign financing. Politicians have to pay close attention to what the polls say and what lobbyists and consultants in the policy community tell them are important issues. Supporting these views can have important impacts on reelections, as money is increasingly the "mother's milk of politics" (Mutch, 1988).

This last point makes clear that there are not only interactions across the three sets of agendas but interactions within each domain. Within the public agenda domain, various interest groups often claim to be the *only* ones speaking "for the people" to convince the media or the policymakers that only *they* are the ones who should be listened to. Influential book authors or prominent nonpolitical leaders write op-ed pieces to try to get others to accept their positions. Coalitions are formed (sometimes among unlikely allies) to increase their influence on the policy agenda. Within the media world, there is some evidence suggesting that there is a synergistic influence among categories. It is often rumored that the major television networks choose stories for the evening news by discovering which issues are given priority by key morning papers such as the *New York Times* and *Washington Post*, or what is being talked about by bloggers that day.

A good example of how conflicting agendas form and get played out could be seen in the early years of the HIV/AIDS challenge in New York City at the beginning of the epidemic.

THE NEW YORK CITY AIDS AGENDA

Agendas and their prominence are sometimes affected by preferences among solutions. Chambré (1999) has noted that the two primary publics with the most interest in the AIDS issue in the United States in the 1980s and 1990s had very different preferences for solutions. Gay men wanted better drugs to prevent the spread of AIDS or to minimize the consequences of the disease. The other key population, intravenous drug users and those concerned about them, instead wanted an increase in the number of free needle exchange programs. The relative dominance of each of these solutions shifted back and forth on the policy and public agendas over time, as did the positions of key players.

The two perspectives—those of gay men and those of drug abusers—rose and fell in their general acceptance by the broader public. The gay men's community sought to increase awareness of the issue and preference for "their" solution through dramatic events and other modes of public advocacy, including picketing and celebrity-stoked fundraising. Their solution was not particularly controversial, although sometimes the tactics used by groups such as the AIDS Coalition to Unleash Power (ACT UP) were viewed as too confrontational and sometimes annoying to potential supporters. Fundamentally, however, arguing for research to find a drug or set of drugs that would cure or at least manage a serious medical condition was well within the "American tradition." At the same time, homosexual lifestyles were becoming significantly less controversial, especially in New York City, where Chambré's case study was done. Pushing the "drug agenda" was acceptable and even widely supported. The major impediments were funding and the state of medical science.

The problem for intravenous drug users was very different. First, they had very few organizational skills and little political influence. Their cause had to be advanced by others acting on their behalf. Second, the course of action they were proposing faced significant opposition at various points because it conflicted with other agendas. On the one hand, it competed with agendas that gave *higher* priority to reducing drug use per se. Needle exchange was seen by many politicians and competing advocacy groups as a tactic that would, at best, keep addicts using their drugs longer and, at worst, would increase the total number of users. Needle exchange supporters also confronted groups that said that this solution, which to a significant degree benefited Hispanic and African American users, conflicted with racial and ethnic agendas.

(Continued)

(Continued)

Many powerful African American leaders argued that, because needle exchange programs typically focused on minority neighborhoods, the programs were stigmatizing African Americans and making drug use a "black problem." Although they later backed down, these spokespeople were influential enough that when an African American mayor, David Dinkins, was elected in New York City, he decided to halt the needle exchange program for a time.

Clearly, it is important to understand the competition among agendas both within and across domains. Some would argue that it is the public agenda that is ultimately the most critical in sustaining an issue and leading to some attention being given to desired outcomes. The media agenda helps to galvanize interest, shape the debate, and carry messages among interested parties. However, the media's ultimate attention to its own audience ratings means that most media outlets will abandon a problem area if it does not get "public traction."

With respect to the other two agendas, public and policy, it is not always clear which will prevail. The policy agenda often progresses parallel to the public agenda because, if the ultimate outcome is mainly a political decision, as we have noted, politicians are reluctant to get too far in front of public opinion; consequently, the public agenda dominates. On the other hand, there are many social problem areas wherein the technical issues are sufficiently great that those in the policy world prevail simply because they know more about the problem and likely solutions.

Public Polls Versus Public Knowledge

How do we track agendas—particularly the public agenda? Daniel Yankelovich has studied agenda setting for more than 40 years, with a particular focus on the roll of public opinion polling. Public opinion polls are often taken by politicians and the media as the definitive measure of the public agenda. Polls are often relied on by policymakers for guidance as the latter seek to make change happen. Yankelovich (1991) argues that this reliance is often ill conceived. He says that where public opinion is to be used as a guide for social action, one should recognize several things. First, there is a difference between "mass opinion" and "public judgment." The former is relatively superficial, inconsistent, and not grounded in any sense of personal responsibility.

Public judgment results when individuals have thought through the issues, understood the action alternatives, and considered the personal sacrifices and other implications of the choices that might be made. In coming to public judgment, there is "more emphasis on the normative, valuing, ethical side of questions than on the factual, informational side" (p. 5).

Second, it necessarily follows that public opinion is not the same as *expert* opinion, nor are they on the same dimension in the sense that public opinion can be considered simply less-informed expert opinion. Public judgment does have informational content, but it is more than that. It is the result of an evaluation of issues in terms of personal relevance. Yankelovich (1991) makes clear that education or public information campaigns—often proposed by advocates as all that is needed to move issues forward—seldom have the major impacts on public judgment that sponsors hope for. This is because critical social issues are less about facts than about the values and sacrifices in play.

Third, Yankelovich (1991) believes there is a methodological reason that polling ought to be suspect. The way that public polls are undertaken (usually by means of telephone or Internet surveys) means that they will measure mass opinion rather than public judgment. Such measures are not likely to be stable. For this reason, Yankelovich argues that they should not be used as a definitive guide for policy choices, although they can more accurately indicate the degree to which people's attention has been aroused.

Stages in the Agenda-Setting Process

Yankelovich (1992) proposes a predictable set of seven stages that transpire as an issue moves up the public agenda from discovery to the point where public judgment has coalesced and the populace is ready for change. The steps he proposes are as follows:

Stage 1: Dawning Awareness. This is the stage at which the public first becomes alerted to a potential social problem and perhaps some suggested solutions. The media play an important role here: reporting new data, presenting vivid examples of the situation, and summarizing speeches or position papers alerting the society to the topic.

Stage 2: Greater Urgency. This second step in consciousness raising occurs when individual members of the public see some personal implications and are ready to consider some responses.

Stage 3: Discovering the Choices. Often at this point, the experts and "policy wonks" will float a number of trial balloons about how to handle the problem. The public will begin to consider these alternatives and evaluate some of the trade-offs to be made with each.

ge 4: Wishful Thinking. Yankelovich (1992) sees this as a stage at which the ⅃blic tends to think it can have it all—a tendency he suspects may have grown more common in the last few decades. At this point, the public has not faced up to the hard choices that will have to be made. For this reason, politicians and other experts may be deluded into thinking that the public is ready for action. Yankelovich cites legislators who enacted both caps on costs and higher premiums for Medicare in 1988, based partly on polls that showed that 69% of older Americans would support a program to address the risks of catastrophic medical costs. It turned out that they were unwilling to bear the higher costs once they realized what they would be, and the legislation was repealed 18 months later.

Stage 5: Weighing the Choices. Up until this point, the policy mavens, reporters, and editorial writers have been doing the heavy lifting in terms of figuring out the concrete benefits and costs of the choices. At this stage, however, the public finally becomes engaged, with people thinking through what a new course of action means to them personally.

Stage 6: Taking a Stand Intellectually. This is the point at which the public will have carefully considered the facts at hand and accepted mentally one course of action. This does not mean that the action is accepted yet emotionally. For example, many businessmen in Western democracies—perhaps the vast majority—would argue that women should have the same opportunities to rise to the top of businesses as men. Still, a significant portion of these same men finds reasons why it is not yet time for such a step for specific women, because it runs counter to the men's lingering preferences for stay-at-home wives.

Stage 7: Making a Responsible Judgment Morally and Emotionally. Yankelovich (1992) says: "Intellectual resolution requires people to clarify fuzzy thinking, reconcile inconsistencies, consider relevant facts and new realities, and grasp the full consequences of choices. Emotional resolution requires that people confront their own ambivalent feelings, accommodate themselves to unwelcome realities, and overcome an urge to procrastinate" (p. 106).

Other researchers have also sought to delineate the stages through which issues move up the broader society's various agendas. It is not surprising that they do not agree on the number of stages or their contents. For example, Rogers, Dearing, and Chang (1991) studied the media coverage of the AIDS issue in the 1980s and concluded that there were four stages in forming the media agenda: the *initial era,* during which there was little attention paid to the issue; the *science era,* during which more attention was paid to assembling the facts around the issue; the *human era,* during which the issue was personalized with interesting cases and stories; and the *political era,* during which the focus became what action was going to be taken to address the problem.

The economist and urbanologist Anthony Downs (1972) suggests that a linear model of public attention to specific social problems is not appropriate—the process is not unidirectional. As we noted in the preceding chapter, public interest is often mercurial and often wanes before anything happens at all. The public gets excited about a topic for a time but eventually becomes bored and moves on to other, "hotter" topics—a phenomenon also found in the media. Downs proposes five stages to this cyclic process.

1. The Preproblem Stage. Problems may well exist for some time before the public becomes interested. To move onto the public agenda, the problem needs what Yankelovich (1992) describes as "awareness and urgency." Downs (1972) argued that many problems are really less serious by the time the public pays attention to them and cites domestic racism, poverty, and malnutrition in the United States as examples. (On the other hand, such a pattern appears not to have affected recent social problems such as obesity, women's heart problems, and AIDS, which have constantly risen in prominence over the last decade.)

2. Alarmed Discovery and Euphoric Enthusiasm. At some point, the issue is "discovered." Downs (1972) argues that, once the public is engaged, there is a period of enthusiasm about finding a solution, emanating from Americans' inherent optimism and belief that any problem can be fixed with a lot of concerted effort and maybe some new technology. This would parallel Yankelovich's (1992) "wishful thinking" stage. It describes well the views of the HIV/AIDS problem in the early 1990s, when there was widespread belief that medical technology would soon find a cure.

3. Realizing the Cost of Significant Progress. With time, the population comes to believe that major problems will take a lot of money to solve (worldwide AIDS), major restructuring (air pollution, global warming), or serious individual or public sacrifices (obesity, racial segregation). Downs (1972) suggests that the major feature of this stage is the recognition that there is an unpleasant connection between the problem and solutions that people may have to make. This would be Yankelovich's (1992) Stage 5: weighing the choices.

4. Gradual Decline of Intense Public Interest. In contrast to Yankelovich's (1992) model of ever-forward progression of individuals, Downs (1972) argues that the realization that a problem will be hard to solve leads to one of three outcomes. Some people will get discouraged. Some will feel threatened by the solutions and so stop talking about the problem and hope it will go away. Others just get bored. Progress may have been made, and people thus conclude that "it is only a matter of time" before the problem is gone—so they can move on to worrying about other matters. This is certainly a challenge for those concerned about smoking or AIDS in the United States in the early 21st century, as many believe (wrongly) that these problems have been successfully managed. It is not unheard of for campaigns to turn to celebrities to keep up interest, as when Elizabeth Taylor speaks up about the continuing HIV/AIDS problem in the United States.

5. The Postproblem Stage. Neglect does not mean that the problem has disappeared or that people are not working on it. It is just that the public has moved on to other topics. The homeless are still with us all over the world, and there are programs and systems in place to help them. However, homelessness is no longer a "hot" issue except perhaps in some countries and some cities in the United States. The same is true of high blood pressure, a longstanding focus of social marketing (Andreasen, 1996). Various medical groups are still concerned about high blood pressure, but there is currently more interest in diseases such as diabetes that are a consequence of the growing rates of obesity.

Issues that do not affect large numbers of people or that are largely outside of their everyday existence (homelessness, ozone depletion, Amazon rain forest destruction) tend to be hard to dramatize and sustain. People are not reminded of them in their daily lives. Issues that have solutions that do not seem feasible or that threaten some important benefits to the majority of the public are likely to be ignored. For example, air pollution may not be a public or political priority if it means stiffer gasoline taxes are needed to improve roads or to subsidize public transportation to combat air pollution. For many, tackling air pollution would mean giving up their SUVs—an undesirable outcome for most.

It also should be pointed out that there are issues that are just dull and boring or that affect only small, specialized (sometimes invisible) segments of the population. It is very difficult to get the public aroused about minor corporate loopholes in the tax system, even though these loopholes can mean significant burden shifting from business to the general public taxpayer. On the other hand, there are "evergreen" issues, such as corporate embezzling, road rage, and airline safety, which affect a majority of people and do not require oppressive personal solutions that would punish individuals directly. These issues also make for dramatic media copy.

It is certainly also true that the public often exhibits shortsightedness and callousness when it comes to addressing social problems. People often fixate on their own issues and ignore or downplay others that are globally very important. There are individuals and groups who are very concerned about the extinction of the snail darter or other rare species in distant locations and want foundations and the government to spend resources to do something about them. At the same time, these individuals may ignore abject poverty, child neglect, and crime in their own cities. They can obsess over highly publicized killings involving actors such as Robert Blake or OJ Simpson or potential child abuse by Michael Jackson and ignore the genocidal murder of thousands of Fur, Zaghawa, and Masalit peoples in the Darfur region of Sudan.

A Proposed General Process
of the Social Change Life Cycle

Although there are a great many options to choose among, it is crucial that we agree on a model timeline for the social change process to guide us for the remaining chapters of the book. Borrowing from Yankelovich and Downs as well as—for the first time—from social marketing theory, I propose the progression outlined in Table 2.1.

Moving an Issue Up the Public Agenda

What are the factors that seem necessary if a social problem is to move rapidly through these stages? Obviously, one needs a solid scientific basis and clearly undesirable consequences. Beyond that, various individuals must take action if there is to be a rapid rise in interest.

Charismatic Spokespeople. A social problem becomes prominent more rapidly when there are high-profile individuals "out front" on the issues. Preferably these will be individual leaders or statesmen with knowledge, competence, talents, communications skills, political and media contacts, cunning, and charisma. Ralph Nader is such a person, and he has been effective in raising a number of critical social issues, starting with his challenges to the auto industry in the 1960s. C. Everett Koop and David Kessler were key figures in alerting us to the problems of smoking and pushing changes in tobacco policy.

Leaders of Coalitions. Solid organizational backing can amplify the spokesperson's messages. Single groups or a few individuals are unlikely to create major change—although they can be catalysts. Coalitions of forces need to be assembled and brought to bear on the crisis. Grassroots mobilization has been effective in environmental protests on the European continent and domestically on the AIDS issue.

Foundation Leaders. For an issue to get traction, studies often must be done, experimental interventions tried out, and conferences and study groups assembled. This is typically the role of foundations and their grant makers. Sometimes they are leaders in forcing societies to come to terms with an issue, as with the Robert Wood Johnson Foundation's efforts in end-of-life care issues and health insurance for children.

Government Legislators and Agency Heads. Major change typically involves legislation and federal or state funding of initiatives. As solutions are identified,

Table 2.1   Stages in the Life Cycle of a Social Change Issue

Stage 1: *Inattention* *to the problem*	The social problem exists, as evidenced by concrete data or dramatic anecdotes, but it has not yet become anyone's concern.
Stage 2: *Discovery* *of the problem*	The problem comes to the attention of individuals or groups (including the media) who think it needs to be addressed. At this stage, initial baseline analyses or measurements will be undertaken. Nuances of the problem will begin to emerge—for example, learning who is most affected by the problem.
Stage 3: *Climbing* *the agenda*	Activists, advocacy groups, individual politicians, investigative reporters, and nonfiction writers raise the volume on the issue. They marshal even more evidence, produce real victims, and potentially raise the guilt level of those not affected. At this stage, funders and potential interveners begin to find the issue sufficiently important for attention and possible action.
Stage 4: *Outlining* *the choices*	Analysts and advocates look at the data and consider how the problem might be addressed. Evidence about causal linkages will be important, as will scenarios for possible intervention.
Stage 5: *Choosing* *courses of action*	This is where debate takes place over the benefits and costs that action and inaction will have on society, victims, and those who have to take action (e.g., donate money, pass laws) if there is to be a solution. Attention will be paid to the efficacy of various solutions. Opposing forces emerge and solidify their positions.
Stage 6: *Launching initial* *interventions*	Foundations or government agencies put money into programs. Organizations mount pioneering efforts and test alternative strategies and tactics. These will involve both downstream and upstream interventions, in which social marketing can play a major role.
Stage 7: *Reassessing and* *redirecting efforts*	With most difficult changes, progress is slow, and there are periods of acceleration, deceleration, progression, and regression. At some point, key figures will feel that it is time to take stock of where the problem stands. The outcome may be a reorientation and resurgence of interventions—or it may not.
Stage 8: *Achieving success,* *failure, or neglect*	After a number of years, the problem will have found some major solutions or will have proven basically intractable and, in the absence of dramatic progress or new data, will "drop off the radar screen." The latter may also be the result of new competition from the latest social problem that captures the public's imagination and drives the "old" problem into the "dustbin of history" (Cohen, 2000).

government agencies typically provide overall guidance, set strategy, and develop monitoring systems. State and local governments then follow up with tailored interventions and policy changes that fit their own culture and their areas of responsibility. In promoting seat belt usage, the federal government raised the issue and created databases. State governments passed specific regulations; for example, in the use of safety belts and safety seats for children and infants. Local governments then set policies and practices for law enforcement.

Journalists, Editors, News Directors. As I have noted, the media helps us think about social issues. Reporters and commentators can provide barrages of data, carry pronouncements by spokespeople, tell stories of victims, and report on test solutions. They can contribute greatly to changes in social norms. At later stages of the change process, the media are critical in delivering information about what exactly individuals need to do and how they can do it (Backer, Rogers, & Sopory, 1992).

These key figures, in turn, are supported by field investigators, epidemiologists, scientists, survey researchers, and the various staff members and volunteers who eventually get into the trenches to make change happen.

Because it is *individuals* who must act at various stages to accelerate the agenda building process, there are, therefore, multiple touch points at which social marketing concepts and tools can play a critical role. Social marketers spend their time trying to understand how to induce target audiences to undertake important behavioral changes. Upstream players in the agenda-setting process are no different from downstream individuals who need to adopt better behavioral patterns. Only their issues are different.

Disjunctions and Distortions in the Agenda-Setting Process

The process by which societies move from discovery of a problem to acting on it is not a straight line. Changes in the playing field are common. New data or new players come on the scene. Coalitions spring up and fall apart. Initial interventions turn out to be wrong-headed or lack impact. Scandals occur, and dramatic events reenergize a flagging cause.

Sometimes the reactions to a problem spread well beyond its origins. In 1996, Europe was hit with an outbreak of bovine spongiform encephalopathy (BSE). Throughout the continent, food safety concerns were significantly heightened, as BSE could lead to incurable brain disease in humans. Many thousands of cattle were slaughtered, and exports of beef to the United States and other countries were cut off. The public's concern over food safety spread to large-scale chicken farming because of anxiety about the amount of antibiotics routinely fed to hens. The concern for food safety then spread to genetically modified food, or "frankenfoods," as the Europeans called them.

A tertiary effect of the BSE scare was its effect on people's confidence in government regulators. In the UK, in the immediate aftermath of the problem, Minister of Agriculture Stephen Gummer was pictured in the media feeding his 4-year-old daughter beef burgers in an attempt to pacify the public. Instead of reassuring consumers, Gummer showed people that public officials charged with food safety was acting with little caution. Officials were further criticized for initially saying that BSE could not be transmitted to humans, which proved to be wrong. This harmed the credibility of UK scientific and agricultural agencies, and the public was said to have felt betrayed (UK Politics: Gummer, 1998). In an attempt to rebuild confidence in Britain's food, the incoming Blair government established the Food Standards Agency in 2000 (Department of Health, Social Services, and Public Safety, 2000).

Issues can get off-track also if committed activists or other key parties distort the seriousness of a social problem or the efficacy of possible solutions out of ignorance or because it suits their own personal agendas. The media are sometimes complicit in this in their quest for sensational stories that produce ratings but very often exaggerate or distort the facts and skew the public agenda.

A case in point is "road rage." In a recent book on public fears, Barry Glassner (1999) noted that, in the mid-1990s, a USA Today story described road rage as "a growing epidemic," citing a AAA report saying that traffic incidents involving personal violence in the U.S. were "up more than 50%." In actuality, the AAA study reported only 1800 such incidents in 1996. Although this was a 50% growth over the 1129 incidents in 1990, it is hardly an increase that should cause great alarm. Such headlines sell newspapers, however. They can also lead to calls for social change.

Air safety scares follow a similar scenario. Americans and the media seem to think that flying on an airplane is a very risky undertaking. Glassner (1999) reports stories in Time headlined "Air Safety—Under a Cloud" and in USA Today describing "High Anxiety in the Skies." He also notes that in almost 90 years of airplane travel, fewer than 13,000 people have died in plane crashes. A person is 10 times as likely to die in his or her bathtub as in an airplane crash. However, crashes make for vivid reporting, tragic human interest stories, and sometimes episodes of bravery and sacrifice. Such stories play out over many news cycles and can reinforce a common fear that flying is quite risky.

Distortions also occur because some social change issues are more controversial than others. Uncontroversial problems often get higher prominence than controversial ones. Fighting the challenge of breast cancer is a good example. Breast cancer charity drives are ubiquitous. There are pink ribbons everywhere, regular road races "for the cure," and dozens of product tie-ins.

Hundreds of companies have created campaigns associating themselves with the problem. Avon has made breast cancer a central social enterprise for its corporation and workforce. Avon's Breast Cancer Awareness Crusade has become one of the most powerful corporate alliance programs ever created. It raised more than $250 million for breast cancer education and research between 1993 and 2002. The Race for the Cure, which it sponsors, now takes place in 100 cities and three foreign countries (Andreasen & Drumwright, 2001).

These efforts and the media activity and promotion that surround them have led to serious public misperceptions about breast cancer risks and about women's health in general. A recent study reported by the American Heart Association found that many Americans—both men and women—have come to believe that breast cancer is the number one cause of death in women. The reality is that the number one killer of women is *cardiovascular disease*. It kills 12 times as many women as breast cancer. Indeed, lung cancer is a worse cancer problem for women, killing almost 60% more women than breast cancer in 2000 (American Heart Association, 2005a).

Similar distortions are present in agendas concerning men's health. It is the case that many people, men and women, think that men have a greater risk of dying from cardiovascular disease than women. In 1980 that was true to a small degree: 4% more men died from this cause than women. Today, 15% more women die from cardiovascular disease than men. The rate of cardiovascular disease among men has dropped significantly since 1980; it has stayed at the same level or even grown slightly among women (American Heart Association, 2005b). As Dr. Nieca Goldberg, chief of the Women's Heart Program at Lenox Hill Hospital in New York, notes, this is a direct consequence of distorted public and policy agendas: "When I was in medical school, when instructors referred to heart disease, they showed slides of middle-aged businessmen clutching their chest" (Grant, 2003). This view was reflected in the common image in the media of a person with high cardiovascular risk as an overweight, Type A, corporate male keeling over one day from a heart attack and leaving behind his unsuspecting and now grieving wife and family. Such stories, however, had their desired effect. Men got the message. They learned how to take precautionary measures, and rates went down.

As Dr. Goldberg points out, however, until barely a decade ago, very little attention was paid to the problem in women, and very little research was done. Women today are unaware that their symptoms can be different from men's, and often they do not realize they are having an attack when it takes place. Similarly, doctors trained many years earlier and family members are less likely to recognize a female heart problem. They may not understand the risk factors that, for example, lead to a rate of cardiovascular death among African American women that is 50% higher than that of white women (American Heart Association, 2005c).

Fortunately, as a result of the actions of many women's health groups, research centers, and physicians, both the public and policy agendas on breast cancer and heart disease are shifting. As a result of these shifting (many would say *corrective*) changes in public awareness and priorities, the National Institutes of Health (NIH) introduced the Women's Health Initiative (now in its follow-up phase), a major 15-year research program to address the most common causes of death, disability, and poor quality of life in postmenopausal women—cardiovascular disease, cancer, and osteoporosis (*Women's Health Initiative*, n.d.).

Framing Social Problems

As we have noted, objective facts are only the starting point for the emergence of any issue on the social scene. The issue then rises or falls on the various agendas, depending, in part, on the motives and interests of the various players (a point we shall return to in later chapters). Objective facts are only raw data until they are given interpretation. The role of many organizations and individuals in the agenda-setting process therefore becomes one of "fact interpreters." For those organizations and individuals with a particular preference for certain outcomes, the process of interpretation becomes closer to what politicians call "spin."

The term *spin* became common during the presidential debates in the 1970s and 1980s, when observers noted that perceptions of who "won" a debate were less a matter of what went on in the debate itself than on how others described it after the fact. This insight led to each party assigning "spin doctors" to buttonhole reporters in the "spin room" after the debates to offer the case as to why their side won. The task of the spin doctor was to take the raw data of the actual debate—words, tone, logic, appearances—and interpret them in ways favorable to his or her candidate.

The more neutral academic term for "spinning" is *framing*. A frame is a context offered for interpreting a set of data. Different people will interpret the same set of facts—*frame* them—in different ways, for one of two reasons. Sometimes (as with spin doctors), they wish others to adopt their frame because it furthers their own policy agenda; they want to spin the data. Sometimes, however, they frame the facts differently because the facts come to them from different perspectives. Take, for example, the data presented in chapter 1 on U.S. income inequality. Liberals would see the data as evidence of the growing disparity between the rich and the poor. They would say that the data clearly show that there are significant imperfections in the economy, corporate America, and the educational system that are biased to benefit those who are already well-off and properly connected and leave behind those who are not so socially well endowed. Their frame of comparison is other countries, such as Finland, Belgium, and Canada, which have done much more to make sure that those at the bottom end of the income spectrum are not so badly disadvantaged. The liberal advocates then call for new social programs to reduce the disparity.

On the other hand, those with a conservative perspective would employ a "relative change" framework, pointing to the evidence on dramatically increased per capita spending power for all households and saying that the poorest citizens are really *better* off. They might also argue that the growing disparity is good news. It is evidence that, in the United States, self-reliance pays off: that those who got good educations, learned the right job skills, and got into growth industries saw high payoffs. They would say that the data show that the free market system really works well. Those who are in the bottom 20th percentile simply need to pull up their socks and do what it takes to succeed. They need to become more self-reliant.

There are other possible "spins" for the same data. Those in the middle of the liberal-conservative spectrum might step in and suggest that, although the data may be reasonably optimistic, one should look beyond "top line" numbers. For example, one might accept the conservative frame and note that the per capita spending power of the poor has actually improved but look further into the data to see whether some subpopulations are worse off in absolute terms between 1970 and 2000. What has happened to the per capita incomes of African Americans or Hispanics? What about seniors? Are there regional differences that leave some states like Mississippi or Louisiana farther and farther behind? Are the folks in rural areas worse off? How about single mothers? The issue here would not be "is there general inequality?" These partisans would argue that the relevant frame is intergroup comparisons—whether some groups are falling behind as others are getting ahead.

Different framing results not only in different interpretations of data but in the ranking of social problems and in the solutions proposed for problems we might care about. Simple labels for social problems can have powerful impacts on the debate about solutions. Consider some of the current hot topics debated in America in the 21st century. Is the issue about

- Gun control *or* gun safety
- "A woman's right to choose" *or* "protecting the rights of the unborn"
- Partial birth abortion *or* late-term abortion
- Urban sprawl *or* urban growth
- Climate change *or* global warming

Gun ownership is a constructive example. In his award-winning[1] documentary film *Bowling for Columbine,* social critic Michael Moore pointed out that annual gun-related deaths in the United Kingdom are 165; in Canada, 68; in Australia, 65; but more than 11,100 in the United States (Moore, 2002). Many people, including Moore, use such data to frame an argument that other countries have learned that gun control is the solution to the problems of crime, spousal abuse, and accidental home shootings. On the other hand, groups such as the National Rifle Association frame the data as positive evidence that individuals in the United States are much better at taking responsibility for their own defense. The NRA also sometimes frames the issue as one of conflicting rights. Members agree that there are "too many" gun deaths in the United States but that any government effort to regulate gun ownership is an infringement on another right guaranteed by the U.S. Constitution: the right to bear arms. In their framing, the value of supporting the Constitution dominates the concerns of those who want less gun ownership and use. Regulation, in this view, would create a different social problem (not adhering to the Constitution) that is more serious than the social problem of what some see as excessive gun deaths.

Objectivists Versus Constructivists

The presence, importance, and dynamics of a social problem can be determined by how data are framed. The structuralist or objectivist approach would argue that a fact is a fact, and although one can pick and choose data, the data are real and just need interpretation. They argue that social problems are real and concrete. They can be measured, for example by assessing the current status of something against some ideal or reasonable standard. This is what the Department of Health and Human Services is doing with *Healthy People 2010*. At the Environmental Protection Agency (EPA), unhealthy air is always determined by comparing scientific measurements against a standard of "unhealthy" defined in EPA regulations.

Constructivists, on the other hand, view social problems as something that a social system contrives or, more narrowly still, that a specific group or agency defines (Spiro, Feltovich, Jacobson, & Coulson, 1991). For example, the EPA air quality standard has six components. One of these defines unhealthy levels of particulate matter in the atmosphere, a standard based on particles that are 10 microns in size. In 1997, the EPA added a daily and annual standard for smaller particles of 2.5 microns in size. The latter was added to monitor finer particles that can penetrate the lungs of children and elderly people suffering from asthma, chronic bronchitis, and other respiratory and circulatory problems. The effect of this change was that the EPA "created" a new social problem for cities that did not meet the new standards. Not only did this new use of existing data create this new problem; the EPA forced cities and corporations to act on it by force of law.

Even if the standard is agreed to, the way data are presented can affect how serious someone perceives the problem to be. Consider the following alternative ways of describing malaria as a worldwide social problem. Which version is likely to create the highest motivation to act?

UNESCO estimates (in 1997) that there are 300,000 to 500,000 cases of malaria around the world.

Ninety percent of the world's malaria cases are found in one region, sub-Saharan Africa.

One million children die of malaria each year.

Children represent half of all malaria deaths each year.

A child in sub-Saharan Africa dies of malaria every 30 seconds.

Which of these frames makes the problem seem most serious—more worthy of the attention of the world community than other health or economic problems? Many readers would agree that the framing implicit in the fifth statement makes the problem much more serious than the routine presentation of facts in the first statement. However, all the statements are ways of framing the same reality.

This example also suggests that problems can seem greater or smaller depending on who is portrayed as the victim. The degree of vulnerability (and size) of the group facing a social problem is often a good indicator of the degree to which a social problem will receive attention.[2] The UN defines vulnerability as "a state of high exposure to certain risks, combined with a reduced ability to defend oneself against those risks and cope with their negative consequences" (United Nations Economic and Social Development, 2001). Historically, children and the disabled have met this test. However, labeling other groups as vulnerable may be specific to a particular time and locality. Thus the elderly may be seen as vulnerable, but in some cultures the standard for "elderly" may be people over 70 and in others it is those over 50. In some cultures, immigrants are a vulnerable group. In other cultures, they may be seen as a *source* of social problems, not victims. Some traits, such as being over 70 or being disabled, are unavoidable conditions. Having a language problem may be seen as only a temporary source of vulnerability.

There is also the reality that social problems rise in prominence not because the objective reality has changed but because our *expectations* have changed. Now we worry about school bus safety, because we expect every child to be bused to school and bused safely. We worry about urban sprawl, because many of us expect to be able to move out to the suburbs and have a crime-free environment. We worry about secondhand smoke, because we think we have defeated *firsthand* smoke! We worry about the "digital divide" in developing countries because we think that computer literacy is the key to a country's development in a wired world. We want prescription drug coverage in Medicare because we are now certain that drugs can keep us illness free and robust into old age.

All of these are concerns that did not trouble us 50 years ago.

Finally, it must be noted that frames can also play a role in assigning blame and implicitly pointing to those who should be responsible for fixing the situation. Sometimes one can detect patterns of blaming within groups of players in the agenda-building process. For instance, Nelkin (1987) and Johnson (1989) have concluded that, in general, the media tend to frame issues in ways that do not threaten the existing social system. Western media gatekeepers see problems as the results of ineptitude, accidents, individual chicanery, and unfortunate events. Seldom is it that they lay the blame on broad social systems, such as capitalism or democracy, or argue that the basic approaches of government agencies are at fault.

Of course, a vast array of vocal protest groups frame the issue as exactly the result of the capitalist system, rampant globalization, or American hegemony (Johansson, 2004; Ritzer, 2004). These groups are especially adept at securing media coverage, but media analysis will, typically, not adopt their framing.

A Balanced Perspective

The preceding discussion makes clear that the existence and importance of social problems and the desirability of various solutions are very much influenced by the way in which information is gathered and framed. How, then, do foundation officers, government agencies, corporations, and individual citizens develop perspectives that will allow proper attention to what is really important and to solutions that are likely to make society better? The ideal solution is to find individuals or agencies without what is often called "a dog in the hunt." Government monitoring organizations, such as the Centers for disease Control and Prevention (CDC), and cross-national agencies, such as the United Nations (UN) and the World Health Organization (WHO), are probably the most reliable sources of raw data that can be assessed when one worries about the spin of activist or doctrinaire organizations. When it comes to assessing possible solutions, one very useful method is carefully setting out alternatives in an unbiased, straightforward manner so that we can choose among them. The latter is a role undertaken by the nonprofit group Public Agenda. To see how they set out alternative frames for 20 or more current issues, see their Web site at http://www.publicagenda.org/issues/issuehome.cfm.

THE PLAYERS

We have seen that social problems rise to prominence on the public, political, and media agendas through a process that involves facts, framing, and interpretations. Social problems become important in Yankelovich's Stage 2 and get acted upon because specific institutions and individuals bring facts to light, frame them in specific ways, and find mechanisms to keep the pressure at a high level until something is done about them. These are the players that collectively control the agenda-setting process.

It is important to recognize who they are, because if 21st century social marketing is to play a role in the agenda-setting process, as I argue it should, it is these individuals who would constitute the target audiences for future social marketing campaigns.

MEDIA GATEKEEPERS

As I have noted, the media typically play a very significant role in agenda setting. They provoke interest in an issue through investigative reporting and so-called muckraking journalism (a term contributed by Theodore Roosevelt). History offers many examples in which the media were major forces of social change. Powerful investigative reports by Woodward and Bernstein led to changes in the relationship between the U.S. Congress and the White House. Financial reporters' exposés of corporate financial mismanagement at Enron and WorldCom led eventually to changes in the way corporations are audited and to the passage of the Sarbanes-Oxley bill regulating financial disclosure. Entire print vehicles, such as *Mother Jones,* and television programs, such as *60 Minutes,* have positioned themselves as prime catalysts in driving social change through investigative reporting. Protess and his colleagues (1991) characterize what they do as "journalism of outrage," the objective of which is "to *trigger* agenda-building processes in order to produce 'reformist' outcomes— policy changes that promote democracy, efficiency and social justice."

The media also dramatize and personalize a social problem, to capture the public's often limited attention span. In the case of Ryan White, the 13-year-old boy who contracted AIDS intravenously and was shunned by classmates, press stories and an ABC movie documenting Ryan's personal story contributed greatly to the country's concern about the issue and their enthusiasm for eventual legislative solutions.

A similar case is the passage of versions of "Megan's Law" in a great many states and current pleas to federalize it. Megan's Law is named after a 7-year-old Hamilton Township, New Jersey, girl named Megan Nicole Kanka. As numerous press and television accounts detailed, in 1994, Megan was enticed by a two-time convicted sex offender promising her a puppy to enter a neighborhood home, where he brutally raped and murdered her. No one in the neighborhood knew of this person's history. Megan's Laws, first passed in New Jersey in the mid-1990s, require the public posting of the names and residences of known sex offenders. A similar federal law was enacted in 1994, named after another child: the Jacob Wetterling Crimes Against Children and Sexually Violent Offender Registration Act. This law requires uniform state registration of sex offenders.

The media also play a role in helping the various participants in a social problem area communicate with each other. Newspapers report on meetings and the results of surveys and policy studies. They give op-ed space or TV talk show time to parties holding various positions on an issue and to the decision makers who must eventually act (or not act). C-SPAN allows citizens to directly observe legislation and conferences on major social issues. Local papers and local TV interview programs help politicians communicate with their constituents about the politicians' stands and the choices with which they want help.

ADVOCACY GROUPS

Advocacy groups take positions on issues that fit with their broad philosophies or other personal agendas. These include political parties, political action committees, associations such as the National Rifle Association, nonprofits such as AARP and the National Association for the Advancement of Colored People (NAACP), and corporate lobbying organizations such as the Pharmaceutical Research and Manufacturers of America that take positions on issues on behalf of their supporters. Foundations with political agendas, such as those controlled by Richard Mellon Scaife, promote solutions with a broad agenda, often characterized as liberal or conservative or fundamentalist. Special-purpose nonprofit advocacy groups spring up around specific issues such as the right to life (as they frame it) that have implications in many policy areas—for example, a pharmacist's right to refuse to sell "morning-after" contraceptive pills. Citizens' groups spring up around one issue or a related set of issues, as was the case for Mothers Against Drunk Driving. Broader-based nonprofits, such as the American Cancer Society, and government agencies, such as the Environmental Protection Agency, from time to time seek to draw people's attention to issues or advocate for specific solutions.

As issues gain traction and rise on the public policy agenda, the number of organizations involved can be significant. Figure 2.1 lists the 71 Web sites available in April 2004 under the Yahoo grouping Directory>Health> Reproductive Health>Abortion>Pro-Life.

Of course, not all advocacy groups are pushing for some new course of action or a new initiatiive. Sometimes groups form to make sure that change does *not* happen or to reverse changes made earlier. The "pro-choice" groups do not want the *Roe v. Wade* Supreme Court decision in the United States to be overturned; the "pro-life" groups want to return to pre-Roe regulations. The Klu Klux Klan and "white supremacist" groups wanted to roll back desegregation in the 1960s, and they often used very violent methods to further their agendas.

DATA MONITORS AND ASSEMBLERS

This group includes policy centers and so-called watchdog groups, universities, foundations, and government agencies, as well as individual faculty

(*Text Continues on Page 56*)

AAA Women's Services: Nonmedical, nonprofit, Christian organization offering local services and national referrals to women facing unexpected pregnancy.

Abortion in Spain: Includes statistics, arguments, and other information.

Abortion Is Murder: Offers information, images, help for crisis pregnancies, political party views, and more.

ACT Right to Life Association: Includes seminar papers and submissions on why lethal injections and abortions are bad for our community.

Alameda Pregnancy Counseling Center: Gospel-oriented, Christ-centered, outreach ministry focusing on pro-life issues and offering pregnancy tests and counseling.

America's Crisis Pregnancy Helpline: National place for pregnancy help and assistance.

American Life League

Baptists for Life, Inc.: Information on pregnancy and abortion, assisted suicide, and euthanasia. Help for churches and individuals forming Biblically based pro-life ministries.

Birthright

Bridge to Life: Nonprofit pro-life organization offering services and resources.

Catholics United for Life: Nationwide organization. Site contains many links to other organizations and sources of interest.

Center for Bio-ethical Reform: Nonmedical organization offers educational material, lectures, and articles.

Central Illinois Right to Life: Seeks to educate, convince, and mobilize citizens to take responsible action in defense and support of innocent human life.

Children of the Rosary: Organizes praying sessions at abortion clinics.

Compassion Pregnancy Center of the Monterey Peninsula: Offering counseling, pregnancy testing, and medical services for women with unplanned pregnancies.

Delaware Right to Life: Pro-life organization.

Democrats for Life of America, Inc.: Advocates a pro-life position within the party.

Elliot Institute: Source of information and research on the aftereffects of abortion and postabortion healing.

Feminists for Life of America: Women's rights organization that opposes abortion and promotes equality for women.

Fort Worth Pregnancy Center: Endeavors to help women by providing a free, confidential pregnancy test; education and information on adoption, abortion, and parenting; and referrals.

Gateway Pregnancy Center: Racially mixed Christian crisis center offering free, confidential pregnancy tests and counseling. Promotes chastity and life over abortion.

Georgia Tech Students for Life

Gonzaga University GOAL: Pro-life student group of the Jesuit tradition.

Gravesend Christians Caring for Life Pregnancy Crisis Center: For women and men facing pre- or postabortion trauma. Includes antiabortion information.

Greater Austin Right to Life

(Continued)

Helping Hand Pregnancy Care Center: Counseling for women in unexpected or crisis pregnancy. Pregnancy tests, postabortion counseling available. There are no medical facilities at this location.

Human Life International: International Catholic pro-life and pro–family values nonprofit organization. In English, French, Spanish, and Polish.

Illinois Right to Life: Pro-life organization offering an abstinence starter kit, information related to life issues, and events.

International Pregnancy Help Center: Offering online crisis pregnancy help, advice, and referrals.

Just the Facts: Site provides information about human development in the womb. Literature and presentations available to schools.

Kansans for Life: Pro-life organization fighting for the lives of innocent babies.

Life: Provides information on abortion and other pro-life issues for students, as well as care and help for women faced with a problem pregnancy.

Life Dynamics: Fighting to return full legal protection for every unborn child from the moment of conception.

Life Education Fund of Colorado: Nonprofit organization promoting pro-life values and alternatives to abortion through television commercials.

Life Matters Outreach: Christian-based, nonprofit organization offering pregnancy testing, pro-life alternatives, parenting classes, and postabortion healing.

Life Pregnancy Care Service: Seeks to give support and counsel to women who find themselves with a crisis pregnancy.

Life Care Services: Provides help (before, during, and after) to those facing a crisis pregnancy.

Lutherans for Life of the Mid-Atlantic States: Helping women in unexpected pregnancies, supporting local pregnancy centers, and educating the Lutheran community on God's gospel of life.

Massachusetts Citizens for Life

Michigan Right to Life

Missionary Catholics United for Life: Pro-life advocacy organization.

Missouri Right to Life

National Campus Life Network: Assists in and contributes to the formation, collaboration, and effectiveness of campus pro-life groups throughout Canada.

National Pro-Life Alliance: Nonprofit organization fighting to end abortion on demand.

National Right to Life Committee

New York State Right to Life Committee: Includes pro-life resources on abortion, euthanasia, adoption, fetal development, abstinence, crisis pregnancy centers, and legislative information.

Ohio Right to Life Society: Topics covered include abortion, euthanasia, infanticide, sexual education, human development, and adoption.

Oneida County Crisis Pregnancy Center

Operation Rescue West

Our Lady of Toledo Shrine: Advocates prayerful, peaceful, practical, pro-life alternatives to abortion.

Pennsylvania Pro-Life Federation: Defending the right to life.

Princeton University—Pro Life

Pro-Life Action League: Protests abortion, promotes sidewalk counseling, and spreads the pro-life message, emphasizing action and education. Headed by Joe Scheidler.

Pro-Life Alliance of Gays and Lesbians

Pro-Life Victoria Inc.: Seeks to educate, promote the pro-life philosophy, and lobby legislators to pass laws to protect the unborn.

Pro-Life Virginia: Christian outreach whose purpose is to save unborn babies.

Pro-Life Wisconsin

ProLife Alliance: UK political party that seeks to secure the protection of the law for all human life from the single-cell embryo stage until natural death.

Prolife.org

Raphael's Refuge: Mission is to build a regional monument to the unborn and to provide counseling for the parents and others involved.

Republican National Coalition for Life

Roe No More Ministry: Antiabortion group founded by Norma McCorvey, the plaintiff known as Jane Roe in the 1973 case *Roe v. Wade.*

Safe Haven: Right to life organization.

Several Sources Shelter: Prolife approach to preserve the lives of the unborn. Provides shelter for expectant mothers and their children.

Student LifeNet: Coalition of pro-life students; campaigns on issues including abortion, euthanasia, cloning, embryo research, and better welfare provision for pregnant students.

Tennessee Right to Life: United against abortion, infanticide, euthanasia, human cloning, and fetal tissue research.

Texans United for Life

Vital Signs Ministries: Christ-centered pro-life agency; offers a Christian point of view on abortion, infanticide, euthanasia, chastity, and other life issues.

Westside Crisis Pregnancy Center: Provides information for women facing unplanned pregnancies, as well as information on prenatal care, fetal development, sexuality, abortion, domestic violence, and related links.

Wisconsin Right to Life

Yuma Right to Life

Figure 2.1   Pro-Life Web Sites as of April 2004

members and researchers. They are the ones to dig into data and monitor trends. They are often the first to notice a problem and bring it to the public's attention. For example, in the 1960s, it was the U.S. Census Bureau that formally defined poverty for us and devised a method with which we can track its ebb and flow for many decades (Citro & Michael, 1995). This important analytical exercise did much to raise awareness of the poverty problem and gave various interveners a common database on which to base arguments and possible solutions. The CDC has played a similar role in bringing our attention to a range of health problems, including ebola, AIDS, and now obesity, simply by documenting prevalence and tracking trends. The World Bank and international agencies such as WHO, the United Nations Educational, Scientific and Cultural Organization (UNESCO), and the Organisation for Economic Cooperation and Development all track the conditions of populations around the world and highlight important disparities. Many of the private groups conduct or sponsor polls on public opinion that can suggest to other players that an issue seems to have traction on the public agenda.

PUBLIC POLICY THINK TANKS

These privately funded groups play an important role in conducting major studies of social problems and often suggest solutions. They also increase the visibility of an issue, through conferences and roundtables in which the issue is described and debated. They are often instrumental in brokering solutions. Think tanks can be found at universities, as part of a foundation, or in nonprofit organizations. Their studies sometimes are designed only to discover a problem and describe its parameters, and they thus serve really as data assemblers. Sometimes their studies are designed to support a particular ideology, a particular framing of an issue, or a particular solution.

Think tanks are sometimes believed to "have their own agendas." For example, the Heritage Foundation (2005) describes itself as a conservative institution:

> Founded in 1973, The Heritage Foundation is a research and educational institute—a think tank—whose mission is to formulate and promote conservative public policies based on the principles of free enterprise, limited government, individual freedom, traditional American values, and a strong national defense.

At the other end of the spectrum is the more liberal Brookings Institution, which describes itself as follows:

> The Brookings Institution, one of Washington's oldest think tanks, is an independent, nonpartisan organization devoted to research, analysis, and public education with an emphasis on economics, foreign policy, governance, and metropolitan policy.

The goal of Brookings activities is to improve the performance of American institutions and the quality of public policy by using social science to analyze emerging issues and to offer practical approaches to those issues in language aimed at the general public. (Brookings Institution, 2003)

INDIVIDUAL AUTHORS, FILMMAKERS, AND DOCUMENTARIANS

Dry reports seldom capture the public fancy. However, talented authors can write books and articles that have dramatic impacts on the public agenda. Over the years, major changes in public consciousness and interest in a particular social problem have come about from such landmark publications as Rachel Carson's (1962) *Silent Spring*, Ralph Nader's (1965) *Unsafe at Any Speed*, and David Caplovitz's (1963) *The Poor Pay More*. In movies, Michael Moore has proved to be a provocative filmmaker, addressing issues of corporate insensitivity, gun control, and war. Michael Spurlock brought our attention to the role of fast foods in the obesity problem with his documentary *Super-Size Me*. CBS producers were the ones to discover and document in vivid detail the Abu Ghraib scandal, and PBS's *Frontline* has won awards for its coverage of global warming.

POLITICIANS

Quite obviously, politicians are in an ideal position to bring the public's attention to an issue, as when George W. Bush sought to get public support for Social Security reform with a 60-city set of speeches in early 2005. Politicians are also often in a position to do something about particular solutions because of their position (e.g., they happen to be the president) or because of their persuasive abilities and access to media. For example, in the 1970s, it was Senator Daniel Patrick Moynihan who brought Washington's attention to the embarrassingly unimpressive appearance of Pennsylvania Avenue, the nation's capital's "main street." Fortunately, as a powerful senator, Moynihan was able to take action to do something about it (Hodgson, 2000). Moynihan happened to serve on the Senate committee that could appropriate the funds so that changes could be made.

Over the last decade, Senators John McCain and Russ Finegold, aided by many analysts and think tanks, again and again highlighted the problems of the federal campaign financing system. In every Congress, they proposed legislation to deal with it, finally succeeding in 2000.

Politicians can also use their power to produce negative impacts. In the 1950s, Senator Joseph McCarthy had extraordinary influence in raising "the Communist menace in government" on the public agenda (Ewald, 1984). McCarthy's efforts were successful in ruining many careers before the falsity of his charges became clear and he was censured by his colleagues and lost office.

CHARISMATIC INDIVIDUALS

People without official titles can also do much to raise the profile of an issue and get it discussed. Mother Teresa was a dramatic symbol of world poverty, especially in the Asian subcontinent. Martin Luther King, Jr., dramatically symbolized and advocated solutions to racial issues, as do Jesse Jackson and others today. Dave Thomas, founder of Wendy's, was an ardent advocate for foster children (like him) and for reform in foster care systems. Magic Johnson has done much to personalize the HIV/AIDS problem in the United States, and Erin Brockovich has been a positive symbol for those seeking to combat big business's environmental pollution.

Social Marketing and Social Agendas

If social marketers are to have a broader role in addressing and ameliorating social problems, it must be with an understanding of how social problems come into existence and are acted on. In this chapter, we have established several important points.

- Social problems typically have their foundation in some sort of objective realty. This reality can be delineated by careful monitoring and research. It often reveals the influence of broad, sweeping social changes or more immediate incidents. Social marketers can influence scholars and researchers to carry out needed documentation.

- Raw data must become "intelligence" to become the basis for social action. The interpretation of data—in contrast to mere summaries—is influenced by the frames imposed by the interpreter. Social marketing can be used to influence those who can advance an issue to stay on message, speak with a single voice, and push in a consistent direction.

- Interpreted data revealing a social problem do not necessarily lead a society (or some part of it) to seek broad solutions. An identified problem is given high or low priority through a process of agenda building or agenda setting. Social marketers can be instrumental in influencing media gatekeepers and others to "promote" an issue as needing solutions.

- There are three critical agendas on which a social problem can hold high or low status: the media agenda, the pubic agenda, and the policy agenda. The three agendas influence each other in complex ways and inevitably need some level of congruence for a mandate for action to emerge. Social marketers, again, can assist those who seek movement in any of these realms by identifying key target audiences, understanding what motivates them to action, and influencing actions that keep them working synergistically.

- Movement up or down agenda hierarchies can be described in terms of identifiable stages. There are key stages at which a careful evaluation of possible courses of action becomes the key to further action. Social marketers need to understand where in this process their skills are best used and where they have to improve their concepts and tools to be more impactful with key players.

- A range of players participates in various stages of this process and plays different roles, including assembling data, advocating outcomes or approaches, and humanizing the drama. These actors represent social marketers' quarry.

Social marketers can also affect agendas through helping others think through various possible courses of action and making eventual choices. This is because most courses of action will involve influencing various behaviors— *and this is social marketing's forte.* These skills are valuable, whether the issue is one of huge proportions, such as the malaria plague in Africa, or smaller, such as the local bridge club's efforts to do something about neighborhood blight. *It is all about behavior.*

Social marketers have another role to play at a critical stage in the agenda-setting process. Yankelovich (1992) notes that "the public comes to focus on choices that leaders offer without insisting upon alternatives to consider. Often the proffered options are not the best choices and not the only ones." In assessing alternatives, social marketers have a potentially important role to play in helping the players understand what actions are or are not likely to lead to real changes in personal behavior. When social marketers find grounds for optimism, a social issue is likely to advance on various agendas toward eventual action and possible resolution.

Sometimes, applying social marketing directly to the problem provides a breakthrough. The challenge of malaria is a good case in point. For years, international agencies sought to reduce the dramatic impact of malaria worldwide through sanitation programs, through citizen education, and by providing rapid treatment of diagnosed cases to minimize interpersonal transmission. Recent application of social marketing concepts and tools holds promise for dramatic impacts on the malaria problem. In 1998, WHO decided to mount a major effort, called *Roll Back Malaria,* that was in part designed to raise the status of the disease on the public and policy agenda, especially in Africa, where it was facing increased competition from the AIDS pandemic. In its Abuja Declaration, WHO and 90 partners agreed to focus on three strategies: more access to rapid treatment, preventive treatment of pregnant women, and widespread marketing of insecticide-treated mosquito netting. The mosquito netting has proven to be highly effective in reducing overall childhood mortality (14% to 29%) as documented in several studies (WHO, 2002).

The WHO strategy is a combination of upstream and downstream approaches involving government, nongovernmental organizations (NGOs), international agencies, and the private sector. The ultimate goal is to create flourishing private sector markets, which have proven significantly lower in cost in delivering mosquito nets and insecticide, especially in urban areas. Still, upstream efforts by governments are needed to reduce taxes and tariffs, and both governments and NGOs need to employ social marketing approaches to stimulate demand. Government and international subsidies for marketing nets and insecticide in poor rural areas are also contemplated. Further details on the Roll Back Malaria program are available at the program's Web site: http://www.rbm.who.int/cgi-bin/rbm/rbmportal/custom/rbm/home.do.

Notes

1. The perceptive reader will note the spin I put on this by labeling the film "award-winning."

2. There are undoubtedly times when the size of a problem seems too large, too intractable to justify dealing with it. One billion people around the world have no permanent home. Where to begin?

PART II

*Social Problems and the
Role of Social Marketing*

3

The Structure of Social Problems

A key to social marketing is picking a behavior. In populations where health problems are rampant, there is a limited amount that one can do. What should come first? In Central America, waterborne diseases were rampant. As a consequence, children suffered from rampant infections, severe diarrheal episodes, and generally weakened conditions that left them vulnerable to many other health problems.

Where to start? Sanitation seemed like a good focus, but should one build better latrines first, replace decayed water systems, teach people better "bathroom behavior," or get more people out of slums and into facilities with decent plumbing? A project funded by the Academy for Educational Development's Basic Support for Institutionalizing Child Survival project decided to start simple. Pick an "easy" behavior that can have a big impact—hand washing! This was something that did not require great training and was likely to be responsive to intense focus. The resultant campaign emphasized the need for hand washing on two occasions: before meals and after elimination.

A great virtue of the program was that it had a role for the private sector. The simple behavior at issue required soap, and major brand marketers were soon convinced that partnering would help their own sales. Good effects on both profits and health were the pleasing outcomes of the joint venture.

W e have already sketched the potential role for social marketers in influencing key individuals who can move social problems up the three key social agendas: public, media, and political. In the next chapter, we will review the basic concepts and tools of social marketing that can be brought to bear and briefly contrast this approach with others. However, we need to have one more building block in place before proceeding. To this point, we have considered the first three stages of the social change process:

Stage 1: Inattention to the problem

Stage 2: Discovery of the problem

Stage 3: Climbing the agenda

We have explored the nature of social problems and how they might emerge from an extended agenda-setting process. We have also begun to consider possible target audiences who could be influenced by social marketers, particularly those who can influence the agenda-setting process itself. We shall return to these challenges in later chapters.

The next crucial stage of the agenda-setting process is Stage 4: Outlining the choices. This is the point at which analysts and advocates look at the data and consider how the problem might be addressed. From a social marketing standpoint, the key questions need to focus on identifying the specific individuals whose behaviors can move a problem toward solution. The identity of these potential targets will vary by problem, of course, as will the linkages between causal forces and possible desirable outcomes.

Experience has shown that, at this fourth stage, there typically emerge maps of the "problem space" that can be used to guide the construction of alternative interventions. That is, there will be patterns and structures for both problems and solutions that can be overlaid on specific cases.

It is difficult to describe how this process would evolve in the abstract. Thus, in much of the remainder of this chapter, we will focus on a specific, relatively new but crucial social problem, childhood obesity, and seek to understand how a program (or programs) of action and intervention (Stages 5 and 6) might be crafted. This real-life problem has advantages in that it involves a class of problems (health) with which social marketing has long experience. Further, it closely involves a wide range of other players, including the private sector, who have had—and can have—major influences on the problem and on future courses of action. Finally, it is a topic that is already receiving high prominence and is likely to result in a range of initiatives in the next decade from organizations such as the Centers for Disease Control and Prevention and the National Cancer Institute.

Childhood Obesity

As I have said, the emergence of a social problem results from an appreciation of both objective and subjective components. In the formation of the "public judgment" that Yankelovich has described, childhood obesity has gone from a state of "dawning awareness" to where there is "growing urgency." Newspapers, magazines, television newscasts, and TV documentaries are replete with stories on the topic that report statistics, offer tips for addressing the problem, and tell dramatic stories of both victims and successes. Books such as Greg Critser's (2003) *Fat Land: How Americans Became the Fattest People in the World* are being written, and government agencies are setting up institutes and programs to address the problem (von Eschenbach, 2004). Research conferences are being held, and foundations are allocating initial funds to programs of action. Talk shows are bringing experts and overweight individuals on the air to discuss the issue and present personal tales of misery and redemption. In 2004, NBC launched a "reality" program in the United States called *The Biggest Loser*, in which overweight people competed over several weeks to see who could lose the most and win a $250,000 prize.

The private sector has rushed to offer products to help us address the challenge. There are weight loss books by Dr. Phil (McGraw, 2003) and exercise books from Oprah's trainer (Greene, 2002). The Atkins and South Beach diets for a time prompted all manner of marketers to offer new "low carb" products (Agatston, 2003; Atkins, 2001). People are learning that trans-fats are bad, and many products (some of which never contained this "bad fat") are touting their fat-friendly composition.

The obesity problem is not limited to the United States (World Health Organization, 2004), although in many countries, the issue is still at Stage 2, discovery of the problem. It is only in this century that China has come to focus on the problem, predicting that 200 million Chinese will be overweight by 2015 (*Obese Chinese Now*, 2005).

In the United States, we are just beginning to outline choices. This involves figuring out the factors driving the problem and what can be done about them. Questions must be framed, and who has responsibility for action must be determined. Nestle's (2002) trenchant book *Food Politics* and Brownell and Horgen's (2004) book *Food Fight* have attacked both industry and government. This prompted organizations and corporations to rush to the media to claim that the problem is not their fault and that they should not be the focus of any future actions that might be damaging to them (see Center for Consumer Freedom, 2002). A case in point is the US Sugar Council, which has loudly proclaimed that sugar has few calories per teaspoon and is a *natural* ingredient! Individuals that use the product in excessive quantities are the real culprits (Revill & Harris, 2004).

The Facts

Evidence about the extent, trends, and impact of obesity is very troubling. Obesity is defined by comparing weight (in kilograms) to height (in meters) and squaring the result. For adults, this calculation is all that is needed to compute each person's body mass index (BMI). A BMI of 25 or higher means that one is "overweight," and a BMI of 30 or more means that one is "obese." For children, the calculation is first compared with a growth chart, which is different for boys and for girls, to yield an age-related, gender-specific BMI. Children in the 95th percentile or above for their age- and gender-specific BMI are classified as obese.

The trends in the number of children who are overweight in the United States are frightening. The proportion of children who are overweight has been growing at an astonishing rate, especially in the last two decades. As shown in Table 3.1, in the 1960s, overweight levels for children were around 4% to 5%. Today, those rates are 3 to 4 times greater, at 16%.

These data parallel similar increases in overweight for adults. According to the Centers for Disease Control and Prevention (2000), an estimated 64.5% of U.S. adults (age-adjusted) are today overweight or obese, and 30% are obese. This is a 65% increase in just 10 years (see also Mokdad, Bowman, Ford, Vincor, & Kaplan, 2001, and Mokdad et al., 2003).

The trends in childhood overweight are not uniform across segments. Some groups have higher rates than others. As shown in Table 3.2 (see Ogden, Flegal, Carroll, & Johnson, 2002), *one in four* African American teenage girls and Mexican boys are overweight, as are one in five African American boys and Mexican girls (ages 6 through 19 years). Similar patterns across gender and race or ethnic groups are found among adults.

Table 3.1   Percentage of Overweight Children and Adolescents (Selected Years, 1963 Through 2000)

Years	Ages 6-11	Ages 12-19
1963-1970	4	5
1971-1974	4	6
1976-1980	7	5
1988-1994	11	11
1999-2000	16	16

SOURCES: National Center for Health Statistics (2005).

Table 3.2   Percentage of Overweight Children and Adolescents by Sex, Age, Race, and Hispanic Origin (1999-2000)

Category	Boys 6-11	Girls 6-11	Boys 12-19	Girls 12-19
African American (non-Hispanic)	17.0	22.8	18.7	23.6
Mexican	26.5	17.1	24.7	19.6
White (non-Hispanic)	14.0	13.1	14.6	12.7
All groups	16.9	14.7	16.7	15.4

SOURCES: National Center for Health Statistics (2004). http://www.cdc.gov/nchs/data/hus/hus04trend.pdf#070

The consequences of childhood overweight are dramatic. First of all, there are serious physical consequences, the most important of which are increased levels of Type II diabetes, sleep apnea, asthma, and hypertension. Very recently, there was virtually no Type II diabetes among children and adolescents. Indeed, it was once known informally as "adult-onset" diabetes. Diabetes, in turn, is associated with higher risk for heart attacks and stroke. The list of other complications of overweight over one's lifetime is long (Stunkard & Wadden, 1993) and includes orthopedic and skin problems and poor female reproductive health (such as menstrual irregularities, infertility, and irregular ovulation).

Perhaps more ominous is the fact that an overweight adolescent has a 70% chance of becoming an overweight or obese adult, a probability that increases to 80% if at least one parent is overweight. If overweight persists into adulthood, there are serious risks of cardiovascular disease and stroke, high blood pressure, diabetes, gallstones, gout, some types of cancer (such as endometrial, breast, prostate, and colon cancers), bladder control problems, and complications during pregnancy.

For many, perhaps the substantial majority of overweight children and teens, a more immediate cost not appearing in the clinical data is significant social discrimination. Peers—especially at that age level—can be cruel. Psychological disorders, such as depression, eating problems, distorted body image, and low self-esteem, are common among overweight children. Richard Atkinson of the American Obesity Foundation says that "obesity is the last bastion of socially acceptable bigotry" (Perl, 2003, p. 8). Research finds that overweight children are more likely to be rejected by high-ranking colleges and, once enrolled, have a harder time getting into top medical schools

(Perl, 2003). When they become adults, obese individuals will find themselves discriminated against as they try to climb the corporate ladder (Huddleston & Perlowski, 2003).

DISSENTING VOICES

Data on the impact of the problem are complex and difficult to reduce to simple numbers. For example, in describing the burden of poor nutrition and physical inactivity, the Centers for Disease Control and Prevention's National Center for Chronic Disease Prevention and Health Promotion estimated in 2004 that "poor diet and physical inactivity cause 310,000 to 580,000 deaths per year and are major contributors to disabilities that result from diabetes, osteoporosis, obesity, and stroke." Although the exact impact is hard to measure, Julie Gerberding, head of the CDC, argues that overweight is, undeniably, a significant health problem and likely to get worse. Indeed, some are predicting that overweight will very quickly become our *number one* source of preventable deaths and diseases (Mercury News Wire Services, 2004).

On the other hand, writer Paul Campos argues in *The Obesity Myth* that the problem is overblown and we should not worry obsessively about being overweight or even somewhat obese (Campos, 2004). Campos argues that the definition of obesity is arbitrary and that there is no clear, indisputable effect of obesity on mortality until one reaches very high levels (in contrast to the case of tobacco, in which the evidence was unassailable). He also claims that there is evidence that those who are mildly obese may, in fact, live longer. People who are somewhat obese but exercise are as healthy as those who are thin but do not exercise.

REFRAMING THE ISSUE

As I have noted, data are not enough to move an issue to the stage at which one outlines choices for action. At some point, there must be intervention by a prominent figure, the mounting of a crusade by some nonprofit organization, or a series of magazine pieces or a dramatic TV segment to give an issue traction. In the case of many public health problems, a key figure is often the surgeon general. In the case of smoking, a landmark step was the January 11, 1964, release of the *Report of the Surgeon General's Advisory Committee on Smoking and Health*. This report resulted, for the first time, in a major government agency and a prominent health authority stating flat out that smoking causes cancer—a claim that the tobacco industry had denied for years. In the case of childhood overweight and obesity, a similar role is being played by Surgeon General David Satcher. In December 2001, Dr. Satcher issued a call to action that stated, in part:

Left unabated, overweight and obesity may soon cause as much preventable disease and death as cigarette smoking. . . . While we have made dramatic progress over the last few decades in achieving so many of our health goals, the statistics on overweight and obesity have steadily headed in the wrong direction. If the situation is not reversed, it could wipe out the gains we have made in such areas as heart disease, diabetes, several forms of cancer and other chronic health problems. Unfortunately, excessive weight for height is a risk factor for all of these conditions. . . . Many people believe that dealing with overweight and obesity is strictly a personal responsibility. To some degree they are right, but it is also a community responsibility. (U.S. Department of Health and Human Service [USDHHS], 2001b, p. xiii)

He was supported in this call to action by then secretary of health and human services Tommy G. Thompson, who said,

Overweight and obesity are among the most important of these new health challenges. Our modern environment has allowed these conditions to increase at alarming rates and become highly pressing health problems for our Nation. At the same time, by confronting these conditions, we have tremendous opportunities to prevent the unnecessary disease and disability that they portend for our future. (USDHHS, 2001b, p. xi)

These statements reflected a major *reframing* of the issue. Until these statements were made, overweight and obesity were too often seen as a personal behavioral problem. Early in the 21st century, the language shifted to calling obesity a "disease" and the rapid rise in rates of obesity as an "epidemic." This reframing took the problem out of the realm of personal "weakness" and idiosyncrasy and associated the issue with other medical problems that deserved maximal attention from physicians, health officials, and community leaders. This repositioning paves the way for changes in physician behavior and, perhaps more important, for potential changes in insurance coverage. Under Dr. Satcher's call for action, childhood obesity is likely to receive a higher sense of priority than adult obesity, in part because of society's sense that it holds responsibility for youthful development. Although adult obesity can be still be seen by many as a matter of personal choice and not society's problem, this cannot said of overweight in children.

Developing Causal Linkages

In Stage 4 of the social change process, a principal challenge in outlining the choices is to understand causation and possible intervention sites. What are the immediate precipitants, and what are background factors that are precursors or contributors to the problem? In the case of overweight, there is general agreement that the immediate causes are threefold: too many calories, too little physical activity, and genetic factors. However, the determinants of the first two conditions, overeating and lack of physical activity, are not as clear. We know that childhood overweight is associated with socioeconomic status, race, and region. We also know that rates are higher in urban areas and for children in low income households and in smaller families. Further, there are suggestions that overweight in children is associated with increased sedentary activity, such as watching television and playing computer games. These factors can reinforce each other. Sedentary lifestyles may be taken up in part because overweight children are ostracized and less often participate in athletic activities. Data about food consumption also do not offer clear causal factors. American children undoubtedly eat more, but they also actually eat less dietary fat and saturated fats today than in the past (Gidding et al., 1996).

The relative contribution of poor nutrition and lack of exercise may vary by racial and ethnic group. Data from the Behavioral Risk Factor Survey indicate that, despite higher overweight rates for African American and Hispanic adolescents, these groups were more likely to attend physical education classes. On the other hand, the same study indicated that both groups were significantly more likely to report no vigorous or moderate physical activity, which may be associated with more television viewing. Thirty-one percent of whites watched 3 or more hours of television per day. For African Americans, the figure was more than double that (68.9%); for Hispanics, it was 47.8% (Barlow & Dietz, 1998; Strauss & Knight, 1999).

Modern lifestyles are also seen as part of a cultural pattern that contributes significantly to the problem. The *Washington Post* magazine portrayed the problem this way:

> As a nation, our modern lifestyle has made us fat. We have the most bountiful food supply, the most powerful food-marketing machine and the most advanced labor-saving technology in human history. We are, as a people, consuming more and ever-larger portions of high calorie restaurant meals and high-fat "convenience" foods, while also becoming increasingly sedentary. As a result, Americans in the last two decades have become virtually the fattest people on earth, exceeded only by some South Pacific islanders. (quoted in Perl, 2003, pp. 9-10)

Setting Out the Options

As those involved sort their way through the data, it is not uncommon as a stopgap measure for authority figures to set out a series of commonsense actions that would seem to have the potential to have a major impact on the problem. In the case of overweight and obesity, the surgeon general has suggested a series of steps to be taken in three areas, as outlined in Figure 3.1.

1. Communication: The Nation must take an informed, sensitive approach to communicate with and educate the American people about health issues related to overweight and obesity. Everyone must work together to:
   - Change the perception of overweight and obesity at all ages. The primary concern should be one of health and not appearance.
   - Educate all expectant parents about the many benefits of breastfeeding.
     a. Breastfed infants may be less likely to become overweight as they grow older.
     b. Mothers who breastfeed may return to pre-pregnancy weight more quickly.

   - Educate health care providers and health profession students in the prevention and treatment of overweight and obesity across the lifespan.
   - Provide culturally appropriate education in schools and communities about healthy eating habits and regular physical activity, based on the Dietary Guidelines for Americans, for people of all ages. Emphasize the consumer's role in making wise food and physical activity choices.

2. Action: The Nation must take action to assist Americans in balancing healthful eating with regular physical activity. Individuals and groups across all settings must work in concert to:
   - Ensure daily, quality physical education in all school grades. Such education can develop the knowledge, attitudes, skills, behaviors, and confidence needed to be physically active for life.
   - Reduce time spent watching television and in other similar sedentary behaviors.
   - Build physical activity into regular routines and playtime for children and their families. Ensure that adults get at least 30 minutes of moderate physical activity on most days of the week. Children should aim for at least 60 minutes.
   - Create more opportunities for physical activity at worksites. Encourage all employers to make facilities and opportunities available for physical activity for all employees.
   - Make community facilities available and accessible for physical activity for all people, including the elderly.
   - Promote healthier food choices, including at least 5 servings of fruits and vegetables each day, and reasonable portion sizes at home, in schools, at worksites, and in communities.
   - Ensure that schools provide healthful foods and beverages on school campuses and at school events by:
     o Enforcing existing U.S. Department of Agriculture regulations that prohibit serving foods of minimal nutritional value during mealtimes in school food service areas, including in vending machines.
     o Adopting policies specifying that all foods and beverages available at school contribute toward eating patterns that are consistent with the Dietary Guidelines for Americans.
     o Providing more food options that are low in fat, calories, and added sugars such as fruits, vegetables, whole grains, and low-fat or nonfat dairy foods.
     o Reducing access to foods high in fat, calories, and added sugars and to excessive portion sizes.

   - Create mechanisms for appropriate reimbursement for the prevention and treatment of overweight and obesity.

(Figure 3.1 Continued)

3. Research and Evaluation. The Nation must invest in research that improves our understanding of the causes, prevention, and treatment of overweight and obesity. A concerted effort should be made to:
- Increase research on behavioral and environmental causes of overweight and obesity.
- Increase research and evaluation on prevention and treatment interventions for overweight and obesity and develop and disseminate best practice guidelines.
- Increase research on disparities in the prevalence of overweight and obesity among racial and ethnic, gender, socioeconomic, and age groups and use this research to identify effective and culturally appropriate interventions.

Figure 3.1   Surgeon General's Recommendations for Combating Overweight and Obesity

SOURCE: U.S. Department of Health and Human Services (2001b), pp. 33-35.

The Surgeon General's outline contains a mix of goals and sensible courses of action, with a heavy emphasis on education. What is important from the standpoint of social marketing is that it implicitly identifies a range of individuals (potential target audiences) who must take action if there is to be progress in fighting childhood obesity. These individuals are both upstream and down. A partial list includes

1. Overweight children

2. Their parents

3. Their siblings

4. Peers

5. School administrators, cafeteria managers, and teachers

6. Health-care workers

7. Physical activity workers (coaches, Scout, Girl Guide, and 4-H Club leaders)

8. Editors and reporters in the print, television, and Internet worlds

9. Television programmers

10. Leaders of nonprofit organizations that work with children

11. Social service workers

12. Restaurant managers

13. Fast food industry leaders

14. Food manufacturers and processors

15. Leaders of weight reduction programs

16. Community planners

17. Legislators

18. Regulators (e.g., Federal Trade Commission, Food and Drug Administration)

Of course, the ultimate goal will be to have overweight children exercise more and eat fewer calories and achieve what the National Cancer Institute calls a better "energy balance." How will this happen? Obviously, a starting point is with the children themselves or with their caregivers. One way of thinking about this is to ask what is necessary for the individual to act and then ask what needs to be put in place for this to happen.

UPSTREAM VERSUS DOWNSTREAM SOLUTIONS

Should one attack the basic problem "upstream" or "downstream"—or with some combination of the two? Larry Wallack argues for the upstream option. He believes that in the past, too many government and nonprofit social change programs focused on the downstream individuals who are carrying out "bad" behaviors (Wallack et al., 1993). Such programs might include many of the antidrug campaigns of the Partnership for a Drug Free America and the Office of National Drug Control Policy, as well as other campaigns that concern seat belt usage and teen pregnancy. However, it is clear that the original objectives of Partnership leaders were to address both downstream and upstream audiences:

> The goal entailed getting commitments for nearly $500 million of free air and space from the media. "Unselling drugs" is complex. It involves many target groups, with very different types of messages needed to reach each (users, potential users, those who influence the behavior of users or potential users, etc.). In order to be effective, the "denormalization of drugs" campaign would consist of multiple messages delivered at many levels over long periods of time. (Backer & Rogers, 1993, pp. 13-14)

This kind of dual focus is obviously needed with respect to overweight and obesity in children. Supporters of upstream alternatives would say that it is futile to focus on the overweight children themselves, because they are the victims of practices by various upstream actors. In addition, downstream approaches should be avoided because these would implicitly blame overweight people as self-indulgent, lazy, lacking in motivation and ambition, and using food as a cowardly way to protect a fragile self-image and compensate for other things missing in their lives. The upstream advocates would say that the problem is with a food industry that promotes extremely high-fat products, such as fried chicken "nuggets" (which appear to be mostly breading), at very low prices ("12 pieces for $1.99") or that promotes "super-sized" fries and soft drinks without raising prices proportionately (so they seem like a great bargain). Other culprits would include school systems that enter exclusive contracts with soft drink companies and promote their sugar-filled products aggressively on school property while preventing the offering of healthier snacks or beverages.

One argument against a purely downstream approach is that it is unfair to expect the individual to act, even if he or she is motivated, because *barriers* in the environment external to the individual make it difficult or impossible to act. We learned this in the 1980s in efforts get women in Asia and Africa to use oral rehydration therapy to prevent children from dying of diarrhea. We found that these efforts were often greatly handicapped by the absence of sanitary water supplies and sanitary containers. Mothers could be trained to mix the oral rehydration solution properly, but they were often stymied by the absence of clean water and supplies—factors outside their control. It was unfair to blame the mothers for not adopting the recommended behavior.

The situation may be similar in the case of childhood obesity. For children in poor families, there is no such thing as a healthful meal prepared at home, because all adults are working and often working multiple jobs. The children's major food sources will be school lunch programs and food they can obtain or prepare themselves. In the latter case, they may simply lack the skills to prepare healthful meals or the ingredients to do so. It is, again, unfair to blame them for inaction.

They may also not get much exercise because their schools lack the funds or the staff to provide exercise activity in class or after school. Their schoolyard may be concrete and tiny and overrun with other kids doing other things. They cannot walk to school because the streets where they might go are unsafe and their caregivers cannot chaperone them. Even where it might be possible to walk to school, working caregivers must rely on the school bus system to take over the burden of getting the kids to and from school on time—and safely.

At home, their neighborhood may offer little help. The Boys & Girls Clubs or YMCA may be too far away and require transportation. The nearest park may also be far away. The streets are typically too high risk during most of the day and too badly lit at night to be used when the traffic dies down. There are not likely to be any safe bicycle paths so the kids can get around on their own. Good behaviors may not take place because they realistically *cannot* take place.

Structuring and Framing the Options

To develop a comprehensive approach to any social problem, it is essential at some point to develop a framework that describes the structure of that problem. Such a framework should not only identify causative factors but also indicate leverage points where those seeking to intervene can begin to take action. Fortunately, in the area of exercise and nutrition, such a framework has already been developed. In the late 1990s, a group called the Partnership to Promote Healthy Eating and Active Living was formed with participants from the government, industry, the academy, foundations, and various advocacy and health groups.[1] Through a series of workshops, interviews, and literature searches, three working groups developed a range of background materials. One group focused on individual factors that lead to overweight and obesity, one focused on environmental and social factors, and one reviewed lessons from the past that could be relevant to addressing the obesity challenge. Their findings and general framework were then published in a special supplement of *Nutrition Reviews* (Partnership to Promote Healthy Eating and Active Living, 2001).

As in the cases of other social change issues, an important early challenge was how to *frame* the problem. The Partnership taskforce decided *not* to focus on overweight and obesity per se. Instead, they set out their mission as "[the promotion of] *healthy eating and physical activity lifestyle behaviors* through a public/private partnership grounded on consumer understanding" (Partnership to Promote Healthy Eating and Active Living, 2004a). Other organizations have sought to frame the issue slightly differently. For example, the National Cancer Institute (n.d.) in the National Institutes of Health is focusing on "energy balance" as an approach to reducing the country's cancer burden due to overweight and obesity.

In the particular area of nutrition, some have framed the desired behavior as *healthful eating,* not weight loss. Advocates tend not to talk about dieting. They do not use language that would imply that individuals should strive for some particular desirable image or optimum behavior. The objective is simply to get individuals *moving* toward improved eating patterns. (This is consistent with sound social marketing in that it focuses precisely on the next desired behavior rather than having individuals develop grand strategies to achieve some long-term goal—although the latter may be motivating for some.)

The language involving physical activity is similarly framed by many groups in terms of *becoming more active*—having a healthy lifestyle rather than engaging in exercise. Organizations such as the Centers for Disease Control and Prevention have avoided using the term *exercise,* as this term is sometimes an impediment to getting individual action. Many overweight people equate "exercise" with gyms and sweating and wearing revealing gym clothing. They often see going to the fitness club as a yuppy affectation and something that would be costly and time-consuming. For many, talk of exercise is perceived as a recommendation that they undertake "a workout." Unfortunately, this perception is implicitly reinforced in the *Healthy People 2010* guidelines for physical activity, which still refer to "exercise" and set as a goal 20 minutes of exercise three times per week.

ESTABLISHING LINKAGES

In their effort to document possible linkages to undesirable behaviors, the Partnership taskforce began by understanding the social changes that have taken place over the last 20 years in America that have promoted unhealthy activity and eating patterns among all adults and children. Among those identified were the following:

• Technological advances that replace human exertion by automatic systems in the human and the job environment. Householders need not do the dishes when they have an automatic dishwasher; need not push a vacuum when they have a RoboVac; need not go to the bookstore or library, shop, bank, or broker's when they can do online everything they would do at these places. In workplaces in developed countries, factory workers no longer do heavy lifting, because such occupations have been exported to the developing world or are being carried out by robots.

• Cars, escalators, and moving sidewalks in malls and airports all reduce the need for walking. Stairs need not be taken when mechanized alternatives are available.[2]

• Schools limit field trips and out-of-school play and sports because they have smaller budgets for facilities and because they are increasingly worried about safety. Parents drive their children to school—even a few blocks—out of the same safety concerns. Budget cuts and pressures for better academic performance have also led to fewer physical education classes and less funding of teams.

• There are more multiearning families and single-parent households, which means family meals are less often eaten together. Busy schedules mean that an increasing proportion of meals are eaten away from home.

• As we have noted, food manufacturers have become more and more effective at producing highly palatable food products with high-fat and -calorie contents and made these products easier to acquire in convenience stores, from vending machines, at check-out counters, and on the menus of fast food chains.

UPSTREAM AND DOWNSTREAM LINKAGES

To structure all of the many influences on overweight and obesity, the first two working groups of the Partnership to Promote Healthy Eating and Active

Living were divided along the lines of the upstream-downstream dichotomy that has framed our discussion to this point. Their challenges were as follows:

> Working Group 1 (downstream): Evaluate how and why individuals make food and physical activity choices and identify the underlying factors that affect these choices.

> Working Group 2 (upstream): Determine how and why environmental and societal factors affect food and physical activity choices.

A major work product of these two groups was a highly complex framework mapping the influences and leverage points where future interventions might be introduced to affect individual behavior. This framework is summarized in Table 3.3.

DOWNSTREAM FACTORS: INTERNAL DETERMINANTS

The left column of Table 3.3 represents the output of Working Group 1, the group concerned with the individual or downstream factors. The first set of factors in the framework includes factors that, in the group's view, constitute the overweight individual's "psychobiological core." These include individual genetic makeup, current physiological status (age, state of health, etc.), self-identity, and predominant needs. These factors are "central to the being of the individual," although (except for genetics) they can shift slowly over the course of the individual's life. This conception of the psychobiological core reflects the fact that eating and exercise behavior are influenced by both what the individual's psyche wants and what his or her physiology seeks and, in the case of exercise, permits. Clearly, as a child becomes more overweight, food needs and preferences will change, exercise possibilities diminish, the person's self-identity changes, and his or her needs become reprioritized.

The second set of factors contains additional internal states that reflect the individual's values and experiences. These are more susceptible to external influence than is the psychobiological core. This second set includes the individual's habits, ethnic identities, beliefs, values, and life experiences. Ethnic identities and values encapsulate norms learned from one's culture and guide what one thinks is appropriate eating and exercise behavior—as well what interventions will be attended to. Hindus, Asian Americans, and American Indians will have different notions about food choices, about how (or if) one ought to exercise, and who ought to be listened to about behavioral changes. Life experiences play a role in teaching individuals what they like and do not like, who they are, and what constitutes their culture. For example, many white teen girls learn that thinness is an important virtue (which may, in the extreme, lead to anorexic and bulimic behaviors); conversely, African

Table 3.3   Framework for Determinants of Physical Activity and Eating Behavior

Downstream Factors—Internal Determinants	Upstream Factors—External Determinants
1. The psychobiological core	1. Behavioral settings
a. Genetics	a. Family
b. Physiology	b. Neighborhood
c. Hierarchy of needs	c. Day care
d. Self-identities	d. Local school
e. Pleasure	e. Food stores
2. Values and experiences	f. Shopping malls
a. Life experience	g. Health club
b. Habits	h. Workplace
c. Ethnic identities	i. Community centers
d. Beliefs	j. Restaurants
e. Values	k. NGOs
3. Relationship to other groups	l. Parks, recreation centers, senior centers
a. Socioeconomic status	m. Transportation methods
b. Educational attainment	2. Proximal leverage points
c. Life stage	a. Family
d. Social roles	b. Food stores
e. Interpersonal relationships	c. Local government
4. Behavioral enablers	d. Developers
a. Knowledge	e. Property owners
b. Sources of information	f. Restaurants, food outlets
c. Convenience	g. Recreation facilities
d. Accessibility	h. NGOs
e. Cost	i. Nonprofit providers
f. Time	j. Community
g. Safety	k. Shopping malls

Downstream Factors—Internal Determinants	Upstream Factors—External Determinants
h. Situation	l. Health-care providers
i. Physical	m. School board and districts
ii. Social	n. Employers
i. Seasonality	3. Distal leverage points
j. Social Trends	a. Political advocacy and lobbying
	b. Food industry
	c. Transportation system
	d. Architecture and building codes
	e. Physical activity and sports industry
	f. Recreation industry
	g. Health-care industry
	h. Education system
	i. Entertainment industry
	j. Labor-saving device industry
	k. Information industry
	l. Government

American girls learn that larger body size means one is healthy and beautiful (Ofosu, Lafreniere, & Senn, 1998). Of course, food preferences and the symbolism of various foods are often highly laden with cultural meanings; arugula and turnip greens are two vegetables that have very different meanings and roles in upper class white households and lower class African American households. Beliefs and habits are included in this ring because they can be considered the residue of life experiences and cultural norms and values.

The group of internal downstream factors comprises dimensions of the individual's relationship to other groups and society generally. These include one's socioeconomic status and educational attainment, social roles (work, family, and community), interpersonal networks, and life stage. *Life stage* reflects the fact that over one's lifetime, one passes through a number of transitions, such as graduation, marriage, divorce, death of a spouse, and so on that can have an important impact on changing one's values, social connections, and even eating and activity behavior (Andreasen, 1994).

The set of internal factors in the framework produced by Working Group 1 encloses a set of factors called behavioral enablers, some of which are highly susceptible to intervention by those seeking downstream behavior changes. Social trends, seasonality, and contextual or situational factors are three enablers that may be taken as "givens." However, the individual's knowledge, sources of information, time commitments, and accessibility to (and the convenience and cost of) eating and exercise options can also be influenced from "outside."

Altogether, for simplification, Working Group 1 summarizes the downstream factors as composing *the individual's lifestyle.*

UPSTREAM FACTORS: EXTERNAL DETERMINANTS

The output of Working Group 2 is shown in the set of factors in the second column of Table 3.3: those that consist of the contextual, environmental, societal, and policy variables that can affect individual lifestyles. These are what we would describe as upstream factors, in that involving them in a campaign requires first influencing other players in the individual's environment. The group divided these into three categories: *behavioral settings,* where people "live their lives"; *proximal* (primary) *leverage points,* which control behavioral environments; and *distal* (secondary) *leverage points,* which may have a more indirect effect on lifestyles. Working Group 2 includes several external settings as both proximal and distal influencers.

Behavioral settings consist of those places where one engages in eating or shopping or where one engages in physical activity. This set is relatively predictable and includes the home, food stores, restaurants, health clubs, workplaces, schools, religious institutions, parks, community activity centers and programs, malls, neighborhoods, health-care institutions, and day care centers. The next set of proximal factors consists of individuals and institutions that can affect these behavioral settings. They include the management and staffs in many of the behavioral settings (workplaces, schools, food stores, malls, etc.), as well as local governments and, most important, family members.

Distal factors, in turn, contain institutions, structures, and potential influencers more conceptually distant but which nevertheless can, often over time, have an impact on the behavioral settings. These include

- Policy advocacy and lobbying groups
- The food industry
- Transportation systems
- Architecture and building codes
- The exercise, physical activity, and sports industries
- The recreation industry

- The health-care industry
- The education system
- The entertainment industry
- The labor-saving device industry
- The information industry
- Government

A SOCIAL MARKETER'S CRITIQUE

The Partnership to Promote Healthy Eating and Active Living's framework is certainly comprehensive in marshalling the diverse internal and external influences on behavioral choice. Its emphasis on individual physical activity and nutritional choices and behaviors is also consistent with social marketing conceptual frameworks. There are, however, several ways in which I believe the model can be improved and made more adaptable to approaches that social marketers might use.

First, there is some confusion in the outputs of Working Group 2 between *institutions* that can be proximal or distal influences and *people* who can be influential. For example, "recreational facilities" do not take actions, but park designers, park managers, city budget directors, and so forth do take actions. "Education systems" are not sources of influence, but teachers, school architects, superintendents, and cafeteria managers are.

Second, there is no attention to *competition*. Certainly the concept of competition is implicit when the two working groups emphasize the need to influence lifestyle choices. There are obviously good and bad choices of eating and activity behaviors. However, there is also competition that might encourage target audiences not to pay any attention to the issue at all. This set would include a wide array of books, products, and Web sites that tout their ability to take weight off with no effort whatsoever. Consider an item that popped up on my computer screen while I was browsing for information for this book (see box).

Suppose we told you that you could lose up to 82% of the unwanted body fat and keep it off forever in just a few months, would you be interested? We certainly hope so.

Have you tried just about every fad diet out there—but nothing seems to work! Then, donet [*sic*] miss this important message!

We invite you to experience the most advanced weight loss product available—C hgh oral spray! We guarantee you to lose weight quickly, safely and keep it off for good forever!

(Continued)

(Continued)

As seen on NBC, CBS, and CNN, and even Oprah, Hgh actually helps to reduce your body fat percentage up to 82% without dieting or exercise! This amazing discovery has even been reported in the *New England Journal of Medicine.*

To check out our REAL life testimonials WORLDWIDE & take advantage of our limited time special offer visit our web site at www .hghr.info

We are the manufacturer & we deliver directly to you! We guarantee you the best quality and lowest price.

Should overweight children or their caregivers see such an ad, it is not difficult to imagine them saying one of two things. First, they could convince themselves that they may not need to worry about the obesity problem because some day they (or their child) will just be able to take a pill and the problem will be solved. This kind of rationalization for undesirable behavior is often used by teens as a reason not to worry about taking up smoking or a reason not to quit if the teen already is a smoker. Antismoking strategists worry that the availability of nicotine patches may cause many teens to think that they can always quit later with virtually no long-term health cost. This is what Bolton, Cohen, and Bloom (in press) call someone's "Get-Out-of-Jail-Free" card. In recent laboratory studies, these researchers found a clear relationship between the availability of such an option and risky behavior.

A third omission is the lack of a distinction between choices that lead to improved activity and eating patterns and choices that lead to *maintaining* those patterns. An excessive emphasis on getting started on a new lifestyle ignores the challenges of reinforcing and shaping the new behavior after it is first adopted. Again, in smoking, interventionists are well aware that getting someone to stop is only part of the battle, given high recidivism rates. The availability of nicotine patches has improved quit rates; without patches, success rates are under 5%. Patches double this, and with other methods, the rate can rise further—but it is still well below 50% (Sajna, 1996).

Finally—and most important—the framework lacks an intervention orientation. It does not outline directly the possible influence points and general mechanisms of influence through which change can operate.

Program Options

The framework in Table 3.3 is simply one way to map a social problem, in this case, obesity. Its principal value is that it identifies both factors internal to the downstream target's psyche and factors that are in the hands of individuals who are in various upstream roles. There are several roles the latter can play. One is to bring about *structural changes that make behavior change unneces-sary.* A past example of this is the design of automatic automobile seatbelts that engage as soon as the ignition is turned on without the individual having to do anything. The approach implicitly assumed that drivers would not act to buckle up on their own and so the system needed to be changed to bring about the desired outcome. Another example is incorporating iodine into salt because people were not getting enough on their own. The second approach is exemplified by regulations prohibiting smoking in public and workplace locations. These structural changes were motivated, in part, by the belief that making it more and more difficult to smoke will get people (reluctantly) to quit.

In the area of nutrition, a similar approach would be to require that school lunches be made up of only healthful foods, with strict portion limits. (However, it takes little imagination to see how an enterprising child would circumvent this strategy.) A more radical strategy for the general population would be to impose regulations on fast food chains that prohibited them from selling certain products (e.g., super-sized portions) to obviously overweight people (not unlike penalties for bartenders who give drinks to obviously inebriated patrons).

A second set of structural changes would be ones that *penalized undesirable behavior.* A structural change to discourage overeating would be a "fat tax" on undesirable foods that would have the same demarketing effect as cigarette taxes on smoking (if obesity costs the country billions of dollars, shouldn't those eating fattening products help defray the cost through taxes?) (*Government unit "urges fat tax,"* 2004).

In the area of exercise, the government could penalize schools that did not provide adequate exercise options for overweight children by cutting specific funding if they failed to do so. An incentive-based alternative to this would be to make the size of school budget allocations partly contingent on a school district's weight loss achievements for their overweight students in the previous academic year (Uhlman, 2003). Systems could be changed so that physical movement is the only way to accomplish some tasks. School parking lots could be closed to students or moved a long walking distance away. Elevators could be restricted to use by the disabled only.

The third approach is to assume that overweight children *want* to lose weight but that one must *remove obstacles* in their way or *provide opportunities* for them to act on their motivations. For example, overweight children know (or can be easily taught to know) what constitutes fattening food and approximately how many calories they ought to be eating each day to lose weight. The food industry currently does not make the former information clear, particularly in fast food chains, so that overweight people can act on their knowledge. Information on food packages or in supermarkets does not focus on calories or fat content; it shouts out "new taste sensation," "new and improved," "be cool, use our product," and so on.

There is no simple way for a child or caregiver to keep track of the calories consumed each day or for each meal or snack. This would be especially daunting when eating out. Suppose, however, that someone invented a scanning device that could read bar codes on products that contained calorie and fat data and, further, suppose that all food manufacturers and all restaurant and fast food outlets were required to have similar bar codes on all their offerings. Motivated people could use the device to keep a cumulative record each day of calories and fat consumed and eventually regulate their intake.

Inventors could help. Suppose we had low-calorie or low-fat foods that really tasted good, as Newman's Own has recently accomplished with trans-fat-free popcorn. Suppose we had electronic games that required physical activity to make them work, such as Metakenkoh (http://www.metakenkoh.com), which requires kids to input data from a pedometer to advance in the game, or EyeToy Play,[3] in which vigorous physical movement is necessary to get a good score? The fourth approach assumes that the child is motivated but will only act if there is widespread *social support* for action.[4] If such support already exists, this could lead to downstream strategies that merely make overweight children aware of the support and encouragement of others. The critical "others" might have to be trained and motivated (upstream) to offer that support. However, the influence of others can be a double-edged sword. They may possibly be sending the wrong signals. It may be that a significant group of "others" is reinforcing unhealthy behavior, motivated perhaps by self-interest. Suppose this group indicates directly or implicitly either that the child is not overweight or that there is nothing wrong with being "a little heavy." David Satcher (2001), the former surgeon general, tells the story of the woman who came to him after a lecture and told him: "It's almost like you're stereotyping when you talk about African Americans and Hispanics having a greater [incidence] of overweight and obesity. It is almost as if people say you're not beautiful when you are overweight or obese" (p. 3).

If cultural norms send an explicit or implicit message that the culture values "bigness," then an overweight child may see no need to change. In the past, groups have said that smoking is cool, that women should not be allowed to vote or to drive cars, and (in the 1700s) that it is OK to own slaves. It can take years and brave advocacy by prominent leaders to bring about needed upstream support.

Social Marketing, Education, and the Law

What is the role of social marketing? Isn't social change possible through other mechanisms, particularly education and the law? If communities need to be mobilized, isn't a powerful education campaign led by charismatic, committed individuals enough to get change moving? If structures need to change, can't we just pass laws or get regulators to be more vigorous in enforcing existing laws?

A useful framework for thinking about the intersection of the various approaches is one adapted by Rothschild (1999) from Petty and Cacioppo (1986) and MacInnis, Moorman, and Jaworski (1991). Rothschild argues that the appropriateness of a particular type of intervention depends on the target audience's *motivation, opportunity,* and *ability to act.* These characteristics determine whether an individual is likely to be *prone, resistant,* or *unable* to behave. Where target audiences—whether downstream individuals or upstream players—are prone to act, *education* can often be the best course of action. Educational initiatives can teach people about benefits and costs of alternatives, acquaint the target audience with the views of significant others (e.g., other spokespeople), list opportunities for action, and, where appropriate, describe skills to give the target audience the self-assurance to act—and keep acting. Education may be sufficient when the target audience has high motivation to act, as in the case of the SIDS educational programs.

At the other extreme, there are many situations in which the downstream or upstream individual does not want to act or defiantly prefers alternatives. In these cases, *the law* may be the best tool—or at least an important adjunct. The law can limit individual alternatives by making them illegal (e.g., smoking restrictions in public places) or by constraining how they may be promoted (e.g., preventing sales of cigarettes to minors). Laws can simply require the preferred behavior (e.g., seatbelt use)—although compliance is another matter. They can increase behavioral opportunities by mandating their availability (e.g., requiring open play space in new residential developments or requiring physical education classes in schools) (see also Seiders & Petty, 2004). Limiting food advertising aimed at children may be particularly valuable. Researchers from the University of Illinois studied food advertising on television programs in 2004 heavily watched by children and concluded the following:

> Convenience/fast foods and sweets comprised 83% of advertised foods. Snacktime eating was depicted more often than breakfast, lunch, and dinner combined. . . . A 2000-calorie diet of foods in the general-audience advertisements would exceed

recommended daily values (RDVs) of total fat, saturated fat, and sodium. A similar diet of foods in the child-audience advertisements would exceed the sodium RDV and provide 171 g (nearly 1 cup) of added sugar. (Harrison & Marske, 2005, p. 1568)

The third set of cases described by Rothschild is ideal for social marketers. In these cases, the challenge is to influence the voluntary behavior of a target audience that is open to change but is reluctant to act, does not see opportunities, or lacks important abilities. I would argue that these are the *vast majority* of cases.

Social marketing, education, and the law, of course, are not mutually exclusive. There are many ways they can work together (Andreasen, 2002). For example, whether the target individual is upstream or down, education could create awareness about the need for change, laws could break down barriers to change, and social marketing approaches could promote the significant benefits and low costs of the behavior, teach skills and build self-confidence, and bring other groups and individuals in to apply social pressure. Social marketing can also fight off any competition for the behavior.

Of course, if serious social change is to happen, there will be roles for all three: education, social marketing, and the law. It would seem self-evident that these approaches ought to be seen—and treated—as complementary. Unfortunately, it seems that too many potential partners see them as competitors and believe one ought to choose one of them as the principal way to proceed. This shortsightedness is often unwittingly encouraged by authors who treat these approaches as somehow antagonistic. This will not be the approach adopted here.

The challenge of influencing legislators and regulators is considered further in chapter 7.

Notes

1. Visit their Web site at http://www.ppheal.org.

2. Indeed, a great many Georgetown University undergraduates routinely take the elevator one or two floors in all of our office and classroom buildings. One too rarely sees them in the stairwells. See also Webb and Eves (2005).

3. EyeToy Play is the name of the disk that accompanies the Sony EyeToy, a computerized camera that works with a television set. To play any of the 12 games on the disk, the player must make a wide variety of arm and leg movements, usually at considerable speed.

4. It may be argued that this is really a downstream approach but one that requires simultaneous upstream action. I would argue that building group pressure is an upstream option, as some (or many) of those who need to act need not be obese or engage in energy-balancing behavior.

4

The Role of Social Marketing

One of the largest social marketing campaigns in recent years has been the youth antidrug campaign of the Office of National Drug Control Policy. The campaign was begun in 1997 as a response to evidence of increasing intentions to use marijuana among youth and lowered perceptions that drug use was a bad thing. The initial request was for a 5-year congressional allocation of just under $1 billion. The campaign proceeded along several fronts, with eight "strategic platforms" for youth and nine for parents. Heavy emphasis was placed on advertising due to a specific congressional mandate, leading many to consider it more of an advertising campaign than a social marketing campaign.

Ads targeting many audiences were prepared by the Partnership for a Drug Free America under the brand "Your Anti-Drug" and placed in paid media rather than relying on the odd placements in which free public service announcements (PSAs) would typically end up. Media ads were backed by extensive Web site development and use.

Much money was invested in tracking systems for the campaign, but managers were disappointed to see a lack of evidence of impact on teen drug use at the end of the 5 years. On the other hand, evidence did exist in other broad-based studies of reduced teen drug receptivity and use, and there was evidence within the campaign that more parents were talking with their kids about drugs.

Despite the lack of observed behavioral impact, much was learned, and Congress refunded the campaign. This time there is to be a specific focus on one drug—marijuana—and on a narrower target, 11- to 14-year-olds (David, 2004; Denniston, 2004).

T o understand in some detail how social marketing can be a powerful tool for addressing the targeting of audiences at various points of the model in Figure 3.3, it is important to appreciate the approach in some detail and to understand where it came from.

History[1]

Social marketing in the 21st century has achieved wide awareness and adoption as an innovative approach to social influence. Although metaphors are often tortured frameworks for understanding historical phenomena, it is useful to think of the growth of social marketing over the past 40-plus years as paralleling the formative years of a person. The field has had its infancy and adolescence, and one could argue that it is just now entering early maturity. As with humans, each of these stages has reflected important conflicts, and the early maturity phase can still be seen as a time during which identity needs to be affirmed and a future career trajectory established (Andreasen, 2002).

THE BIRTH OF THE FIELD

Many marketing historians trace the first suggestions that marketing might be adapted to challenges other than promoting goods and services for the profit of commercial corporations to an article by a sociologist, G. D. Wiebe, in the 1950s (Wiebe, 1951-1952). Wiebe was concerned that marketing was not being applied to such problems as "selling brotherhood like soap." However, this notion did not really obtain traction until the mid- to late 1960s and early 1970s, when the Vietnam War and social unrest caused many sectors of U.S. society to rethink their social obligations. Harvey (1999) posits that social marketing as a field of practice had its origins with the promotion of family planning in India in 1964. This early effort focused on marketing of Nirodh condoms, with the assistance of major private sector marketers such as Unilever and Brooke Bond Tea Company, who did much to secure wide distribution of the new low-cost nonprofit sector product. This venture was soon followed by a number of significant social marketing efforts over the next decade, primarily involving the marketing of family planning products and services in a wide range of countries and with considerable success (Manoff, 1985).

It is not surprising that these first baby steps in social marketing involved relatively simple products and that the principal marketing tools were conventional promotion and distribution. These were challenges that would not seem at all strange or difficult to marketers. The fact that these product introductions met a huge, pent-up market demand (for a while at least) strongly reinforced the belief of social activists that they had discovered a potentially very powerful social force.

This nascent movement did not escape the attention of the academic community (Elliott, 1991). In 1969, Philip Kotler and Sidney Levy first argued that marketers were too narrow in their view of the field. Rather, they asserted:

> Marketing is a pervasive societal activity that goes considerably beyond the selling of toothpaste, soap, and steel. . . . [An] increasing amount of society's work is being performed by organizations other than business firms . . . [and] every organization performs marketing-like activities whether or not they are recognized as such. (p. 10)

This oft-cited article did not sit well with the scholarly establishment at the time. Luck (1969) argued that the "broadening" of marketing was taking the field well beyond where it properly belonged, because marketing obviously only involved *markets,* and this meant buying and selling. Broadening the field, these scholars asserted, would divert attention from critical issues and encroach on other disciplines. Bartels, a marketing historian, later stated that this debate suggested that the field was facing an "identity crisis" and needed to decide whether marketing was defined by its technology (the Kotler-Levy position) or by the class (or classes) of behaviors towards which it was directed (the Luck position) (Bartels, 1974; see also Kotler, 1972).

Because Kotler saw marketing as a technology, he and his colleague Gerald Zaltman (1971) explored what it would mean to apply the technology to social issues, in which case, they suggested, it could be called "social marketing." Thus the new field was given a name for the first time.

This period of initial academic thinking and attempts at definition caused two kinds of confusion that would plague the field for the next two decades. First, it tended to confuse practitioners—both for-profit and nonprofit— about three potentially distinct topics: *nonprofit marketing, social marketing,* and *socially responsible marketing.* Second, the definition that Kotler and Zaltman proposed for social marketing made it common to confuse it with just plain "social advertising," public relations, or, most simply, mere education.

CHILDHOOD

The growth of social marketing, except within the world of family planning, was relatively slow until the mid-1980s. Marketing academics shifted their social focus elsewhere. Their academic research became concerned with what has been called "the dark side" of the marketplace (Hirschman, 1991; Magnuson & Carper, 1968): problems of consumer exploitation, discrimination against disadvantaged consumers (Andreasen, 1975), inadequate market regulation, environmental degradation, and the like (Wish & Gamble, 1971). During this period, collections of essays on social marketing appeared (Fine, 1981, 1990) but tended to conflate the many possible meanings of the term. The first textbook, by Kotler and Roberto, did not appear until 1989.

In my view, practitioners were held back in diversifying their applications by the early association of social marketing with the marketing of (relatively simple, straightforward) products. Indeed, the most common use of the term in the 1970s and 1980s was to refer to "contraceptive social marketing" programs, in which the transaction not only involved products but also happened to involve money payments, albeit very small, by target audience members—a form of transaction that would assuage early critics such as Luck and Bartels. Marketers were venturing out into the wider world, simply doing what they knew best. Unfortunately, this early focus precluded other organizations and agencies from seeing social marketing as applicable if there was not a currency transaction or if no product changed hands.

The limited expansion was, I have argued, also partly attributable to Kotler and Zaltman's (1971) original definition of social marketing. As restated later by Kotler and Roberto (1989), the definition said:

> The term "social marketing" was first introduced in 1971. . . . Since then, the term has come to mean a social influence technology involving the design, implementation, and control of programs aimed at increasing the acceptability of a social idea or practice in one or more groups of target adopters. (p. 24)

This definition made it difficult for those in areas such as health communication, health diffusion, and health education to understand how social marketing was in any important way different from what already concerned them (Hastings & Haywood, 1991, 1994; Hill, 2001).[2] If social marketing had a goal of "increasing the acceptability of a social idea," then how was this different from many programs based on communications and education that were the goals of health educators and communicators?

The Kotler-Zaltman definition also made it hard to distinguish social marketing from "socially responsible marketing," in which the issues were how marketers could change consumer attitudes so that they would treat the environment or minorities better and how commercial marketers could be induced to desist from evil practices. This confusion is evident in Lazer and Kelley's definition of social marketing in a 1973 readings book titled *Social Marketing:*

> Social marketing is concerned with the application of marketing knowledge, concepts, and techniques to enhance social as well as economic ends. *It is also concerned with the analysis of the social consequences of marketing policies, decisions and activities.* (p. ix, emphasis added)

ADOLESCENCE: THE BEHAVIORAL BREAKTHROUGH

After an extended "identity crisis," it might be said that social marketing finally recognized its true nature in the 1990s when a number of leading scholars and practitioners came to the realization that its essence was not changing ideas but *influencing behavior*. A frequently cited version of this new definition is found in my 1994 article in the *Journal of Public Policy & Marketing*:

> Social marketing is the application of commercial marketing technologies to the analysis, planning, execution, and evaluation of programs designed to influence the voluntary behavior of target audiences in order to improve their personal welfare and that of the society of which they are a part. (Andreasen, 1994, p. 110)

This definition helped distinguish the field from its disciplinary competitors—that is, social marketing was not about mere education or attitude change, except to the extent that this would lead to the intended *influence on behavior*. This positioning of behavior as the "bottom line" of social marketing had other benefits. It made it clear that the ultimate criterion of effectiveness is behavioral influence—although, as Hornik has recently reconfirmed, such influence is often extremely hard to detect and attribute to precise causes (Hornik, 2001). In practical contexts, the new definition also allowed various team players to see their roles as contributing in various ways to this ultimate goal—and not fighting each other over which way was best.

On the scholarship side, the focus on behavioral influence directed researchers and thinkers toward more intensive evaluation of various behavior influence theories and models (e.g., Prochaska & DiClemente, 1983) and the creation of testable propositions about them (e.g., Maibach & Cotton, 1995). The evolving behavioral science conceptualizations and research then fed back to practitioners as frameworks within which they could craft and integrate program elements.

A third benefit of the new definition was that it made clear where social marketing stopped and other approaches were more appropriate. As noted in the previous chapter, Rothschild (1999), for example, carefully distinguished marketing as a clear alternative to education and the law. In simple terms, he argues that education may be all one needs in simple social situations where information alone will achieve the desired ends (e.g., putting babies on their backs to prevent SIDS). Alternatively, where consumers are extremely reluctant to act—or reluctant to act if others are allowed to avoid the behavior—then the appropriate intervention is the law. Social marketing covers everything else (Rothschild, 1999).

Fourth, this new definition made clear the intersection between social marketing and "socially responsible marketing." To the extent that, by the latter term, one means *behavior* that is socially responsible, when one is focused on making this behavior happen, this is the proper domain for social marketing. However, if one is merely concerned with documenting abuses or arguing policy, this is not where social marketing is relevant or useful.

The final benefit is that it makes clear how social and commercial marketing are similar and why there ought to be few barriers to adopting virtually all concepts and tools from the commercial sector into social marketing. A moment's reflection will make clear that the ultimate measure of success for *commercial* marketers is the influencing of behavior—sales, repeat patronage, favorable word of mouth, cooperation in joint marketing ventures, and so on. As Sergio Zyman (1999) argues: If you do not "move the needle"—that is, influence behavior—you are not being a good marketer.

EARLY MATURITY

There is considerable evidence that social marketing has now moved beyond adolescence into some kind of early maturity. Consider the following example.

On the Conceptual and Theoretical Side. Several general textbooks have been published (Andreasen, 1995; Donovan & Henley, 2003; Kotler, Roberto, & Lee, 2002), along with several specialized social behavior marketing books (Siegel & Doner, 1998) and workbooks (Weinreich, 1999). Chapters devoted to social marketing are now included in nonprofit marketing textbooks (Andreasen & Kotler, 2003; Sargeant, 1999) and health communications readers (Glanz, Lewis, & Rimer, 1999). A journal entirely devoted to the area, the *Social Marketing Quarterly*, was founded in 1994. There are now several annual social marketing conferences, one of which dates back over a dozen years. One of the first of these conferences produced a frequently cited collection of social marketing papers (Goldberg, Fishbein, & Middlestadt, 1997). Social marketing centers and associations have been established in Scotland, Canada, Australia, and Poland, and social marketing training programs have been held in several parts of the world. The Social Marketing Institute was established in 1999. Several summaries of best practices are now finding their way into the scholarly and practitioner literature (e.g., Alcaly & Bell, 2000). There is now a book devoted to social marketing ethics (Andreasen, 2001).

On the Practice Side. Social marketing approaches have been adopted by a wide range of U.S. federal agencies, most prominently the U.S. Department of Agriculture (5-a-Day program), the Office of National Drug Control Policy, and the Centers for Disease Control and Prevention, as well as state and local governments and a significant number of nonprofit organizations (see examples at http://www.social-marketing.org). The Joint United Nations Programme on HIV/AIDS (UNAIDS) has invoked social marketing as a primary tool in its fight against AIDS, and the World Bank has conducted distance learning sessions using social marketing concepts. Requests for proposals for social influence programs at government agencies and foundations now frequently require social marketing components and evidence of social marketing capabilities.

A number of major consulting organizations, most prominently Porter Novelli, the Academy for Educational Development, and the American Institutes for Research, have emerged as leading social marketing consultants, abetted by a growing number of smaller consultancies, such as Equals3 and the Sutton Group. Major advertising and public relations organizations, such as Fleishman Hillard, Burson Marsteller, Golin/Harris, and Ogilvy Mather now claim specific social marketing capabilities. Senior executives with "social marketing" in their titles have begun to appear. Applications of social marketing have grown significantly beyond North America and the UK, with particularly innovative work going on in Australia and New Zealand (Donovan, 1999; Donovan & Owen, 1994; Stannard & Young, 1998). The social marketing listserver maintained by Georgetown University now has more than 1200 participants.

With the turn of the century,[3] the field has slowly begun to embrace potential roles beyond downstream behaviors, as discussed in earlier chapters. In 2002, Gerard Hastings and Rob Donovan issued a call for social marketers to "embrace a broader perspective that encompasses not just individual behavioral influence, but also the social and physical determinants of that behavior" (p. 4). The rationale for urging attention to "upstream" interventions was becoming obvious. First of all, as noted in this book and in the work of Hastings, Macfayden, and Anderson (2000) and Goldberg (1995), many problematic behaviors are strongly influenced by environmental factors beyond the control of the individuals who exhibit problematic behaviors. Second, elements in the upstream environment often inhibit change even when target audiences are motivated to take action. For example, if sidewalks are not lit, police protection enhanced, or bike paths paved, urban residents may find it very difficult to exercise. If condoms and birth control pills are not available in remote regions of Kazakhstan, women will find it very difficult to practice birth control.

Third, as Smith (2000) argues, changes in structural conditions may make individual behavioral influence unnecessary, either because behavioral problems are avoided (e.g., the cigarette industry is dramatically inhibited) or because problematic behaviors are no longer dangerous (e.g., air bags protect real dummies who neglect to wear seat belts, iodizing salt in the Philippines prevents goiter). A final reason for addressing upstream factors noted by Goldberg, Sandikci, and Litvack (1997) is that social norms and role models can have critical influences both for and against desired behavioral influence, as in the reduction of violence in hockey.

Behavior Change Versus Behavioral Influence

In many settings today, academics and practitioners tend to refer to social marketing as all about "behavior change." In truth, such is probably the focus in the majority of social marketing campaigns around the world. However, it is also clear that many social programs have as their goal the *prevention* of behavior. The Office of National Drug Control Policy wants teens not to use drugs. The American Legacy Foundation wants teens not to smoke. The National Domestic Abuse Hotline seeks to prevent abuse of partners, spouses, children, and the elderly.

I argue here for the adoption of a more generic term—*behavioral influence*—although I recognize that many will continue the earlier locution. At least the focus remains on behavior.

Essential Elements of My Approach

As it has evolved today, social marketing has a number of key elements that I and others have suggested are essential components. Various versions of these principles are available in other sources (Andreasen, 1995; Andreasen & Kotler, 2003), but it is useful to restate them here for those who are new to the field or need a refresher.[4] This information is also critical as a foundation for the chapters that follow.

I argue that there are three principal features in a solid social marketing approach:

- The proper mind-set
- A sensible process for carrying out social marketing campaigns
- A set of concepts and tools that make the process effective

THE PROPER MIND-SET

One of the most important characteristics that distinguish great social marketers from others seeking social influence is their slavish attention to target audiences. This is fundamental wisdom in the private sector. Private sector marketers are painfully aware that it is their target audience members—their customers—who determine their success. Marketers can have great, award-winning advertising campaigns, clever packaging, competitive pricing, and all the other seeming hallmarks of good marketing. If target audience members do not buy their burgers, fly their airlines, or choose their brand of paper towel, however, they are not successful. Managers will not be rewarded, and their firms will not be favored in the investment marketplace.

The same audience-centered mind-set ought to infect all social influence programs, but it often does not. All too often, programs and their sponsors are "organization centered" rather than audience centered (Andreasen, 1982). The principal reason for this is that they *really* believe in the social change they are seeking. They really believe that everyone should recycle, that corporations should stop contributing to global warming, and that people should wear seat belts, exercise more, never smoke, and never take mind-altering drugs. This commitment is admirable, but it too often gets in the way of being an effective change agent.

An organization-centered mind-set unfortunately very often leads campaign planners and managers to think of the target audience as *the enemy*. These planners and managers are convinced that the lack of success of any attempt at behavioral influence is the target audience's fault. Two explanations are typically offered for target audience inaction:

1. *Ignorance.* The target audience simply does not appreciate the many benefits of the action being recommended.

2. *Character flaw.* If the target audience does know of the benefits of the behavior (not smoking, wearing a seat belt, maintaining a better energy balance) but still does not take action, then they must be weak, excessively macho, vain, lazy, selfish, or have some other inherent flaw. This perspective causes the organization-centered campaigner to see recalcitrant overeaters, stubborn lobbyists, distracted media gatekeepers, and selfish parents as "old-fashioned" or "pig-headed," to view politicians as "bought" and public servants as "lazy bureaucrats," and to assume reluctant allies are too fixated on their own agendas.

An organization-centered mind-set has a number of implications for how a campaign tries to bring about individual change:

1. There is a tendency to rely almost exclusively on communications approaches. If the problem with the target audience is assumed to be their ignorance or lack of motivation, then one's challenge is to make the case better. One needs better position papers, cleverer ads, or a new brochure to tell the story more effectively. Scare tactics are invoked to get the target audience to take action or not take an undesirable action. The basic idea is that, if you communicate the right information in the right way, the target audience will do the right thing.

2. An organization-centered perspective also is frequently associated with a simplistic view of the target audience. The audience is "them"—the people standing in the way of success. They are one monolithic group. Diversity among target audience members is largely ignored, or audiences are segmented into simplistic demographic groups—Southerners versus Northerners, African Americans versus Hispanics, city dwellers versus rural inhabitants.

3. Research tends to be downplayed, as the organization-centered person "knows" what the problem is (those pesky target audience members).

4. Competition tends to be ignored. The campaigner is fixated on his or her cause and flogs it relentlessly.

The right mind-set, of course, is audience centered. The target audience member is the one who ultimately determines success. Therefore, the challenge is to understand where this audience member is "coming from" and respond to this learning. Further, an audience-centered social marketer thinks that, if an approach is not successful, it is not the target audience's fault. It is quite probable that the social marketer does not understand the audience well enough to create effective strategies. This usually means reexamining the research, planning, and execution process.

THE SOCIAL MARKETING PROCESS[5]

If one is going to bring about some important change in a target audience member, it is critical that one have a careful process for carrying out one's campaign. The steps for the process are as follows (see also Figure 4.1).

Listening

Because social marketing is fanatically audience centered, it is essential that campaigns begin with a thorough understanding of the target audience they seek to influence. Campaign planners must know "where the audience is coming from"—what do audience members think of the offer implicit in the campaign, what do they see as the benefits and costs, what do their friends think, and do they think they can actually carry out the behavior that is being recommended? Marketers must also know as much as they can about the competition the campaign faces from the target audience's point of view. What are the alternatives, and why are they attractive? Where are their weak points? This

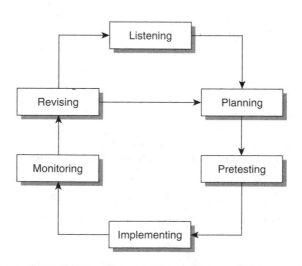

Figure 4.1   The Social Marketing Campaign Process

type of research is often called *formative research*. One of the most common causes of failure in social marketing campaigns is inadequate attention to the "listening" stage (see Andreasen, 2002).

Planning

Next, campaign planners must translate their learnings about the target audience into concrete programs of action. These programs typically will involve crafting an "offer" or exchange that will contain motivating benefits appealing to the target audience, minimize the costs (both monetary and non-monetary) that could inhibit behavior, feature communications that "talk" effectively to target audiences about the offer, and provide a mechanism that will make it feasible and easy for the audience to act. Planning will also entail setting goals, timelines, and responsibilities and making sure that systems are in place and coalitions formed to actually carry the effort out.

Pretesting

Probably the second biggest mistake in campaign planning and implementation is in not pretesting key elements of the plan with the target audience. Planners often think that they have learned enough at the listening stage and are clever enough to translate those insights into an effective program. However, target audiences are the ones who will decide the program's fate and often will *not* have the reactions to program elements that the planners thought they would. A vivid example of this is the campaign of a major U.S. government agency that sought to increase the number of women getting mammograms by telling them about the factors that heighten a woman's risk of getting breast cancer. The campaign planners neglected the pretesting step and were puzzled when the campaign resulted in a *decrease* in the desired behavior. An evaluation study carried out *after* considerable time and funds had been spent revealed that (a) the target women learned the risk factors very well (i.e., the campaign was a great *educational* success) but (b) many women who were intending to get a mammogram passed it up because they did *not* have the risk factors. Unfortunately, the risk factors accounted for only 10% of all breast cancer cases. Clearly, if the campaign managers had only done a few simple pretest interviews using their campaign materials, they would have quickly learned the folly of their approach and saved themselves significant amounts of time, money, and embarrassment.

Implementation

Once adjustments have been made based on the pretest results, the next step is to actually launch the campaign, putting in place all of the four "P"s (product, price, place, and promotion) that marketers in the private sector emphasize. A key requirement here is making sure that control mechanisms are set. Without such controls, campaigns can wander off target, elements get neglected or underused, and goals are missed.

Monitoring

Campaigns never turn out as planned. Competition does not stand still. Target audience members change, often as a result of early elements of the campaign. The environment has a tendency to develop unexpected hurdles, such as budget cuts or a health scare. For these reasons, it is essential that campaigns have a clear tracking system to monitor program performance along most key dimensions. Is the right audience being reached? Are they moving forward and acting as intended? Are they even being reached by the program? How are they responding to various program elements—is the offer understood and valued? Answers to all of these questions provide the critical clues that tell campaign managers what needs to be done in the next step.

Reexamine and Revise

Monitoring data may suggest a return to either the listening or planning stages. The data may show that key target audience member segments are not "getting" the message—they do not see the benefits that the campaign intended them to value. They think the behavior is too costly in some fashion, or they are somewhat interested in the behavior but are just not acting. All of these findings suggest that management has failed to really understand the target audience, and they must go back to "deep" listening if they are to succeed. On the other hand, new listening may not be necessary if the problem is mostly a matter of coordinating campaign elements so they reinforce each other and do not conflict. The problem may be a matter of emphasis; some markets are getting too much attention and other markets too little. In all cases, the campaign managers must remember to continue to *pretest* their new ideas. Once a campaign is well under-way, there is a natural tendency for campaign staff to think that now they really, really know target audience members and "are sure" how they will react. Too many horror stories from the field have convinced me that such an attitude can effectively sabotage an otherwise well planned campaign—one that would have benefited considerably from greater attention to midcampaign program pretesting.

It is important to recognize that I use the term *campaign* here in a very broad sense. It is not restricted to formal campaigns with careful planning documents, lots of meetings, budgets, evaluations, and so on. A campaign can be as simple as one person's efforts to lobby a congressional staff member through a series of visits. It could be a single meeting to induce a potential partner organization to adjust its efforts to reinforce the campaign's own approach. The principles apply whether there is an audience of one or an audience of thousands. It applies if one is addressing people one never meets or a single person one comes face-to-face with. Getting a boss to raise a budget or a staff member to work on a weekend is also a social marketing campaign, just as the multi-million-dollar Office of National Drug Control Policy antidrug effort is a social marketing campaign.

CONCEPTS AND TOOLS

If one is to be fanatically audience centered, then the first step, listening, becomes the key to much of what follows. How does one become an effective listener?

I have written about research methodology at some length elsewhere (Andreasen, 2002). There, I emphasize two points about listening research. First, there are many low-cost and effective approaches to carrying out such research (Andreasen, 1983), which will be comforting to campaign planners with limited budgets. Second, it is critical that the listening research be *useful*. This means (a) making sure that it will lead to specific campaign decisions—specifically, that it is not merely "exploratory" or a fishing expedition, and (b) making sure that it is guided by some conception or framework about how target audiences might go about undertaking the behaviors on which you are focusing.

The last point is especially critical, because, without a framework for inquiry, the campaign manager can only *hope* for insights that will guide proper interventions. In my own work, I make extensive use of three conceptual frameworks, which focus on (a) "Stages of Change," (b) the "BCOS Factors," and (c) Competition.

Stages of Change

The behaviors to be influenced in any social marketing campaign are very likely to be what commercial marketers refer to as "high involvement" (Celsi & Olson, 1988). This means that the audience typically thinks about them a lot, engages in a careful search for information, and often agonizes over the best course of action. It follows that high involvement behaviors do not come about quickly; they evolve over time. One does not go overnight—or even in a few months—from being overweight or obese to being a conscientious dieter and regular exerciser for a lifetime. Villagers in the developing world do not adopt new sanitation practices as the result of a single lecture from a government health worker. Legislators do not change their positions on important issues after a single conversation or a daylong hearing. Teens do not decide never to smoke because of a few classroom slides of diseased lungs.

One of the valuable insights from social science research is that the process of influence in high involvement behaviors over time can be divided into stages. Also, as research by James Prochaska and his colleagues (e.g., Prochaska & DiClemente, 1983) has made clear, campaigns can be made more effective if they tailor interventions to the stages at which target audiences are found. The social marketer's challenge should not always be getting an immediate behavioral response but moving target individuals through the various stages. Each stage has its own specific implications for strategy and tactics.

The number of stages—and their labels—depends on the behavioral influence goal. In the case where one seeks behavior *change,* there are a number of stage model options (see, e.g., Maibach & Cotton, 1995). Many use five stages, as suggested by Prochaska and DiClemente (1983). In my own work, I have adopted a four-stage model that collapses their separate Preparation and Action stages into one for simplicity and mental portability. The stages and their brief implications are as follows.

Precontemplation. At any point in time (especially early in the agenda-setting process), there will be a great many members of a target audience who are not thinking at all about the behavior in which the social marketer is interested. This may mean they have never heard about the desirability of the behavior (e.g., they do not know there is a vaccine for a particular disease that is sickening and killing their neighbors). In other cases, they may have heard about the behavior but have concluded that they are not interested. This may be because there are social pressures strongly opposing the behavior, including religious or cultural proscriptions. They may think it is just not appropriate for someone like them (e.g., it is a "Western idea" in an Eastern culture). Then again, they may simply be comfortable in their present behavior (e.g., sticking to their usual diet and exercise routine).

Contemplation. This, of course, is where most marketing is done, and it is where most marketers expect to encounter the target audience. It is the stage at which the target audience is thinking about the behavior. Audience members are weighing the costs and benefits in the exchange, considering what others who are important do or do not want them to do, and forming a sense of whether they can actually carry out the behavior. I make a distinction between Early and Late Contemplation:

- *Early Contemplation.* At this point, the target audience is just beginning to think about the behavior. Here, the benefits and costs will be a central focus. Benefits will be especially important, because, if target audience members do not see significant *personal* benefits, they are unlikely to go farther in the process (unless there are very strong social pressures to do so).
- *Late Contemplation.* At this point, target audience members are well along in considering the option and are moving toward action. They are no longer

dwelling on the benefits—they pretty much know the potential. They worry more about the costs. It is not uncommon that what once seemed like a really good idea becomes less appealing as the time for action draws near, costs become more salient, and other obligations grow in importance.

Preparation and Action. As a campaign gains momentum, a great many members of the target audience will be at the stage where they have thought through the behavior and are ready to act, but they will not yet have taken that first step. Sometimes this is a matter of a lingering sense of self-doubt, but sometimes it is simply a lack of opportunity or the need for some final push. A valuable focus here may be bringing about trial behavior of some kind.

Maintenance. Some campaigns are successful if people only act once. More often, however, they need target audience members to continue the behavior indefinitely, often for a lifetime. The National High Blood Pressure Education Program focused much of its early effort on making target audience members aware of the problem of high blood pressure, getting them worried about its effects, and getting them to take preventive action. However, in the later years of the multiyear campaign, monitoring research showed managers that many high blood pressure sufferers were discontinuing the desired behaviors—in part because prevention behaviors offered no personally observable benefit. As a consequence, the campaign added a focus on keeping people doing the desired behavior.

The Maintenance stage involves two broad kinds of situations. First, there are Maintenance behaviors that are simply repetitions of previous behaviors, such as remembering to get a flu shot every year or always putting a baby on its back to prevent SIDS. These behaviors require that target audiences store important information and possibly develop some cuing system to repeat the behavior. The social marketer can play a role here by finding ways to provide regular stimuli, such as the American Cancer Society's annual Great American Smokeout (for more information, go to http://www.cancer.org/docroot/PED/ped_10_4.asp?sitearea=PED).

Maintenance in many other areas involves more profound changes in individuals. To become a regular exerciser or someone who stops smoking or doing drugs requires deeper changes in self-image, values, attitudes, and even personality. A person who does not do drugs is a different person from the individual who did drugs before. It is not just a matter of remembering not to do drugs. One must become someone different. The challenge in these circumstances is obviously much more dramatic.

Behavior Maintenance: Promoting the Status Quo. The Stages of Change are somewhat different when the real goal of the campaign is *conscious inaction*—getting a teenager *not* to smoke in the first place or an angry spouse *not* to use violence to settle an argument. At any point, individuals not now engaging in an undesirable behavior can be found in one of three states: Precontemplation, Contemplation, or Maintenance. There is no Preparation and Action stage. The three segments can be characterized as follows:

- *Precontemplation.* Here, individuals are not remotely considering the undesirable activity. They could not imagine why anyone would smoke, abuse their spouses, engage in risky sex, or starve themselves to "look glamorous."
- *Contemplation.* Here, target audience members are thinking about the undesirable behavior—binge drinking, not paying child support, or committing a crime. They have not yet done so. It is possible to further divide this group into three subsegments: (a) *The intrigued,* individuals vaguely contemplating the undesirable behavior but not yet close to acting; (b) *potential switchers,* individuals who find the alternative attractive and perhaps worth exploring for the first time; and (c) *defectors,* individuals who once engaged in the undesirable behavior and gave it up but are tempted to take it up again.
- *Maintenance.* Here, as in Precontemplation, one is committed to not taking up a behavior, such as smoking. This group came to this position after contemplating it or perhaps even experimenting with it.

A social marketer's goal with respect to these three stages is different than in the case where behavior change is sought. Although the goal is to move people in Contemplation to Maintenance and to keep people in Maintenance, the goal is *not* to move Precontemplators forward. One is perfectly happy that they stay that way—although savvy marketers will be alert for competitive actions (e.g., from the tobacco industry) that could draw Precontemplators over to "the dark side."

The BCOS Factors

In the Contemplation stage, target audience members are thinking in a tentative way about the proposed behavior—either something new and good or something new and *bad.* What, then, do they contemplate? What are the forces that are likely to drive them toward actually undertaking the good behavior and sticking to it or committing themselves to not undertaking something society considers undesirable (see also Rothschild, 1999)? Rothschild (1999) and MacInnis, Moorman, and Jaworski (1991) offer a useful starting point. They note that behavior will take place if three conditions are met: motivation, opportunity, and ability. That is, targets will act if they want to and believe they can. The relevant literature suggests that one can reasonably distill these drivers down to four elements that I call the *BCOS* factors:

- Benefits (motivators)
- Costs (demotivators)
- Others (either motivators or demotivators)
- Self-assurance (perceptions of opportunity and ability)

The first two factors are the ones that are the most frequent focus of marketing texts in that they emphasize the role of *exchange*. One way to think about the behaviors in any social influence campaign is that they require the target audience to make a trade, or exchange, between benefits and costs. Audience members have to give up some costs and, in return, get some benefits. In the private sector, the costs are typically money and time, in return for which one gets a desired product or service. It is the same in the social sector. However, in the latter world, it is often hard to portray benefits such as those one gets from recycling or eating less red meat. The costs of the exchange might include such things as pain (in an inoculation, a blood donation, or drug withdrawal), embarrassment or loss of self-respect (getting tested for Alzheimer's), and guilt (reporting a suspected child abuser). The challenge for the social marketer is to reduce the costs if possible and, if not, create a compelling package of benefits to overcome important costs. This can be a daunting challenge.

Behavior is not driven solely by the benefits and costs that compose exchanges, however, although attention to these components alone may be sufficient to bring about considerable success. Behaviors can—and are—strongly influenced by *others* in the target audience's environment. We all know of occasions when we made our own benefit-cost calculation and came up with the best choice for us personally and then did something entirely different because someone else wanted us to do so—for example, our significant other, our boss, or our children. Many people try drugs or cigarettes because others "make them" do so. The force of interpersonal social pressure can be a very powerful influence, both for and against the social marketer's campaign. If key groups or individuals do not consider a social issue important or do not support a particular course of action, it will be difficult to get the media's attention or to get politicians to become involved. Even though particular individuals think the behavioral choice is desirable, they will not act if their peers or members of their reference set seem to be opposed to it. Thus the "other" factor can work *for* or *against* a marketer. Clever marketers learn to bring social pressure to bear when it helps and minimize it when it hurts.

Finally, even if the benefits of a particular behavior exceed the costs and even if social pressures are strongly favorable, target audience members often still do not do what we want. Considerable experience has shown that the missing factor is what Albert Bandura (1986) refers to as "self-efficacy" but which I have chosen to call *self-assurance*. (I have learned from experience that Bandura's term, although academically precise, is very hard for students and practitioners to grasp and therefore employ on a regular basis.) Self-assurance is simply the individual's belief that he or she can actually make the behavior happen (Perry, Baranowski, & Parcel, 1990).[6]

This last component is easiest to recognize in the case of smoking and dieting. A significant proportion of all smokers and obese individuals (at least in developing countries) are quite convinced that the benefits of the quitting or dieting will exceed the costs. Further, they know that others who are important to them (e.g., their spouse, their children) want them to "do the right thing." They do not act because (sometimes based on their past experience) they simply think they cannot succeed. If the marketer in these cases adds another benefit or "shouts louder" about existing benefits through a clever communications program, these still will not bring about the desired change. The marketer needs to provide skills training or support mechanisms that will cause the target audience member to believe he or she can actually succeed.

Competition

The passion that many social marketers bring to their campaigns or other intervention efforts sometimes causes them to ignore the competition they face. For most campaigns, there is very real competition. Sometimes the competition takes the form of individuals or organizations trying to get their own behavior adopted (e.g., their news story on the front page, their bill passed in Congress). In other cases, it is just the status quo that is offering some important competing benefits that the target audience member does not want to give up. Thus the teenage drug dealer who is the target of a drug cessation program will be thinking: "Why should I give up all this money, the girls, the cars, the clothes, and my cool reputation in the community?" If the social marketer does not pay attention to this competition and what the competition is offering, the campaign will not succeed. Often, behavioral influence is really about "beating the competition."

In many situations, specific organizations—even entire industries— constitute the competition. The tobacco industry spends upwards of $12 billion a year to get people to smoke (although they say that their campaigns only promote brand choices). McDonald's and Ben & Jerry's urge us to indulge ourselves in fattening foods. The drug dealer offers the vulnerable individual a free hit "just to see what it's like." Real organizations and such individuals merit direct confrontation.

Other Valuable Marketing Concepts

There are other very valuable, "big" concepts to be adopted from the commercial sector to make social marketing more powerful. The following are several that I have found very useful, and they will play a role in our discussions later in this book.

SEGMENTATION

It seldom makes economic or tactical sense to treat a target audience as one monolithic community. There are a number of reasons for this. First, a "mass marketing" approach ignores the considerable variety within most target audiences and underestimates the likelihood that they will clump together strategically meaningful ways. Second, given this variety, a single approach is either so broad as to be ineffective or is it targeted at one dominant group and not meant to meet the interests and needs of a great many other valuable targets. Third, given this variability, it is also likely that some target audience members will be more appealing than others, and some may deserve to be ignored altogether.

Thus, in principle, an optimal strategy is one that aims the most appropriate approach (e.g., a relevant, impactful message and behavioral option) at each target individual or group and that spends no more campaign resources than the segment merits (which might mean zero). The one-strategy-fits-all approach defies market reality, private sector experience, and the need to optimize small budgets. Further, modern technology, especially in developed countries, permits "segments of one" through use of the Web or direct mail. (Readers need only recall their last visit to the supermarket, where the cash register spit out cents-off coupons tailored to their just-completed purchase behavior.) Amazon and Netflix are Web sites that similarly tailor messages and pop-ups to individuals, based on past browsing behavior.

Commercial marketers have developed a rich array of bases for segmentation, ranging from relatively straightforward demographic and behavioral measures (e.g., past practices) to sophisticated psychographic and lifestyle profiling. When mixed with information on the vulnerability of target audiences and the costs to reach them, these frameworks can yield sophisticated budget allocation models and insights for creative strategy (see Andreasen, 1995).

BRANDING

Branding has a long tradition in the private sector, from its early role as a way of differentiating and promoting unique products such as Ivory Soap and Coca-Cola. In recent years, branding ideas have found their way into the nonprofit world. Nonprofits such as the Boys & Girls Clubs of America and the American Cancer Society have learned that their brand is quite valuable and can be a key element in their efforts to bring about social influence.

Individual social marketing campaigns can also be branded, as in the case of the "Just Say No" and "The Anti-Drug" campaigns of the federal government or the "truth®" campaign of the American Legacy Foundation. Brands are more than labels or logos. They can also develop personalities (Plummer, 1985), captured by spokespeople (the Maytag lonely repairman) or fictional characters (Tony the Tiger, the Taco Bell Chihuahuas). Brand personalities have been developed in the social sector as well. Most Americans know McGruff the Crime Dog, the Crash Test Dummies, and Smokey Bear, who have all proven to be powerful spokescharacters for their issues.

THE 4 PS

Commercial marketers think of the key elements of any strategy as the "4 Ps": product, price, place, and promotion. Social marketers and nonprofit organizations have translated these elements as follows:

- *Product:* The package of benefits that a recommended behavior offers to the target audience. As in the private sector, the benefits may come from specific products (condoms) and services (inoculations), or they may comprise the psychological and social benefits of "mere behavior," such as the sense of accomplishment from quitting smoking or working out.
- *Price:* The cost that the target audience perceives it will have to pay when undertaking the behavior. These include monetary, psychological, and sociological costs, as well as the cost of foregone alternatives (e.g., continuing present behavior).
- *Place:* Creating opportunities to act at particular times, in particular places, and thorough particular modalities.
- *Promotion:* Communicating about and urging the behavior with a variety of "messages," including visual images sent through a variety of channels, including the Internet.

Extensive consideration of the 4 Ps is usually found in nonprofit marketing texts (Andreasen & Kotler, 2003).

COBRANDING AND COMARKETING

Commercial marketers recognize the value of partnering with other organizations and other brands to achieve sales and positioning objectives. Breyer's Ice Cream contains M&M's, Snickers Bars, Reese's Pieces, and Oreo Cookies. Cereals feature film characters from major studios and from children's TV.

Nonprofits have also recognized the value of cobranding. Dreyer's Ice Cream has partnered with the Girl Scouts to produce Thin Mint Ice Cream to raise money for the Scouts. The American Cancer Society partnered with Nicoderm to promote greater levels of smoking cessation. Some of the best known long-term partnerships have involved the Advertising Council. The Ad Council's historically memorable campaigns have given us such timeless phrases, images, and slogans as the following:

- The toughest job you'll ever have (Peace Corps).
- A mind is a terrible thing to waste.
- Only you can prevent forest fires.
- Take a bite out of crime.
- Friends don't let friends drive drunk.

The Advertising Council continues to be an effective partner in social marketing campaigns. Because their work is often so dazzling and memorable, however, there is sometimes a danger that exciting ads will lead campaign managers to neglect marketing's other three Ps.

Transferring the Frameworks

I shall return again and again, in the chapters that follow, to these basic frameworks for effective social marketing: the audience-centered mind-set, the six-step planning process, the Stages of Change, BCOS factors, and the concept of Competition. I will argue that these frameworks offer powerful guidance to those seeking to craft behavioral influence programs and interventions in a wide variety of areas that once were not considered social marketing's proper "turf."

First, we shall consider how social marketing might help a change agent set priorities (Stage 5 in the social influence process described in chapter 2).

Notes

1. The material in this section first appeared in Andreasen (2003).

2. Ironically, it was the public health community that would soon become very important to the growth of the field in the 1990s.

3. This section is drawn from Andreasen and Herzberg (2005).

4. Those who have read my book *Marketing Social Change* (Andreasen, 1995) may wish to skip this section.

5. This section is drawn from Andreasen (2004a).

6. Some researchers make a distinction between two kinds of self-assurance. First, there is the person's sense of his or her ability to actually undertake the action. Second, there is the perception that the action will actually work. My own view is that the latter is incorporated in the individual's perceptions of the likely benefits of the action. If people do not think an action is likely to work—or is likely to work in some odd fashion—they may not consider some or all of the benefits likely to take place.

5

Setting Priorities in Social Marketing

In October 2004, the Bush Administration announced $100 million in new grants to support orphans and vulnerable children as a part of the president's $15 billion, 5-year Emergency Plan for AIDS Relief. In a press release, the U.S. Agency for International Development noted: "In 2003, more than 15 million children worldwide under age 18 had lost one or both parents to AIDS. By 2010, it is estimated that more than 25 million children will have lost at least one parent to AIDS. Each U.S. grant will provide care and support to orphans and vulnerable children affected by HIV/AIDS in at least two of the 15 focus countries of the President's Emergency Plan. The focus countries, which are home to more than 50 percent of HIV infections worldwide, are: Botswana, Cote d'Ivoire, Ethiopia, Guyana, Haiti, Kenya, Mozambique, Namibia, Nigeria, Rwanda, South Africa, Tanzania, Uganda, Vietnam and Zambia. The U.S. Agency for International Development will oversee the programs" (U.S. Agency for International Development [USAID], 2004).

One may ask, why these countries? Are they chosen because they have friendly, stable governments? UNAIDS has prioritized countries for aid that have "Three Ones"—one comprehensive national AIDS framework, one national AIDS coordinating authority, and one monitoring and evaluation system. What if the countries that are most affected by the crisis do not meet these standards? Why is the United States spending money on children who do not have AIDS at all? Shouldn't money go toward prevention? If we focus on *prevention, should we emphasize populations such as men who have sex with men, who are at higher risk, or populations that have more "emotional weight," such as pregnant, AIDS-infected mothers, who might pass the virus on to their children? Should it matter how much a particular target group is likely to respond to behavior change efforts, or would this criterion lead to discrimination against particular racial or ethnic groups?*

Finally, what of those who already have HIV/AIDS? So-called drug cocktails to minimize the effects of the disease are available but very costly. Some governments, such as that in South Africa, say they cannot afford to buy them even though pharmaceutical companies have recently agreed to reduce the cost. Should UNAIDS step in? If so, where does this leave the orphans and the HIV-infected pregnant mothers?

Priorities and Agendas

By the end of Stage 4 of the agenda-setting process, some sort of map of the social problem has been developed and a sense of the various points at which one might address the problem has emerged. Typically, the options are divided into upstage and downstage interventions. At Stage 5, the challenge is to begin to choose among the various courses of action. This is the point at which various government agencies, foundations, nonprofits, and socially involved corporations debate the relative costs and the efficacy of various solutions. Often such debates are carried out in workshops, conferences, and—if the issue is controversial, as with social security reform—in the media. Stage 5 is also the point at which opposing forces emerge and solidify their positions.

Of course, eventually some group or set of individuals will have to take action. The agents could be specific interest groups with broad mandates, such as AARP, or with narrower purviews, such as Mothers Against Drunk Driving. They could be specific nonprofit organizations, such as the American Cancer Society or the Nature Conservancy. They could be a corporation, such as Nike or Timberland, or a quasigovernmental organization, such as UNESCO, the European Union, or WHO. They could be a local, regional, or national government agency such as the Centers for Disease Control and Prevention or the Food and Drug Administration, or a legislative body such as the U.S. Senate. They could be a foundation or philanthropic organization, such as the Robert Wood Johnson Foundation or the Bill and Melinda Gates Foundation, with a portfolio that supports particular interventions.

Critical roles in setting priorities are often played by foundations; think tanks such as the Heritage Foundation, the Brookings Institution, or the

American Enterprise Institute and academic institutions such as Harvard, Johns Hopkins, or Georgetown University. They can assemble available data and conceptual frameworks and point to critical gaps in our understandings. They can convene major players to be educated in this knowledge or to debate alternatives. They can assemble the options and sharpen the discussion. An important role in setting out policy options is often played by Public Agenda, a quintessential Stage 5 organization.

What will take precedence? What will be tried? Certainly, entrepreneurial organizations will seek approaches that apply their own skills to the problem independent of any general consensus. Government agencies will emphasize public information campaigns. Nonprofits will want to work with their own constituencies, with skills they have already developed. Foundations with particular missions will have approaches to which they naturally gravitate. Some will fund interventions; some will fund training or research for others who want to intervene. Some will have specific target audiences they want to influence, such as the poor or the elderly.

The most difficult challenge among the various options is faced by organizations relatively unconstrained by history or budgets (although there is never enough money for most problems). Such organizations might be the large foundations, such as the Robert Wood Johnson Foundation, and big agencies, such as the Centers for Disease Control and Prevention. Given a complex problem such as childhood obesity, with a complex, diverse array of factors that may be addressed to bring about change (as outlined in chapter 3), where should they begin? How can social marketing help them set these priorities?

First of all, we need some criteria for choosing among options. Clearly, a good intervention is one that has a major impact on the ultimate undesirable behavior and that is cost-effective and lasting. The problem, however, is complicated by a number of issues implicit in the discussions in chapter 3:

1. Having an initial impact and having a lasting impact may not be the same thing.

2. A successful initial innovation far upstream from the "final audience" may require many other links to fall in place and other parties to "step up to the plate" for, say, an upstream action (e.g., a change in school menus) to ultimately change downstream behavior (e.g., a child's eating patterns).

3. One intervention may be successful only if another parallel intervention is also undertaken and is effective. Changes in school menus may only be effective if there are also changes in caregivers' advice, cooking, and household snacking behavior.

In each of these cases, it is critical to understand (or at least predict) how different players in the system will react. One useful framework for considering possible options that is widely used in the commercial sector is *scenario forecasting* (Scearce & Fulton, 2004; Schwartz, 1996). This approach begins with the present status and recognizes that there are many pathways into the future. Some of these pathways are influenced by the actions we take, some by the actions others take, and some by broad forces that are not directly under anyone's control (such as changes in the local economy).

Scenario forecasting efforts typically begin with present circumstances and have several stages.

1. Through interviews, secondary research, and internal brainstorming, the forecaster specifies what will be "givens" about the future and what are critical unknowns. The "givens" comprise a set of assumptions and the "unknowns" comprise critical elements whose probabilities will eventually have to be estimated. For example, suppose the (hypothetical) Andreasen Foundation was deciding whether to pursue school-based, nonprofit-based, or local government–based approaches to increasing teens' physical activity in a specific community. One set of givens may be the probable future economic status of each of these domains—for example, the level of the school budget, local nonprofit charitable receipts, and local tax revenues. A critical unknown will be the probable enthusiasm and creativity of each of these sectors in carrying out programs the foundation might fund.

2. The forecaster next attempts to specify a reasonable set of pathways into the future, constructed of decision points and outcomes. For example, the choice to pursue a school-based approach may meet with high, medium, or low enthusiasm. The Andreasen Foundation then has a decision to make: what to do next. For example, if school enthusiasm is weak, the foundation could consider (a) increasing its pressure on the schools, (b) redesigning its approach, or (c) abandoning the approach and doing something else. These choices then have their own behavioral outcomes. On the other hand, if school enthusiasm is strong, there may be several variations of in-school programs to choose among, each with different possible outcomes. Articulating the pathways may seem very complex, but planners will typically stop when the endpoints seem adequate to helping the organization make key decisions—for example, whether the Andreasen Foundation should go with schools, nonprofits, or government.

3. The forecaster next needs to make probability estimates for each of the outcomes of each decision. For example, what is the probability that nonprofits will have high, medium, or low enthusiasm for carrying out exercise initiatives that the Andreasen Foundation will support?

4. Then some value for each end state needs to be assigned. This is easier if the outcomes are all in the same units (e.g., the percentage of teens exercising). However, it is more complex when they are in different units (e.g., more exercising versus better eating). Ideally, the outcomes should be specified in a common numeric. Suppose, however, that one were choosing between exercise

and nutrition initiatives. What is the relative value of having 10% of overweight Hispanic girls eating significantly better diets, as compared with a 20% increase in hours of physical exercise by preteen white boys? As discussed later, the task of valuing these outcomes can be a major activity all its own. Discussion about these value choices can often reveal important schisms in priorities among managers and funders and can prove more valuable to the enterprise than the scenario model itself.

5. Along the way, it is desirable to eliminate implausible branches. For example, an assessment of the change organization's strategic capabilities may cause it to forego certain options. For example, a decision point may be marked by this question: Do we segment by race and ethnicity, by lifestyle, or by gender? The social influence organization may decide that it simply lacks the capability to pursue the race and ethnicity option, either because its knowledge base is poor or because its own experience is limited and it does not want to bring in a partner.

6. A typical consequence of a carefully done scenario-planning exercise is the realization that one does not know enough to forecast probabilities at certain points. Although in many cases collective internal wisdom may be adequate, in other cases, an investment in further research may be wise before choices are made.

Ultimately, the scenario-building process creates a set of stories about the way the future may unfold, which helps in choosing first steps. An important value of the process is that it forces the organization to think much farther down the road than it normally might do. In my experience, far too many change agents are too eager to get their initiatives on the road. Often, scenario-building causes them to realize that they must face serious issues of capacity building if they want to pursue particular pathways. As several observers of the nonprofit world have observed (Bradley, Jansen, & Silverman, 2003; Letts, Ryan, & Grossman, 1999), nonprofits are notorious for neglecting to build capacity for future initiatives. They often feel that funds devoted to longer term investments in staff, systems, knowledge, and facilities will take away from core mission goals of delivering programs, creating initiatives, and making change happen. However, most serious social problems, such as overweight and obesity, are highly complex, involve a great many potential players, and are very long term in focus. Capacities that an organization may have now may not be what is needed in 5 years. The environment may change, target audiences may learn and grow, issues may rise or fall on various agendas, and competitors may come and go. Without scenario planning, twists and turns in the future can leave social influence agencies blindsided by events and unprepared to cope. Capacity building is one way to prepare for such eventualities, and scenario planning helps organizations think about potential capacity-building requirements.

Corporate and Social
Approaches to Choosing Alternatives

Trying to tackle an emerging social problem with behavioral approaches that have not been tried before is in many ways similar to the challenge faced by corporations when they consider whether to introduce a new product or service. In such situations, corporations are likely to ask a number of questions:

1. *Market size:* How big is the potential market for this innovation?

2. *Segments:* Who makes up the primary market segments for the innovation?

3. *Strength of demand:* How strong will demand be (e.g., what price might people pay)?

4. *Innovativeness:* How radical is the innovation we are proposing? Is it just a "brand extension" or the creation of an entirely new category (consider the Segway)?

5. *Skills required:* Do we have the skills and know-how to bring it to market? If not, can we easily acquire such skills?

6. *Investment level:* What investment in skills and capacity will we need to make?

7. *Cost per transaction:* What is the probable cost per transaction (i.e., how much will it cost to deliver the product or service)?

8. *System support:* How supportive will distributors and other partners be?

9. *Competition:* What competition will we face initially and later if the innovation is successful?

Each of these factors has a parallel in the domain of social influence:

1. *Market size:* How many people will be affected if this approach is successful?

2. *Segments:* Who is most likely to respond immediately, who will take longer, and who is pretty much "hopeless" in the near term?

3. *Strength of demand:* How motivated are people likely to be to take the recommended action?

4. *Innovativeness:* Are we asking people to do something they have never done before (Africans getting immunized) or something that is a small adjustment (putting a baby to sleep on its back)?

5. *Skills required:* Is this something our organization knows how to do (e.g., distribute family planning products in remote areas), or is it something with which we have little experience or success (e.g., using the Internet to reach Asian seniors)?

6. *Investment level:* What funding level is needed for basic infrastructure, background research, and so on?

7. *Cost per transaction:* What are media costs of reaching mothers to tell them about SIDS? How much does a diet clinic for the poor cost? How costly is it to get mosquito nets into shops in rural Tanzania?

8. *System support:* Is this a go-it-alone venture, or are there others poised to help?

9. *Competition:* How tough are the alternatives to the behavior we want (not smoking or stopping dealing drugs)? Are there competitors on the horizon (e.g., charlatans promising quick weight loss with herbs or yoga) that we need to worry about? Is competition static or dynamic?

Despite these similarities, there are two important differences in goals between the sectors. First, there are differences in the calculation of end-state outcomes. In the commercial sector, the objective is to maximize return on investment (ROI) to stockholders, measured in dollars. In the world of social influence, the parallel is to maximize the welfare of society at large.[1] In the commercial sector, maximizing dollar returns means attracting many customers, enticing them to come back frequently, but spending as little of the corporation's resource as possible to achieve these outcomes. Dollars are fungible. Getting one customer to buy (over his or her lifetime) at a certain cost and price is as good as getting any other customer to buy.

In the world of social influence, outcomes are measured in improved lives of target audiences and the societies of which they are a part. All target audiences are not the same, of course. It is sometimes the case—for example, in some economic analyses of social problems—that target audiences are treated as fungible. However, most societies, as well as the nonprofits, foundations, and government agencies that implement their will, have explicit or implicit notions of who is most and least deserving of "social help." In the obesity context, social thinkers might argue that reducing childhood obesity is more important than reducing adult obesity. They might give lower priority to an obese middle class white kid and higher priority to an overweight minority kid who has had a tough life, faces lots of hurdles, and has few resources with which to fend for him- or herself.

The fact that different segments have different implicit value to a society is a complicating factor in setting social priorities because choosing social innovations means choosing whom to help. The economist might argue that the criterion ought to be cost-effectiveness. That is, one should target "low-hanging fruit"—those easiest to reach and most likely to be responsive. Thus one should target obese, middle class kids with two working, educated, nonobese parents. Economists would say that a foundation or nonprofit social influence organization would get more lifetime social change by focusing on this segment rather than aiming at obese minority kids in poor homes with obese single parents. However, many social influence agents would argue that these are the wrong metrics. They consider it their obligation to help the most in need of help; those who are (to continue the metaphor) higher on the tree.

The second important difference in goals between the commercial and social sectors is reflected in the point that marketing strategy in the private sector is almost totally aimed at final consumers. There will be occasions in which corporations focus on recruiting allies for their efforts, and sometimes, especially in the developing world, they have to work to remove regulatory barriers to preferred courses of action. In the main, however, their decisions about strategies are totally focused on the final consumers. Is marketing mix A better than marketing mix B in achieving maximum profits through sales for segment 1? Is a strategy aimed at segment X likely to yield more profits than a strategy aimed at segment Q? In the main and in most industries, the criteria are in terms of near-term sales.

In the social sector, choosing strategies for major social change is complicated by the fact that such change typically will be a long time coming, and the best course of action right now is to focus upstream rather than on the "final consumers." Rather than aiming at overweight and obese kids, one must choose among campaigns aimed at schoolteachers, writers for *Parent* magazine, Yahoo Web page designers, fast food menu designers, and neighborhood police patrols. These interventions may differ widely in (a) how easy it is to change the specific target audience (how low the fruit is hanging) and (b) how likely it is that the change in the upstream target audience will precipitate or facilitate later changes needed to get a bottom-line "final customer" impact.

Thus the goal of any specific social marketing effort may be a specific set of near-term behavior changes in a specific (often upstream) target audience. However, choosing whether to green-light such an effort requires complex consideration of probable impacts down the line on a social problem that has surfaced. Again, scenario planning can be useful here.

Other Issues in Priority Setting

SOCIAL MARKETERS AND PRIORITY SETTING

Organizations and funders cannot make judgments across alternative interventions without having agreement on what would constitute ideal—or at least satisfactory—social influence. When a social problem initially is identified, it reflects some level of dissatisfaction or despair about a given set of static conditions or trends. There is too much poverty, too many African children are dying needlessly, or there is too much global warming or medical malpractice. These global statements are important starting points, but they are not very helpful when one must choose among courses of action.

I would argue that better conditions do not come about *unless we influence behavior.* Therefore, outcome measures ought to always be couched in terms of behavior: the number of target audience members in X group doing Y behaviors within Z timeframe. This does not preclude establishing secondary outcome objectives, such as specific communications goals, that might reasonably be expected to lead to behavioral influence. However, these secondary goals should not be used *instead* of behavioral goals. It is tempting to do so, because they are often easier to track and because one would like to believe that people who have the right knowledge and the right attitude will surely do the right thing. It is an approach often relied upon by those with strong communications backgrounds. One value of involving social marketers in the process of setting social influence objectives is their insistence on the centrality of behavioral goals.

The majority of the objectives described in *Healthy People 2010* (CDC, 2000) meet this social marketing criterion. The goal statements implicitly say that to get healthy people, we need target audiences to change their behavior (or keep desirable present behaviors) so that by 2010

- Only 12% of adults have smoked in the last 30 days
- 100% of the population has health coverage
- 90% of pregnant females get prenatal care
- 85% of adolescents exercise 20 minutes three times per week
- 50% of those with depression get treatment

However, not all of the *Healthy People 2010* goals are in behavioral terms. Some state outcomes such as "0% will be exposed to secondhand smoke" or "9.2 vehicle deaths per 100,000." Had a social marketer been present, he or she would have said: "If you do not give me behavioral objectives, I cannot help you decide what programs to choose and how to implement them."

SOCIAL MARKETERS AND UPSTREAM PRIORITIES

The complex portrait of the obesity problem reproduced in chapter 3 clearly sets individual behavior change as the bottom line. We cannot consider ourselves successful unless we get adults, teenagers, and children to take actions to exercise more, eat differently, or, if they are already eating and exercising appropriately, maintain healthy patterns throughout their lifetime.

However, as the earlier discussion predicted, the portrait also makes clear that there are many other actors in the upstream problem environment who have important roles to play. There are three such roles in the problem domain:

1. *Enablers.* These are individuals who must act if downstream individuals are ever going to change their behavior and stick to it. Depending on the downstream segment, these could include
    a. Caregivers, who have an important role in meal preparation, meal scheduling, standard setting, and "enforcement" of TV watching, computer game playing, and exercising

    b. School cafeteria planners, who must make healthful meals available

    c. City planners, who must create play spaces and opportunities

    d. Law enforcement officers, who have to make existing play and exercise environments safer

2. *Motivators.* These are individuals who could act to encourage, teach, coach, and reinforce target audience members in their good behavior. These could include

    a. Teachers and sports figures

    b. Community organization leaders and workers

    c. Celebrities

    d. Relatives (parents, brothers, sisters, uncles, aunts, grandparents)

3. *Partners.* These are individuals in organizations who must use their own resources to help change norms, provide behavioral opportunities (e.g., in the workplace), provide useful information, provide incentives, and otherwise *contribute* to program implementation. They include

    a. Corporation leaders

    b. Media writers, producers, and editors

    c. Government officials and administrators

    d. Nonprofit CEOs

    e. Academics

In establishing a broad social change program, leaders may set behavioral objectives with respect to any of these groups or a cascading set of goals that sequence attention to various enablers, motivators, and partners over a multiple year period depending on when and where their role is most critical. Although the choice of which parties need to be tackled first and which later is difficult, the scenario-planning framework described earlier in this chapter can provide an excellent framework for thinking this through. Close monitoring of other potential interveners can also narrow choices.

SOCIAL MARKETING AND SEGMENTATION

I have told many audiences that, too often, behavior change initiatives do not adequately exploit the power of segmentation approaches. Sometimes programs do not segment their target audiences at all, perhaps arguing (especially if they are a government agency) that they must cover everyone. Others, when they do segment, tend to use the most accessible and seemingly obvious segmentation measures—gender, ethnicity, location—even though these may not be predictive of appropriate interventions.

Both these shortcomings hamper campaigns from achieving their maximum impact. This is for two reasons. First, as noted in chapter 4, segmentation allows marketers to allocate resources more efficiently. That is, by assembling often simple sets of information, marketers can decide to allocate a disproportionately large share of effort to segment A and a disproportionately smaller share of effort to segment B and ignore (for the moment) segment C altogether. This is obviously much smarter than allocating resources in direct proportion to a segment's size, which is what one is implicitly doing if one does not segment. Pursuing a single global strategy means that one is assuming that everyone in the target audience merits the same attention. Rarely is this good management.

The second value of segmentation is that it allows one to consider spending resources in different ways for different segments, independent of the amount of resources one is using. Tailored interventions are more likely to "speak" to the segment in ways that will achieve greater progress toward behavior influence goals than would an approach that treats everyone the same. This, of course, is a lesson that lobbyists learned decades, maybe centuries, ago. One could send a mass electronic mailing to all relevant congresspeople concerning some issue, but one is guaranteed to have much greater effect if messages speak to each recipient in terms of his or her own needs and the needs of his or her constituency.

It is the first aspect of segmentation that is relevant here. Given a target market—either an upstream target audience (e.g., school principals) or the downstream target audience (e.g., overweight or obese children)—planners need to make judgments about whom to target and how much in the way of resources to apply to this group.

In chapter 5 of my 1995 book, *Marketing Social Change*, I proposed a set of criteria that a social marketer could apply to market segments to help prioritize them for future behavior influence efforts. This approach presumed that planners had figured out some way to divide up all possible target audiences—for example, for school principals, dividing them into segments according to (a) region, (b) rural or urban setting, (c) public or private, and (d) presence or absence of significant Hispanic and African American populations. Given a matrix of possible targets, there are two sets of factors to consider. First, there are general factors estimating the size of the need and the likely impact of the program. In targeting schools, these factors are as follows:

1. *Size of the market segment.* How many people are there in each segment who might be addressed in the prioritized effort? How many schoolchildren are there in Eastern urban private school systems, how many in rural Appalachian public systems, how many in West Coast communities with large Hispanic populations, and so on?

2. *Prevalence of the problem behavior.* What portion of the schoolchildren in the segment are overweight or obese or likely to become so?

3. *Severity of the problem behavior.* Of the children who are overweight or obese or likely to be, what are the likely physical and psychological costs if nothing is done?

4. *Relative inability to cope with the problem.* Are the school districts aware of the problem, and do they already have programs to deal with it? Are the local parent-teacher associations (PTAs) likely to bring about change or resist it, perhaps citing other priorities? Are their budgets adequate to the challenge?

5. *Likelihood of responding favorably to an initiative.* Are the school administrators concerned about the problem? Do they give evidence of eagerness for help?

The last factor is dependent on a program's ability to influence each target segment. Thus a second set of factors needs to be considered:

1. *Segmentation cost.* What might it cost to address the challenge in each segment? Other things being equal, one would want to put more effort into (for example) white Eastern urban schools than into African American rural Southern schools, simply because the cost to reach each principal and student is lower.

2. *Sensitivity to possible program tactics.* Segments that are farther along in the Stages of Change are more desirable than those that are farther back. Those for whom the BCOS factors are clear and competition is light are also more desirable.

3. *Organizational capabilities.* Organizations differ in their ability to influence different segments. If an organization has had past success in reaching rural Hispanic populations in other markets, it ought to give such segments higher priority than segments in which it is less confident of its ability to make behavior influence happen.

Using the Three Frameworks

How might one analyze sensitivity to possible strategies? A social marketer would ask the following questions about each potential target audience and behavior:

1. What do we know about where the target audience stands with respect to the behavior changes of interest? In the case of a new behavior involving obesity, what stage is the audience in?
   a. *Precontemplation:* not yet thinking about doing anything about the obesity challenge (e.g., a doctor not ready to intervene with obese patients, a TV producer unwilling to consider a documentary, parents not willing to try to shape their child's behavior, corporate executives unwilling to change their product or promotion)
   b. *Early Contemplation:* beginning to think about the benefits to themselves of changing behavior to address the obesity problem
   c. *Late Contemplation:* seeing the benefits as positive but focusing now on costs and what others are doing
   d. *Preparation and Action:* having decided to proceed and either needing help in getting going or having taken first "baby steps"

e. *Maintenance:* having begun some desirable behavior changes but in need of reinforcement and, in many cases, further shaping of new behavior patterns.

2. How many target audience members are there in each microsegment (e.g., doctors in Precontemplation, parents in Maintenance, etc.)?

3. What are the BCOS factors that we can identify as needing to be addressed before movement along the stages can take place? Are there benefits that need to be emphasized or costs that need to be reduced? What are the social pressures for or against the behavior? Are there group influences that can be brought to bear to make positive change? Are there self-assurance issues? Do the segment members feel they lack skills or knowledge that might keep them from acting?

4. What competitive challenges do we face? Is the lack of behavior a matter of inertia, or are there other environmental or organizational pressures promoting the present status or an alternative future status that competes?

To understand these factors and potentially feed them into a scenario planning exercise, priority setting requires some form of "listening" to the target audiences. This can involve interviews, reading of secondary sources, focus groups, conversations with experts, or any number of other formative research approaches. It often requires considerable imagination and creativity, particularly if it is difficult for the target audience to envision anything other than the status quo. For example, it may be hard for an obese woman with five children, no husband, and no full-time job to list the factors that might lead her to begin regular exercise or to cook healthier meals. Careful probing will be essential and imagination will be needed on the part of the researcher to identify the appropriate challenges.

Ultimately, it will be highly desirable to carry out quantitative field studies to nail down exact numbers for these factors. Qualitative methods are wonderful for insights into Stages of Change, BCOS factors, and Competition, but one would like to have estimates of how many target audience members are in which Stage of Change, considering what BCOS factors, and facing what competition. Collecting such data in the form of knowledge, attitude, and practice studies has a long tradition in public health (Harvey, 1999). As the reader might expect, I would recommend that future such studies pay more explicit attention to the frameworks set forth in this book.

ESTIMATING STAGE TRANSITIONS

The Stages of Change model raises a thorny problem in priority setting. A key premise of the stages approach is that one ought to tailor strategies to where one finds the target audience and seek to move that audience to the next stage. That is, for a given target audience, the short-run goal might be to move it from Precontemplation to Early Contemplation, not to immediately get Preparation and Action. Of course, the ultimate goal is to get everyone through to the final stage, but experience shows that individuals get stuck in stages, regress, and proceed to the end point at different paces.

How does one factor this problem in when setting priorities? How does one decide how much effort to put into trying to move segment B3 to Stage 3, as opposed to moving segment G16 to Stage 2?

Fortunately, private sector marketing has addressed this kind of problem with what are known as "switching models" (Meyer & Kahn, 1991). These models were developed to help marketers understand the likelihood that a customer in a given state (e.g., having bought their brand on 5 out of the last 10 purchase occasions) is likely to stay in that state (sticking with the last brand purchased) or switch behavior (e.g., move to some other brand). To my knowledge, these models have not been applied to a social marketing context. In a social marketing context, one would like to know the following for each segment: (a) Given that an audience member in the segment is at Stage Y at time t, what is the probability that he or she will move to Stage Y + 1 at time $t + 1$? and (b) What is the probability that, if that audience member moves to Y + 1, he or she will move on to later stages and eventually be fully compliant with our preferred behavior?

Transition Matrices

One way of thinking about this would be to develop a set of transition probability matrices for each segment that would capture the probability of moving from Stage Y to Y + 1. For example, suppose one were planning a school-based program for Hispanic families designed to secure long-term improvement in their diets (arbitrarily, say, a 25% reduction in the consumption of products promoting bad cholesterol and 30% reduction in sweeteners). A transition matrix for a hypothetical 10,000 individuals might look like Table 5.1. Their starting position (time t) is in column 1. The numbers in bold type running down the diagonal represent the probabilities of someone being unaffected by the campaign (staying exactly where they are). Each number *below* a bold number represents the probability of regressing one stage.[2] Each number above a bold number represents progress, including leaping ahead more than one step. The final column ($t + 1$) yields the status of the audience after one period—say, a year. To estimate the distribution in subsequent periods, one need only multiply the $t + 1$ distribution by the transition probability matrix again and again.

These probabilities can be a useful forecasting and allocation tool. But where does one get these numbers? I would argue that they can be filled in by knowledgeable planners, adapted from comparable programs, or intuited from the concrete results from field data (if the program has been in place for a time

Table 5.1   Hypothetical Transition Probability Matrix

Number of Individuals at t	Stage	1_{t+1}	2_{t+1}	3_{t+1}	4_{t+1}	Number of Individuals at t+1
6850	1_t	**0.8**	0.13	0.05	0.02	5701
2210	2_t	0.1	**0.55**	0.21	0.14	2177
710	3_t	XXX	0.1	**0.42**	0.48	1126
230	4_t	XXX	XXX	0.09	**0.91**	997

NOTE: Numbers in bold type indicate the probability of a person being unaffected by the campaign.

and the correct behavioral tracking data are developed). They can also be adjusted to reflect the competencies of the social marketers. That is, a particular organization or program might be especially good at getting action—for example, moving people from Stage 2 to Stage 3. The probabilities could be adjusted accordingly. Alternatively, one may know from experience with similar programs that Strategy A will have difficulty getting target segment P beyond Contemplation, whereas with Strategy B and target audience Q, there is likely to be a lot of backsliding, especially after Stage 3, initial action. The matrices are a vehicle for making explicit this experience.

What might the future look like? Simply multiplying the end states $(t + 1)$ by the matrix again and again allows one to estimate the number of individuals arriving in Stage 4 at each time period. For example, given the assumptions in Table 5.1, one can develop forecasts for each out year, as in Table 5.2.

The model allows one to estimate the number of years it will take to achieve some goal level of accomplishment, such as 50% of the target population reaching stage 4. In this case, this target would not be reached until Year 7.[3]

Is This Too Complex?

By now, readers may be throwing up their hands, saying: "These approaches to priority setting are far too complex and too time-consuming, require too much nonexistent data, and make too many assumptions that are just guesses." There are four rejoinders I would offer to suggest that the process of estimating the relative payoffs for various social marketing interventions is not impossible. (a) Although the task may be daunting the first time, future planning cycles will be greatly simplified. (b) Analyses can be carried out as a joint project of

Table 5.2   Forecasts for Out Years

Stage	t	t + 1	t + 2	t + 3	t + 4	t + 5	t + 6	t + 7	t + 8	t + 9	t + 10
1	6850	5701	4779	4028	3410	2898	2470	2112	1810	1557	1343
2	2210	2177	2051	1880	1696	1518	1355	1211	1084	975	882
3	710	1126	1305	1386	1422	1436	1440	1439	1436	1431	1427
4	230	997	1866	2707	3472	4148	4734	5239	5670	6037	6348

many funders or government agencies or by a think tank or university. Public policy programs at universities have a long history of such exercises. (c) It is an infinitely better basis for social influence planning than more simplistic alternatives, such as funding people, institutions, or programs with good track records; funding whatever is "hot" sociologically or economically; or acquiescing to the idiosyncratic preferences of funding sources. (d) The approach implies a monitoring framework that, if adhered to, will yield much more in the way of valuable tracking information for program adjustment in the inevitable case that interventions do not work out quite as planned.

Notes

1. Because social influence involves programs by specific organizations, an alternative formulation would be to maximize the returns to an organization's supporters. The supporters could be individual donors, government agencies (and, indirectly, taxpayers), or corporate partners. These supporters might be said to have different preferences for outcomes (e.g., different populations they wish to see changed). A discussion of these possibilities is beyond the scope of this book.

2. I am assuming here that no one goes from Stage 3 or 4 back to 1 or from 4 back to 2.

3. If actual data for this program exist, the matrix yields potentially interesting diagnostic information. For example, a manager could ask the following questions: (a) Are the diagonal probabilities equal, declining, or increasing? If decreasing, this would suggest that the behavior seems easier as one moves from stage to stage. If increasing, one might conclude the opposite. (b) Is some diagonal value significantly lower than others (or in comparable programs)? This might suggest that there is a bottleneck at that point that deserves special attention. (c) Are the probabilities of *regressing* high? If people are falling back at various points, this might suggest the need for a program component reinforcing the present stage, as well as urging continued movement forward.

PART III

Upstream Applications

6

Beyond Downstream Interventions: Influencing Communities

Sex workers in most parts of the world are major conduits for the transmission of the HIV/AIDS virus. They are highly likely to be victims themselves. Sex workers in bordellos present a promising venue for social change because they constitute close communities. In many programs, the goal is to have the sex workers insist that clients use condoms. However, success is often impeded by the sex worker's fear that other workers will not be so demanding and will steal their clients.

Several years ago, under the leadership of Michael Ramah, Porter Novelli initiated a project in Tijuana that deeply involved the sex workers in a bordello in creating a social marketing campaign to be aimed at themselves! A highly effective tactic was a series of novellas featuring a sex worker named Maritza. The girls in the bordello helped choose Martiza's clothing and hairstyle. They identified four prototype clients (the Executive, the Macho Guy, and so forth) and helped concoct narratives that would show other girls how to deal with each type.

Finally, they all agreed not to defect from the project by giving in to client demands.

B eginning with this chapter, we shall look at how social marketing concepts and tools can be used to influence critical upstream behavior. As discussed briefly in chapter 3, a major argument raised by critics of social marketing in the past is that we have focused entirely too much on those individuals who are engaged in, or likely to engage in, problem social behaviors—the downstream approach. One cannot deny that ultimately downstream targets have to be influenced, but critics argue that reliance solely (or largely) on those targets' voluntary behavior is (a) unfair to the individuals and (b) often not cost-effective for the society when compared with alternatives.

Indeed, there are a great many actors upstream in the "problem domain" who could play a role in long-term solutions to social problems (National Cancer Institute, 2003, pp. 9-10; see also McLeroy, Bibeau, Steckler, & Glanz, 1988). Getting them to act is often a precondition to giving downstream audiences the motivation, ability, and opportunity to do what society wants. There are also times when upstream inaction is sought. An improved society may result when legislators do not repeal environmental protection laws, when police ignore minor building code violations in a makeshift playground, or when a media gatekeeper refuses to print unsupported charges against a desirable social change program.

It is also often the case that upstream players acting individually at some point must become a *community* that supports change. Social problems rise to prominence when there are many people speaking out about the fact that they need attention. Specific programmatic options only get funded when they are broadly supported, and specific changes will not take place unless a number of people act collectively. For example, school lunches are not likely to change or remain permanently changed unless a significant group of parents gets behind the program. Parents in one school system are likely to feel more emboldened if they know parents in other school districts are mounting similar campaigns.

Communities of actors are also important to give "cover" for potentially controversial actions. For example, a school administrator may not conclude that it is "safe" from a career standpoint to implement a radical change in school policy or planning (e.g., eliminating candy and soda vending machines) until he or she hears that other administrators are taking such actions. The first administrator may see it as career suicide to do otherwise.

The cover provided by joint action is often particularly important in the commercial marketplace. There are undoubtedly many managers in the private sector who would like to take socially desirable actions. When a desired action has the potential to leave their firm vulnerable to losing market share or incurring costs that competitors continue to avoid, managers may be understandably reluctant to act. If a fast food chain wants to *boldly* proclaim the calorie and fat content of its offerings, it may fear that consumers will rush to competitors who are not so forthcoming about how high calorie (or fat laden) their offerings are.

We shall turn to the special problems of influencing legislators, business people, the media, and other specific groups in later chapters. Here, we shall focus on the challenges to getting action on the part of ordinary people.

Social Marketing for Community Response

Community is defined here as any group that (a) shares common interests and (b) can be identified (at least in theory) as a specific group by outside observers (e.g., social marketers) for potential interventions. Community contact and involvement in pursuing social improvement has a long history in the United States. Alexis de Tocqueville (2001) in the 19th century saw community bonds of mutual support as one of the essential characteristics of the new American nation. As he wrote in *Democracy in America:*

> Americans of all ages, all conditions, and all dispositions constantly form associa-
> tions. They have not only commercial and manufacturing companies, in which all
> take part, but associations of a thousand other kinds, religious, moral, serious,
> futile, general or restricted, enormous or diminutive. The Americans make associ-
> ations to give entertainments, to found seminaries, to build inns, to construct
> churches, to diffuse books, to send missionaries to the antipodes; in this manner
> they found hospitals, prisons, and schools. If it is proposed to inculcate some truth
> or to foster some feeling by the encouragement of a great example, they form a
> society. Wherever at the head of some new undertaking you see the government in
> France, or a man of rank in England, in the United States you will be sure to find
> an association. (p. 106)

What de Tocqueville observed were face-to-face interactions among neighbors, churchgoers, and participants in civic institutions such as fire companies and food co-ops. These same groups exist today, augmented by a large array of formal associations such as PTAs, chambers of commerce, Elks, and Rotary Clubs, which have arisen to serve specific local community needs or personal needs for friendship and camaraderie. However, a major difference between today and de Tocqueville's time is that most of us are part of communities in which there is no physical contact. There are communities in cyberspace chat rooms. Bloggers send e-mails to like-minded readers. Many communities are really matters of self-iden-tification. Young people see themselves as bikers or "fashionistas," some Wisconsin natives are Green Bay Packers cheeseheads, and some Los Angelinos are Lakers fans even though they never have attended a game.

Members of a community will identify themselves as such and know how to detect kindred souls. However, they may differ significantly in the depth of their identification. One person may be a die-hard, rabid, lifetime Republican; another is someone who simply votes Republican when the party has the better platform. The former may list "Republican" as an important point of self-definition, whereas for the latter, it is only one of the traits he or she possesses, and perhaps a fleeting one at that. For the former, being a Republican very much expresses who this person is—his or her self-image, values, and preferences (Amos, Gray, Currie, & Elton, 1997).

Communities can serve as reference points for individuals' opinions and behavior. They form their views of the president of the United States based on what their senator says or what Jay Leno or Rush Limbaugh is telling them. Their teenage daughter may see herself as the "Paris Hilton type," and her boyfriend may dress like Fred Durst of Limp Bizkit when going to a club. Thus communities may be formally organized or not; have direct, indirect, or no contact with each other; and be composed of permanent or temporary participants. Most individuals belong to several communities and will have different levels of commitment across these alternatives. Some communities require formal membership (e.g., AARP, National Rifle Association), but most do not. They can be large or small, specific or vague—a community can be a bridge club or everyone in the world concerned with global warming. Social group identity often implies the identification of an "out group," as well. Athletes disdain "nerds"; fashionistas are not housefraus; Red Sox fans are not Yankees fans.

In the present context, we are simply assuming the existence of a "community" that has the capacity for action. It can play a role in addressing some social problem. This excludes communities that are merely personal labels (e.g., Baby Boomers) and in which there is no implication for social action.

Communities have often been the focus of downstream campaigns, in which they are treated as market segments. For example, in 1998 and 1999, the U.S. Bureau of the Census was eager to increase the participation of minority groups in the 2000 Census. Advertisements were aimed directly at the Hispanic population as a whole, and at the same time, various specific upstream Hispanic organizations were recruited as allies in bringing the message to their specific members and associates and helping these individuals learn how to fill in census documents. This effort was particularly successful, increasing overall census participation to 67% from a predicted 59% rate (Vigdor, 2004).

A TAXONOMY

To give some structure to the discussion, it is useful to set out the major forms communities might take.

   A. Externally defined communities
      1. Geographical communities—neighborhoods, apartment buildings
      2. Political communities—boroughs, towns, states, countries
      3. Workplace communities—both formal (committees) and informal (teams) (see Handy, 1988)
      4. Demographic groups—particularly ethnic and racial groups

B. Membership communities (formal or informal, paid or unpaid, but involving some degree of choice and commitment)
   1. Mutual interest communities—stamp clubs, bridge clubs, book groups, religious organizations, electronic discussion groups
   2. Mutual assistance communities (people banding together to help each other)—Alcoholics Anonymous, professional associations, business associations, labor unions, many Web communities (e.g., the Mac Users Group)
   3. Political groups
   4. Social service communities (people banding together to help others)—readers for the blind, funders of many nonprofit organizations
   5. Advocacy communities—National Rifle Association, AARP, ACT UP
   6. Fellowships (people seeking friendship and camaraderie)—Rotary Club, chatrooms on the Web, neighborhood coffee clubs

C. Personally defined communities
   1. Lifestyle communities—bikers, golfers, opera lovers
   2. Values communities—religious people, conservatives, environmentalists
   3. Opinion communities—progun, prochoice

Communities may be the focus of campaigns and the basis of segmentation. Finding and reaching a community depends on its basic type. If it is externally defined, there undoubtedly are public databases that will help one approximate where that sort of community would be found (e.g., a specific set of zip codes, a list of industries). On the other hand, without further research it may be difficult to know what sort of campaign approach would be effective with such a community. By contrast, membership communities are often ideal. They can be precisely pinpointed. They have clearly defined positions on many social issues. With their organization's assistance, they are reachable.

Personally defined communities are a mixed bag. On the one hand, their lifestyles, values, and opinions provide excellent hints on how to "talk" to them. However, they are probably the most difficult to locate and reach. It is in just such situations that expert advertising executives can be most helpful. They are masters at finding ways to create messages, visual images, and storylines that alert some personally defined group to the fact that the marketer is speaking to them. (Spokespeople who represent such communities are also valuable at sending signals to the intended community.)

Roles for Communities

Communities can play one of six kinds of roles in bringing about social change. First, they can be the *implementers or catalysts for* a social initiative. For example, MADD was formed by a group of women who had lost children because of drunk drivers and who set about together to change laws about drinking and driving. Foundations are also often implementers addressing new social challenges.

Second, communities can be *intermediaries,* through which an initiative can reach other groups. The media community would be a specific example, as would senior management in an industry or in a specific company who are gatekeepers for workplace initiatives. Third, they can be the *targets* of social change campaigns themselves. Fourth, communities can be *allies.* Many social campaigns initiated by one group, organization, or individual will seek to involve other groups as a way to leverage their own resources and increase creativity. Thus a local Boys & Girls Club wishing to clean up a neighborhood or get city hall to install a traffic light may seek business partners, workplace volunteers, and religious institutions to help achieve its aims. Partnering with allies may be the only way an initiative can go to scale.

Fifth, communities can be *social influencers.* Communities are often very important in determining the norms that specify which behaviors are acceptable or unacceptable. They communicate in overt and symbolic ways the values and standards that target audiences are expected to use in deciding on behavioral choices. This group usually contains opinion leaders who can bring direct interpersonal influence to bear on defined target audiences.

Finally, communities can be *competitors* for a specific social change initiative. It may be that they oppose the initiative's goals, believe it is too high on the social agenda, think that other issues are more important, judge the proposed solution as impractical, believe the leaders of the initiative to be misguided or evil, or, in extreme cases, believe that the initiative or its objectives (e.g., "a woman's right to choose") are just plain bad for society.

In the case of obesity raised in chapter 2, some communities of relevance would be (a) implementers (Centers for Disease Control and Prevention, American Dietetics Association, Robert Wood Johnson Foundation), (b) targets (teenagers, African American women, factory workers, members of AARP), (c) allies (sports associations, companies with related products, such as Weight Watchers and Nike), (d) intermediaries (schools, workplaces, all media), (e) social influencers (sports figures, movie stars), and (f) competitors (segments of the food industry, such as the Sugar Council).

Community-Based Social Marketing

There are three broad approaches to community-based social marketing that have appeared in past social marketing literature (McKenzie-Mohr & Smith, 1999). One is to treat *community as a segmentation variable.* That is, one can launch social marketing strategies in the Hispanic community that are different in quality and intensity from strategies for the Asian community. The key distinction is that different communities require different kinds and levels of treatment. Community-based segmentation strategies can often secure significant benefits in terms of effectiveness, because messages, channels, delivery systems, and products and services can be more narrowly tailored to "speak to" specific targets.

A second approach is to consider *community as a geopolitical designation.* That is, a community is a place. There are many logical reasons for aiming social marketing campaigns at places. First, it is easiest to define physical space, and residents in those physical spaces are likely to have a great deal in common. Green and Kreuter (1991) argue for a broad role for geopolitical communities in many kinds of social change strategies, stating that "decisions on priorities and strategies for *social* change affecting the more complicated lifestyle issues [which is certainly the case for childhood obesity] can best be made collectively as close to the homes and workplaces of those affected as possible" (p. 15). They argue that "the most appropriate center of gravity for health promotion is the community" (p. 15). One can also make the case that focusing on one or more political entities can yield significant cost economies. It is much more cost-effective to mount a campaign in Des Moines, Iowa, with a specific set of institutions, media outlets, and array of partner organizations than it is to develop a national strategy aimed at a geographically dispersed Asian community. These advantages are major reasons why AARP pilot-tested a campaign to promote greater physical activity among seniors in two geopolitical communities (Richmond, Virginia, and Madison, Wisconsin) that have very different demographics and lifestyles (Novelli, 2004).

Enthusiasm for treating community as a geopolitical focus was sparked in the 1960s and 1970s with the success of a number of family planning programs in Asia and Africa that sought to bring about change at the village level (Cuca & Pierce, 1977). Village communities were also the focus for many child survival programs (Hornik et al., 2002).

In the United States and abroad, cities and other political jurisdictions have been the target for major interventions related to heart-health issues, including the Stanford Heart Studies (Farquhar et al., 1985; Flora, Maccoby, & Farquhar, 1991), the Minnesota Heart Health Program (Viswanath & Finnegan, 2002), the Pawtucket Heart Health Program (Lefebvre, Lasater, Carleton, & Peterson, 1987), and the North Kerelia (Finland) project (Puska, Tuomilehto, Nissinen, & Vartainen, 1995).

These first two approaches in the marketing literature—communities as segments and communities as places[1]—are mainly downstream approaches. The goal is to focus on a defined set of individuals who are exhibiting (or might exhibit) problem behaviors. The third connotation is the one I shall focus on here. It is treating *communities as interveners.* It argues that, for many important social changes, communities need to be mobilized and take "ownership" of a challenge for anything lasting to take place. Typically, a wide range of changes will have to take place simultaneously for anything significant to happen. To have major impact, media, politicians, businesses, and civic groups need to pull together to set up programs, change laws, publicize issues and alternatives, and create momentum. The broad objective is for the community to increase motivation, opportunity, and ability among its constituents.

Getting communities to intervene is a matter of *social mobilization*. Fraser and Restrepo-Estrada (1998) define it this way:

> Social mobilization can be defined as a planned process that enlists the support and active involvement of any and all sectors within a society that can play a role in achieving an agreed social objective, converging the interest and actions of institutions, groups, and communities towards that objective, thereby mobilizing the human and material resources to reach it, and rooting it in society's conscience, particularly in the community to ensure its sustainability. (p. 69)

These authors cite UNICEF's efforts in the 1980s and 1990s to address child survival issues as a good model for this approach. Appropriately, they make clear that behavioral influence is the key:

> In practice, UNICEF's objectives depend upon changing aspects of people's behaviour. These changes may include parents having their infants fully immunized, or boiling drinking water, or giving oral rehydration salts to children with diarrhea, or allowing their daughters to attend school.
>
> In addition, the changes needed also include modifying government policy, or persuading national or provincial planners to give greater priority and budget resources to child survival and development, or improving the social skills of health workers, or changing the way journalists and media producers perceive and report on social issues. (Fraser & Restrepo-Estrada, 1998, p. 69)

CHOOSING COMMUNITIES

If we are to apply our frameworks to communities, we need to ask: On which community or set of communities do we want to focus, and what do we want it to do? A first question is, then: Is there a community *at all?* Citizens of a city or state are organized; neighborhoods usually are not. The Rotary Club is organized; high school smokers are not. The first challenge for a social marketing program may have to be creating (mobilizing) the community. The next question is: Is there a structure through which mobilization can take place? All formal organizations have structure and identification. A neighborhood has a structure; people with AIDS do not. If we need to create a structure, it is important to know whether potential members personally identify with that community. Frequent flyers recognize that they are part of that community

Table 6.1   Alternative Communities

Type	Formally Organized	Structured	Members Personally Identify	Examples
Type I: Organized	Yes	Yes	Yes	Cities, workplaces, AARP
Type II: Not organized	No	Yes	Yes	Neighborhoods
Type III: Not structured	No	No	Yes	AIDS victims, poor people
Type IV: No membership	No	No	No	Potential cause communities

and could be mobilized to bring about changes in airline practice or Federal Aviation Authority regulations. On the other hand, those upset about land-mine use around the world may not feel that they are in a community. These considerations yield four possible kinds of target communities (Table 6.1).

Organizing and Structuring Communities: The Challenge of Mobilization

Many social scientists argue that change will be more effective if those who will need to take action are involved in the planning of interventions. This is a position strongly advocated by the Rockefeller Foundation and its Communication Initiative (1995). The foundation and groups such as the United Nations and World Bank believe that community involvement is especially appropriate for the developing world. It is a rationale that is partly scientific; specifically, empirical evidence suggests that change is more likely to occur if there is community involvement and ownership of the approach (Minkler, Frantz, & Wechsler, 1982-1983; Zapka & Dorfman, 1982).

There is also a second, less obvious reason for promoting community involvement in strategy development. This is a matter of ethics. Many social change advocates strongly believe that lifestyle changes should not be "imposed" from outside of any community. In part, this is because many past community-based initiatives have been forces for both good and evil. One can think of social revolutions in France and the United States and union movements throughout the world that were forces for social improvement and explicitly involved the development of community social capital

(Putnam, 2000). On the other side of the ledger, the rise of the Taliban in Afghanistan and al-Qaeda in the Muslim world have proven that community building can have distinctly negative impacts.

If a community is not organized (Type II, III, or IV), mobilization is needed. This challenge is often referred to as grassroots mobilization (Caldeira, Hojnacki, & Wright, 2000). McAdam, McCarthy, and Zald (1996) wrote that the secret here is what they call "micro-mobilization." In their view, issues get addressed because small groups—sometimes subgroups within an existing organization—become upset or motivated enough to get together to address a social problem. This is particularly the case when they will play an implementing role.

McAdam et al. (1996) identify several features critical to the emergence of a community activist movement:

1. Geographical proximity: The easier the physical interaction, the more likely a group can coalesce.

2. Prior organization: If a group of individuals has gotten together to address some other issues (e.g., school performance or neighborhood safety), those individuals are more likely to feel like a group.

3. Prior success: If a community has tackled an issue and seen progress, it is more likely to feel emboldened to act in concert again.

4. Perception of "an enemy" (a competitor, in our terminology): As Saul Alinsky (1972) noted, if a community feels that someone, some organization, or some political entity is doing something injurious to it, it will want to respond. (This, of course, was one of the reasons that youth in Florida became involved in the Truth antismoking campaign. Campaign leaders emphasized to young Floridians that they were being manipulated by the tactics of the tobacco industry and ought to rebel.)

5. A sense of isolation: If a community is not tied to other communities (particularly those that support the status quo), it is more likely to act as the only one that will look out for its own interests. Further, isolation will lead to less concern for the interests of opposition groups.

6. Broad consensus for the need for action: If the issue has moved up the community's agenda, action is more likely, particularly if members feel relatively deprived compared with others.

There are a number of approaches to assessing a community's readiness to become involved. Edwards, Jumper-Thurman, Pleasted, Oetting, and Swanson (2000) suggest looking at existing effort levels, amount of community knowledge on the issue, leadership capacity, climate, and resources.

Good examples of community empowerment are the various efforts at developing microcredit programs in the developing world (Rahman, 1999).

These programs seek to alleviate poverty by making available very tiny loans to poor people who normally would have no access to credit. These loans are then used to start small enterprises that can grow to support the borrowing family and perhaps eventually an entire village. Thus a farmer might get a $100 loan to buy a fertilizer spreader that will increase the productivity of his small plot of land, or $50 might be given to a woman to purchase a cell phone that she rents to neighbors who pay to make local or long distance calls.

A major secondary benefit of many of these microcredit programs is that they can go a long way toward building social capital and heightened community self-efficacy (Bandura, 1995). Programs often require villagers to make loan decisions collectively. In the process, they learn to meet, organize, and come to collective agreement, and, perhaps most important, they learn that their efforts can make a difference. The impacts on other issues are often particularly pronounced when women are brought into the process. Previously disenfranchised or marginalized, women come to recognize their own capabilities and potential impact. The new social capital will have become highly potent.

A Social Marketer's Approach

How would a social marketer approach the challenge of community mobilization? In this and the next three chapters, I suggest how a social marketer might address various kinds of upstream challenges. These challenges are often considered the purview of professionals with other kinds of skills and training—community organizers, political scientists, or media advocacy specialists. In this book, I am not arguing for the superiority of a social marketing approach over these alternatives, only the possibility that it may offer fresh perspectives. I do believe that social marketing, with its simple focus on behavior (any behavior), is sufficiently flexible to be used in a great many very different application areas. I am even tempted to argue that one does not need to immerse oneself deeply in all sorts of other methodologies—social marketing may be all one needs. Whether such a bold claim will prove true depends on how the ideas in this book are accepted, used, and broadened even further. Before proceeding, let me revisit the essence of a social marketing approach.

Precisely determine the behavior or set of behaviors that you seek to influence. This implies both specificity and a set of metrics that will identify progress and ultimate success or failure. *Premise #1:* Social marketing is all about behavioral influence.

Carefully select the target audience(s). This can be a process involving segmenting the market, choosing focal targets (e.g., "low-hanging fruit"), and deciding how much effort to allocate to each. *Premise #2:* Social marketing strategically targets carefully selected audience segments.

Listen to the target audience. This can mean formal research, expert advice, informal conversations, and lots of background reading. *Premise #3:* Social marketing starts with understanding the target audience as deeply as possible.

Use formal frameworks to conduct the listening step and then design specific courses of action. The three key frameworks that I use are the Stages of Change, BCOS, and Competition models. *Premise #4:* Social marketing is guided by clear theories about why target audiences might carry out and maintain the desired behavior.

Pretest program elements with the target audience and frequently track results through monitoring. *Premise #5:* Social marketing religiously relies on the target audience for guidance on what should work and, later, what is or is not working.

Craft programs that are not just advertising or communications but aggressively employ what private sector marketers call the 4 Ps. *Premise #6:* Social marketing features integrated marketing strategies to make the desired behavior fun, easy, and popular.

Expect to engage in many midcourse corrections. Programs never work as planned. The environment changes. The success of the intervention itself brings about change. Communities evolve. What worked initially is almost never appropriate in years 2, 3, and 4 (maybe even in week 2). *Premise #7:* Social marketing follows the private sector maxim of *ready-fire-aim.*

Applying a Social Marketing Approach

TARGET AUDIENCES AND BEHAVIORS

Creating or mobilizing a community to bring about change requires that someone—often many "someones"—must take action. Social marketers would emphasize that one begin by being very precise about the behaviors sought by any mobilization effort. Should the goal be radical reform or incremental change? Should the desired behavior be one with few competitors or one that is more challenging to vested interests or other groups' agendas? Will the behavior have many allies or require that one go it alone? Are there case studies from other communities to provide templates, or is this a new-to-the-world approach? Clearly, simpler options make mobilization easier, and because success is more likely, simple options may empower a group to seek bolder alternatives later. Of course, the downside is that simple, safe goals may postpone action on more fundamental problems and even derail an agenda altogether as communities become content with what they have achieved.

It is important to state that the choice of behaviors is ultimately not the social marketer's responsibility. In many ways, we are "hired guns." Give us behaviors and we will help you make them happen. We can offer insights and predictions about what behaviors are more likely to be changeable, but ultimately the goals need to be defined elsewhere.

Once the behavioral outcomes have been defined (e.g., getting school cafeteria managers to change menus or high school coaches to provide exercise options for obese kids), one needs to identify target individuals who can coalesce the group and move the agenda forward. Strategies and tactics have to be planned, community members identified, speeches given, meetings held, followers energized, and so on. Often a good place to start will be with members of an existing organization. Parents in the PTA might help set up a subcommittee to become active on nutrition issues; an association of high school coaches might take on exercise-related initiatives. Where a social change may confront vested interests, it will be profitable to recruit groups that feel aggrieved. For example, a religious or racial minority might be willing to take up obesity issues if it can see these issues as another example of "establishment" discrimination.

Of course, making all this happen requires leaders. A good place to find such leaders is among participants in past social movements. Activists often like to stay active and use their organizational skills to build something new.

Once the behavior and potential target audiences have been identified, what should the social marketing campaign do to move the issue forward? Here, our three basic models can be helpful to planners.

Stages of Change

Given that there are a great many community groups (or potential community groups) one might target, how does one choose? In my experience, it is likely that careful listening will find communities in one of the four stages I use to frame social marketing plans. Precontemplators will not be thinking about the problem. Contemplators will be thinking about doing something but will not yet be prepared to act. Some community groups will already be embarking on tentative actions. Finally, for long-standing challenges, there may be a few groups that are already undertaking important social changes but need to be reinforced to maintain their motivation and energy—and perhaps be a catalyst for others.

Precontemplators. In my experience, Precontemplators are probably not thinking about some desirable social change in a serious way for one of two reasons related to the agenda-setting process described in chapter 2. First, they may be ignorant of the need for *any* new initiatives in that they are unaware that there is a social problem. For them, the agenda-setting problem has not passed from Stage 1 (inattention) to Stage 2 (discovery). Alternatively, they may not be taking an action because they believe that the problem does not apply to them or is not particularly serious, or that solving the problem would not benefit them.

In the case of childhood obesity, families with overweight children who might be mobilized to collectively take action may think that there is no need for action. They may say:

1. The problem will take care of itself: "Our kids will outgrow it." "It's just a stage." "People are just exaggerating the problem."

2. It's genetic and beyond our control: "People like us are always overweight, so there is nothing that can be done."

3. It's not really a serious problem; there are only minor consequences: "Our kids may face a little kidding on the playground, some restrictions in activities, but it's nothing serious."

4. Our community norms favor overweight people: "We like people to be a little heavy—too many skinny models are distorting what is a good body image."

5. No one else seems worried; why should we be?

6. Even if we wanted to act, there is no really effective method of dealing with the problem: "Look at Oprah; she goes up and down in weight all the time!"

For potential target communities at the Precontemplation stage, it is important to ascertain the strength and role of each of these explanations and begin to identify what strategies might lead to movement to the Contemplation stage.

Contemplation. For those community members who have begun to think about the problem, it is important to understand how they are actually contemplating involvement in a community initiative. Here, the BCOS factors and the concept of Competition will become particularly helpful.

Benefits. If target audience members are in the Early Contemplation stage, we need to identify the benefits that someone might see from joining a community initiative. The literature suggests that there will be two classes of important benefits. The first is the potential that the *outcome* of the social campaign will lead to personal benefits for the participant. These can include a sense of personal meaning through trying to help others. The second set of benefits flows from participation in the group itself. (Remember that influencing a behavior is likely to mean joining a group dealing with the behavior; certainly it will mean being actively involved in a community dedicated, at least in part, to some social change.) Many individuals can see important benefits from social interactions with others. Camaraderie is, by itself, rewarding, and through community involvement, a person can make business or social contacts with future payoffs. People can exert leadership skills and perhaps gain community respect. Community involvement can take up time in lives that often have little content—for example, among retired seniors. It can lead to romantic attachments or identify future jogging partners.

Costs. As individuals see benefits, they inevitably contrast them with the possible costs of action. These costs may include time spent working on the community enterprise and perhaps monetary outlays for babysitters or transportation to meetings. There will be the anticipated frustration of endless meetings and indecision. There will be concerns about feeling like a "sucker" when they could have reaped the benefits without the effort. Contemplators may worry about confronting competitors, being shouted at, losing friends, or feeling that they are on the wrong side of an issue. They may also worry that nothing will ever happen, and they will have wasted their time on the project.

Others. The influence of others will, of course, be very influential in the Contemplation stage. On the negative side, opposing groups may try to pressure Contemplators not to join, because it is the wrong side. They may taunt potential members as "suckers." On the other hand, others can be a positive force—the main instigators of joining. One joins because one's friends belong or because someone one admires belongs. This point is illustrated in Everett Rogers's (1995) summary of research on who participated in the 1964 Mississippi Freedom Summer project and who withdrew (see also McAdam, 1986):

> By far the best predictor of going to Mississippi was having a strong network relationship with other participants or to a Freedom Summer activist. Having a close friend who withdrew from the project influenced a [study] respondent to also withdraw. Some of the withdrawals resulted from the opposition of parents or other adults. (Rogers, 1995, p. 312)

Malcolm Gladwell (2000) has suggested that the growth of social causes (and their organizations) can be thought of as "epidemics." Change comes about through a contagion of ideas that runs through social connections. People hear about the need for social change, see one or two people acting in some relevant way, or catch a newspaper or TV snippet describing the initiative. Participants may see small successes, and they pass the word on to others. Momentum (contagion) builds until major social change takes place. Gladwell cites dramatic drops in the New York City crime rate as the result of little changes in better policing behavior, small declines in crack cocaine use, and the aging of the population. Decreases in crime suddenly accelerated, causing, for example, a 64.3% drop in the number of murders in just 5 years.

Sometimes it is important that leading personalities bring their personal pressure to bear on a new venture. For example, for many years, corporate America, with a few exceptions, avoided addressing the HIV/AIDS issue. A corporate community was formed in 1998: the Global Business Coalition on HIV/AIDS. As recently as 2001, it had only 17 members; however, in June 2003, organization membership was up to 117, including some of the world's largest businesses, and a major awards event at the Kennedy Center for the Performing Arts attracted the likes of Colin Powell, James Wolfensohn, and the CEOs of DaimlerChrysler, Viacom, and Coca-Cola.

Partly, the change was the result of the intervention of several key corporation executives who recognized the effects of the epidemic on their own workforces and the significant benefits they might reap if action was taken. Several individuals played major parts in this turnabout. First, President George W. Bush pushed for a $15 billion commitment to battle AIDS around the world. Second, important conservative leaders such as Jesse Helms and the Reverend Franklin Graham indicated their support for efforts to battle the problem. As Richard Holbrooke, the current CEO of the coalition, said, these two "made it safe for conservatives to support massive AIDS efforts" (Roberts, 2003).

Self-Assurance. For individuals to move on to actual participation in a community effort, they must feel that they can make the participation actually happen. For many, this is a matter of finding the time. For others, it is not simply the time involved but the worry that such time will be wasted. It is for this reason that researchers and theorists studying community mobilization place great emphasis on building what they call community *empowerment* and community *capacity.* Both of these concepts, of course, really refer to creating self-assurance at the community level. In social marketing, we emphasize *individual* self-assurance, but of course there comes a moment when the community as a whole must develop enough communal self-assurance that action will finally move forward (Bandura, 1995).

Competition. Here we are talking about competition for the target audience's time and attention. People have other challenges in their lives, other things to worry about. A poor mother may want to earn more income through a microcredit program, but she is conflicted because she has sick children and a husband who is off working in another country. Volunteers have many alternatives—church work, coaching softball, fundraising for the United Way, working in a soup kitchen, and so on. The challenge for the social marketer is to (a) recognize the prime competitors that potential recruits might face, (b) assess the benefits people might see in pursuing these alternative choices, and then (c) provide arguments that the social marketer's package of BCOS factors is superior to those of the competition. Sometimes it can be argued that working on your issue can empower the community so that it can be even more effective in dealing with its issue.

Action. To get individuals to the point where they act, social marketers, as always, must find ways to emphasize the *benefits* mentioned here (and add new ones), reduce as many *costs* as possible, bring positive *social pressure* to bear and fend off negative social pressures, and, finally, find and communicate *easy ways* to make the behavior happen. With respect to the latter, we are blessed by the fact that much more organization and planning can now be done—even worldwide—through the Internet.

The Internet allows the formation of Type IV groups, those without organization, structure, or identification. Electronic contagion can create new, sometimes temporary coalitions focusing on particular issues. In the 1990s, the Internet proved itself to be a very powerful tool, allowing Amnesty International to create a community (network) of advocates called Fast Action Stops Torture that linked individuals and organizations around the world to bring attention to cases of human torture. Such ad hoc community pressure was believed to have played a major role in securing the release of a Kurd who had been tortured by the Turkish authorities in the 1990s (Wallace, 2000). More recently, Internet communities have sprung up because of disasters; for example, in the early efforts in December 2004 to deal with tsunami relief in South Asia.

It is important at the Action stage to get target audiences *started* on the behavior. Target individuals need to go to a first meeting or rally, visit the Internet chat room for the first time, or write a first letter as part of a campaign initiative. Tactics at this stage should be full of "how-to" information—places to get information, sites for rallies, Web sites to search, 800 numbers to call, and specific individuals to speak to. Once target audience members have taken the first step, they may begin to see themselves as part of the community focused on the social marketer's issue—changing their self-perception from that of disinterested outsider to "one of those fighting the good fight."

Maintenance. The challenge for social marketers focused on joiners is to make sure that real benefits are delivered. Recruits need to feel that belonging leads to more respect, more camaraderie. They need to have their sense of self-assurance heightened and rewarded. They need to feel personally the reinforcement of others. As with any behavior, intrinsic and extrinsic rewards can be powerful sustainers. It also can be helpful to have an "enemy." The research literature makes clear that confrontation (or anticipated confrontation) is a strong builder of group solidarity and continuing commitment.

Social Norming

A major outcome of community mobilization can be the change of community norms. One way of thinking about social marketing mobilization goals is that one wishes to make a new set of behaviors the community norm. In the case of childhood obesity, social marketers may seek a norm that says that everyone—not just those who are overweight—must act to bring about changes at the school, Burger King, the playground, and so on. In future, everyone must talk about childhood obesity; we must urge our legislators to make new rules about school lunches and get school administrators to make such lunches better. We all must develop a social norm that *requires* physical education classes and a norm that says that caregivers have family mealtimes with healthy menus. Family norms should put strict limits on children's time at the computer or game console.

In many social change situations, a social norms approach makes considerable sense. Almost two decades ago, Solomon and DeJong (1986) reviewed much of the initial findings in the literature on AIDS and concluded: "More than any other recommendation, we urge that AIDS risk-reduction strategies focus on establishing a social climate in which people feel that it is the norm and not the exception to adopt AIDS risk-reduction behaviors" (p. 314). They argued that major changes in a society's approach to smoking or drunk driving did not occur until there was widespread agreement that, for example, smoking was bad and smokers ought to have fewer rights. Similarly, direct confrontations of drinking drivers was possible only after it was widely accepted that drinking and driving was potentially lethal and thoughtful partygoers ought to select one of their participants to be the "designated driver." Certainly, it is now much more acceptable for bartenders to refuse service to inebriated patrons than it was a decade ago.

A powerful argument for a community norming approach to many social problems is that norming involves multiple influences and multiple behaviors. Often (as in the case of childhood obesity) we are not dealing with single behaviors of single individuals. We are dealing with lifestyle patterns strongly influenced by other individuals and institutions in the target community's environment. For needed changes to take place, all of these parties must accept the need for change. Individuals are much more likely to act if they believe that their friends and colleagues support the behavior and if some have already undertaken it and provided role models! Change will be slower if target audiences—both upstream and downstream—think that the community norm is inaction.

The media can play an important role here. New norms will be diffused more rapidly if opinion leaders speak out for them and political leaders support the new behaviors (e.g., by supporting antismoking laws). Fortunately, as community norms change, it becomes more palatable for political leaders to speak out and propose or adopt needed structural changes. This, in turn, sets the stage for other individuals to act.

One of the domains in which social norming has received considerable attention is in the area of drinking and drug use by college students (Wechsler, Davenport, Dowdall, Moeykens, & Castillo, 1994; Wechsler & Kuo, 2003). The problem of binge drinking on campuses has caused great concern in the last decade, particularly when it has been linked to the deaths of college students. Research showed that part of the problem was that a great many students believed that binge drinking and heavy drug use were very common among their fellow students—and therefore they ought to mimic this behavior to fit in. Media reports of wild parties and vandalism undoubtedly contributed to this perception, as, probably, did the bragging of fellow students. However, research showed that substantial majorities on all campuses were not bingeing. As a consequence, many student service coordinators mounted campaigns to inform students that their perceptions of student norms were simply wrong.

These campaigns differed dramatically from traditional student education campaigns that emphasized the evils of drugs and alcohol. The goal was to change the social norms concerning this critical behavior.

For example, at Western Washington University, baseline data from 1993 to 1996 showed a relatively constant level of high-risk consumption (i.e., bingeing) of around 34%. However, students believed that the figure was much higher. The university then began a "mass media social norms-based social marketing campaign" in 1997 and reported a decline in high-risk consumption to 27%. A subset of students was tracked the following year (i.e., after they were exposed to two waves of marketing) and had a reported further decline, to 22%. Before the campaign, the percentage that thought other students drank heavily once a week was 84%. This figure dropped to 45% the next year. (*What Campuses Are Doing*, 2003).

Results from other campuses report similar effects, and there are similar social norming approaches in high schools (Thomas, 2002). Although plans are being made to spread the approach to more campuses and to more topics, such as smoking and drunk driving, there are reviews that suggest that social norming approaches have not been effective (Wechsler, Nelson, & Lee, 2003).

The Role of Change Agents

Individuals make change happen. Change agents play powerful roles in community building and social change. Thus they are important targets in a social marketing campaign to mobilize a community. Change agents may be individuals who already have high community status, such as ministers in African American communities, leaders of medical associations, reporters at the *New York Times* or the *Washington Post*, or secretaries of education in various states. They may also be individuals who are known to be early adopters of new ideas and practices.

Over the years, social scientists have conducted a vast number of studies on the innovation adoption process. Perhaps the best known formulation is found in the work of Everett Rogers (1995). Rogers suggests that, for a range of innovations, one can divide the population into five groups. Change agents are in the second group (in respect to time), the "Early Adopters," which is the key group. Those in this group are the "Opinion Leaders," who, in turn, influence the next group, the "Early Majority."

Gladwell (2000) has a different view of how social change comes about. He suggests that "social epidemics" can emerge from any place in the social and economic pyramid. There are three kinds of roles in Gladwell's framework. The first group he calls "Connectors." These are the ones who spread social contagions. They are conduits of ideas and trends. These are the people with large Rolodexes and lots of people on their "Buddy List." They are the charity organizers who know all the right people to call. They are the professors with hundreds of students with whom they keep in touch. They are the football coaches who can always round up 10 people to clean up an unsightly vacant lot. They are your cousin who is the one who knows what everyone in the family is doing at any given moment and what they are planning to do next.

A key feature of connectors, identified in the work of Granovetter (1978), is that they work through many, many "weak ties." We all have *strong* ties to other people much like ourselves. Thus if someone in our group supports a new community initiative, others like us will soon be supporting it also. Little effort is needed to diffuse the idea among our friends because of our strong ties. However, people who have weak ties with more distant groups are the ones who can really accelerate change. Gladwell (2000) cites Paul Revere as one of our best known connectors.

The second group in Gladwell's (2000) trinity is the "Mavens." These are the specialists in information or ideas who bring new knowledge to the connectors for the latter to pass along. Mavens like to know things. They often specialize. They are the ones who know about the best movies to see and where the best clothing bargains are. They are the parents who read the health literature and attend university lectures on child development. They are the doctors who keep on the cutting edge of drug therapy and surgeons who study all the latest findings on nanotechnology. The reason these people are key is not just that they know a lot but that they are eager to tell others. They are akin to Rogers's (1995) opinion leaders: They want the knowledge to spread. Connectors are their allies.

The last group is the "Salesmen." Mavens just collect and provide information and connectors just pass it along. But as Gladwell (2000)—*thinking like a social marketer*—notes: "For the social epidemic to start . . . some people are actually going to have to be persuaded to do something" (p. 69). Without salesmen, there is no "tipping point"—the information does not lead to the wildfire of word-of-mouth epidemics and the creation of action communities. Gladwell believes that a crucial quality that makes people good salesmen is their upbeat, positive approach to change. They are able to create "emotional contagion" to get others to support their views and their actions. They are the key builders of social coalitions that we need for important social changes.

When identifying target markets in the social marketing process, one must pay particular attention to these potential group dynamics and specifically seek out the names of people who can play Gladwell's three key roles as change agents in community building.

Note

1. Places can, of course, also be thought of as segments in a national campaign.

7

Structural Change: Influencing Lawmakers and Regulators

Bosnia-Herzegovina (BiH) is a central European country that was created out of a region of the former Yugoslavia and reorganized after armed conflict in the mid-1990s under the Dayton Peace Accords. The signing of the accords in 1995 was immediately followed by significant involvement of hundreds of international organizations and nongovernmental organizations (NGOs) trying to create political, social, and economic stability and promote growth in this new, ethnically complex political entity. However, after much initial enthusiasm, by 2003 much foreign aid was drying up. The country found itself with an official unemployment rate of 40%, a fragmented market (the 3.5 million inhabitants were now divided into two separate entities), gross domestic product per capita of only US$1800—among the lowest in Europe—and limited foreign direct investment.

The lack of economic development was traced to dozens and dozens of annoying laws and regulations that discouraged the growth of private entrepreneurship. To attempt to change this climate, a team from the World Bank under Benjamin Herzberg created "The Bulldozer Project" to bulldoze 50 constricting rules—not entire regulations, just small clauses and addenda that caused problems. The team chose this route to make change easier and less politically threatening for the politicians. They marshaled wide support among small entrepreneurs by promising that small reforms had a high chance of succeeding. This meant that the entrepreneurs' time wouldn't be wasted on a fruitless quest. Because the entrepreneurs *were united, the politicians could see that changing the small laws and regulations would mean votes and perhaps campaign support in future (Andreasen & Herzberg, 2005).*

The campaign succeeded in securing 50 reforms in 187 days. Plans were immediately made to "bulldoze" another set of laws in the following months.

P roblematic social behaviors can often only be addressed after upstream structural changes are made that give downstream target audiences the opportunity and ability to act as desired. In the case of obesity, this means changes in schools, playgrounds, fast food menus, and the like. In this chapter, we shall focus on two groups whose behaviors are central to structural change: lawmakers and regulators. This is because removing upstream causes of undesirable behavior or impediments to social change often requires the creation of specific penalties for noncompliance or specific incentives for compliance. Penalties and incentives, of course, first require specific individuals to take action to create them. In the case of incentives and penalties, there are three potential targets for such actions: lawmakers, law implementers (regulators, police), and private parties.

Lawmakers

Lawmakers can legislate needed incentives or penalties or otherwise change an unsatisfactory legal environment. An unsatisfactory legal environment means that, for example, the present level or type of incentive or penalty is inadequate to stimulate the desired behaviors from institutions in the problem environment, especially those antagonistic to action. Thus federal or state governments may need to withhold funding from schools that do not offer physical education classes. Companies may need to be fined under new city ordinances that bar smoking anywhere on company premises. Mayors in villages in Africa may need to be put in jail for sanitation systems that are below a desired level of quality and availability.

The World Health Organization has considered several changes in domestic laws to fight obesity around the world (Lawrence, 2003). They propose three regulatory approaches:

1. Using pricing controls on foods: imposing tariffs, providing domestic subsidies, or imposing or increasing domestic taxes on particular food commodities

2. Restricting the supply of particular foods: banning their import, prohibiting domestic sale, or requiring certain composition standards

3. Mandating labeling requirements for foods sold in the domestic market, such as having labels contain warning statements, nutrient claims, and more useful nutrition information panels

Getting such laws enacted by specific countries or cross-border institutions such as the European Union is not a trivial challenge.

Law Implementers

The creation of laws and regulations is, of course, only one step toward social change. Even if new laws are passed or new regulations put in place, there will be no impact unless regulators and other implementers act and act vigorously. Unfortunately, social histories are replete with stories of laws that were ignored or applied unevenly. Depending on political connections, some "villains" are subject to draconian interventions and other targets are given favorable treatment. In many parts of the world, this disparate impact follows rampant bribery and kickbacks.

When a law is established for an existing agency to implement, the practical effects are typically spelled out in guidelines. For example, the U.S. Federal Trade Commission has a mandate to prosecute "unfair competition." What is meant by that depends on who is on the commission and what its current guidelines happen to be.

Nestle and Jacobson (2000) note that since 1952, when the American Heart Association cited obesity as a major cardiac risk factor, more than 30 guidelines on the topic have been published by various government agencies and private organizations. (The most recent set of Dietary Guidelines for Americans, from the U.S. Department of Agriculture and the U.S. Department of Health and Human Services [DHHS], is at http://www.health.gov/dietary guidelines/). However, the authors conclude that "typically, these guidelines focused on [downstream] individuals and tended to state the obvious. . . . Only rarely did such guidelines deal with factors in society and the environment that might contribute to obesity" (p. 14).

Nestle and Jacobson (2000) propose a number of legislative and regulatory changes to reduce the prevalence of obesity, often mimicking approaches taken over the years to reduce tobacco consumption.

1. Ban commercials for high-calorie products from school television programs.

2. Require and fund daily physical education and sports programs in primary and secondary schools, extending the school day if necessary.

3. Require calorie content information in chain restaurants and on soft drinks and snacks sold in movie theaters, convenience stores, and other venues.

4. Restrict advertising of high-calorie, low-nutrient foods on television shows commonly watched by children, or require broadcasters to provide equal time for messages promoting healthy eating and physical activity.

5. Require print ads to disclose calorie content of food advertised.

6. Restrict high-calorie food offerings in schools outside of cafeteria meals.

7. Provide incentives for Food Stamp users to consume healthful foods.

8. Require training programs for health-care workers that include the principles and benefits of healthful diets and exercise.

9. Provide funding and other incentives for bicycle paths, recreation centers, swimming pools, parks, and sidewalks.

10. Provide guidelines for changes in zoning regulations to encourage physical activity (e.g., auto-free zones).

11. Levy city, state, or federal taxes on soft drinks and other foods high in calories, fat, or sugar to fund campaigns to promote good nutrition and physical activity.

12. Remove sales taxes or provide other incentives for the purchase of exercise equipment.

13. Provide tax incentives to encourage employers to provide weight management programs (p. 20).

Many of these recommendations involve new laws, as well as new forms of implementation.

Private Enforcement

Implementation of laws and regulations is in the hands of legislators and bureaucrats who want to bring about change. Such laws and regulations can also be used by private parties to bring about social solutions. In the case of tobacco, private lawsuits by individuals and nonprofit organizations kept the issue before the public for many years. Their example led attorneys general from dozens of states and cities to bring their own lawsuits to recover the social costs of tobacco use to their constituents (Glantz & Balbach, 2000). The funds generated by individual settlements and as part of the multiparty "master settlement" agreement provide huge amounts of money for social marketing campaigns to use in working on smoking issues downstream. The American Legacy Foundation continues to use such funds in their efforts to reduce smoking levels even further (American Legacy Foundation, 2004).

The tobacco lawsuits had an important secondary effect. The litigation released thousands of tobacco company documents that made it possible for social marketers to cast industry practices in a highly unfavorable light (Glantz,

Barnes, Bero, Hanauer, & Slade, 1996; Glantz, Slade, Bero, Hanauer, & Barnes, 1996). Kersh and Morone (2002) argue that such questionable tactics are ideal ingredients for turning a personal issue into a social and political one. It helps mobilize communities.

Private class action lawsuits are another means of using the law to bring about social change. One of the most vigorous proponents of this strategy is John Banzhaf III, a professor of public interest law at George Washington University. In the 1980s and 1990s, Banzhaf brought dozens of lawsuits against the tobacco industry through his organization, Action for Smoking and Health. In addition, he sued to force broadcasters to provide time for antismoking ads and to make airlines offer nonsmoking sections (and eventually total bans on smoking on domestic aircraft). He and his students have brought actions on other issues as well, seeking more toilets for women in public places, smoke detectors in airplane lavatories, increased safety on school buses, clearer warnings on birth control pills, greater roles for African Americans on television, and new police procedures for dealing with spousal abuse (Banzhaf, 2004).

Recently, he set his sights on the fast food industry. Banzhaf brought lawsuits against McDonald's and other fast food chains, charging that they deliberately induce customers to take up unhealthy behavior for the firm's own economic gain. Banzhaf has already won $12 million from McDonald's and $3 million from Pirate Booty, a snack food company. In a June 2003 certified mailing to Burger King, Kentucky Fried Chicken, McDonald's, Taco Bell, and Wendy's, Banzhaf (2003) argued:

> This letter will put your corporation on legal notice of a growing body of evidence that foods of the type served at your fast food restaurants may produce addictive-like effects, and of the consequent need to consider posting a health warning or other appropriate informational notice to avoid potential legal liability. . . . [T]he legal duty to warn or inform customers does not arise only when possible evidence of harm is conclusive and generally accepted by the scientific community. Rather, it occurs whenever information might be relevant to a reasonable person making a purchasing decision. . . . [S]everal courts have held that cigarette manufacturers may be held liable for failing to disclose that their products might produce addictive effects, even though the general health dangers of smoking were so well known as to be regarded as common knowledge.

Banzhaf organized an Obesity Lawsuit Conference at Northeastern University in Boston in June 2003, at which 120 attendees discussed the possibilities of suing fast food companies and other parties over this issue. Banzhaf proposed attacking those school boards that have exclusive contracts with companies such as Coca-Cola and Pepsi as promoting poor consumption and offering few healthy choices for students.

Professor Banzhaf may be having an effect. In the summer of 2003, Chancellor Joel Klein of the New York City public schools, the country's largest school system, ordered that candy, cakes, donuts, and soda be removed from all public school vending machines. He also recommended the elimination of beef ravioli, potato salad, and macaroni and cheese from school lunches if they cannot be made with lower levels of fat. He insisted that tacos and chicken nuggets be offered in low-fat versions. Other recommended changes included requiring juice (e.g., in vending machines) to be 100% fruit, more whole wheat in bread, fewer canned vegetables and more fresh and frozen, more fish options, fewer mayonnaise-based salads, and offering soy-based chicken and burger substitutes. The New York City Council subsequently promised legislation to both strengthen the guidelines and lock them into place (Goodnough, 2003).

The industries in the crosshairs of private litigation are not unmindful of the effects of past suits on the tobacco industry. Many fast food restaurant chains are rapidly increasing their array of "healthy" offerings (Horovitz, 2003). The food industry also has legislative allies. Republicans in Congress passed legislation in March 2004 barring class actions against the food industry that accuse the industry of causing the "obesity epidemic." Speaker Dennis Hastert of the House of Representatives was quoted as saying: "We as Americans need to realize that suing your way to better health is not the answer. Trial lawyers need to stop encouraging consumers to blame others for the consequences of their actions just so they can profit from frivolous lawsuits against restaurants" (Hastert, 2003).

Social Marketing and Legislative Change

If upstream structural change encounters resistant or reluctant executives or managers, new legislation may be needed to restrict bad behaviors and incentivize good behaviors. How would a social marketer go about securing such legislation? Again, the principles developed throughout this volume apply, as does the use of the three fundamental strategic models: Stages of Change, BCOS, and Competition.

The interjection of social marketing ideas into the realm of legislation and governance may strike some as overreaching. In the Philippines, Professor Ned Roberto (2002), an early pioneer in social marketing, faced considerable criticism when he sought to publish a manuscript applying social marketing ideas to governance. His objective was to introduce formal research and other "listening" methods into the legislative process to make governors and administrators more responsive to constituent needs. However, when he showed his manuscript to three friends, they said, "What are you crafty social marketers doing in local governance?" One added (jokingly), "How dare you!" (Roberto, 2002).

As you are aware by now, my perspective is that social marketing is valuable whenever one has a behavior to influence. I believe the application to legislative behavior is reasonable even if some do not welcome this extension and perhaps political scientists and others find it to be "poaching" where we do not belong. Social marketing is appropriate if the goal is to induce someone in power to create, lobby for, or vote for specific legislation to bring about a desirable social change. It is also appropriate for motivating a bureaucrat to implement new or existing laws or regulations that would contribute to increased social welfare.

Influencing legislation and legislators has typically been the exclusive domain of lobbyists—a profession with a long tradition (Goldstein, 1999; Kollman, 1998). As I note later, these professionals have much experience and insight into how the legislative process works. Many of the techniques and strategies they use are compatible with a social marketing approach. Our models and frameworks are flexible enough to guide efforts aimed at this kind of upstream behavior, especially for the many smaller organizations, especially at the local level, that cannot afford lobbyists (see deKeiffer, 1997). Even when a social change organization can afford a lobbyist, however, social marketing can provide managers with a framework for reviewing what the lobbyists propose.

Just how would a social marketer approach a legislative influence challenge?

BEHAVIOR AND TARGETING

Let us assume that there is a possibility of passing a U.S. federal law that would make federal funding available for each state that passes regulations requiring 1 hour of physical education for every student at every school level at least three times a week. The law would provide funding for teachers and assistants to cover the newly mandated programs. The social marketer's behavioral challenge is to identify and approach senators and members of the House of Representatives from both parties who can secure the law's creation, introduction, and passage.

Given this clear behavioral goal, a first step would be to segment the target audience into potential supporters, opponents, and "undecideds." The Stages of Change model provides a useful way to think about this.

Precontemplators

Many legislators will be unaware of the issue or the possibility of some legislative or regulatory solution. Others will be in Precontemplation because they consider it a nonissue; although it is perhaps socially important, they believe other competing issues take priority. They may also believe that other legislators will kill it in committee or otherwise make sure it does not rise to the level where the Precontemplator has to deal with it. To move these people forward, social marketers will have to move the issue up the media and public agendas.

Talk shows are often excellent vehicles at this point. The real challenges will arise as Precontemplators move to the next stage.

Contemplators

There will be Early and Late Contemplators among legislators for any issue that has been on the public agenda for a time. The challenge will be to move both groups rapidly toward Preparation and Action. The time frame here can be months for "hot" issues or *years* for "evergreen" issues such as environmental protection or nuclear waste disposal, which come up year after year. Once an issue rises in prominence, the BCOS model can help develop approaches to specific congresspeople, senators, or (later) town council members contemplating action.

The key is to "listen" to various potential targets and assess how the BCOS factors might work for and against potential legislative action. This listening activity, of course, is the stock-in-trade of professional lobbyists, who spend as much time as possible with potential targets in their offices, at social gatherings, in the gym, or on the golf course to learn what their "hot buttons" are and what issues or factors are perceived as toxic. Secondary data on legislative interests and priorities are also available from past voting records in the *Almanac of American Politics* and in detailed records available from every federal House and Senate committee. For national issues, additional insights can be gained from speeches made by congresspeople, Google searches on the Internet, and conversations with others in Washington or in the legislators' home districts who have worked with them on campaigns, committees, or other public commitments. Party affiliation and party positions on the proposed legislation will also help guide social marketers toward audiences likely to be sympathetic.

Once a set of target candidates is identified, the next important challenge is to pinpoint possible points of influence. To see how this might work, let us speculate how the BCOS factors would help prioritize approaches to three hypothetical senators: Sally Brown from California, Aaron Fielding from Louisiana, and Oscar Hernandez from New Mexico. In each case, the important requirement is to understand the BCOS factors as they might be perceived *by the senator.* It is less important how the legislation affects the American citizenry than it is what it does for the *senator.*

Before proceeding, let's paint a portrait of each senator.

• Sally Brown, 62, is a lifelong Democrat from the northern part of California. She has been in the Senate for 16 years and will be up for reelection in 2 years. She is likely to face a well-financed, downstate, conservative Republican and may have to go through a Democratic primary race against a rising Hispanic politician, the mayor of Fresno. She has one married daughter and three very young grandchildren. In the past, she has focused on foreign affairs and has developed a reputation as extremely knowledgeable about Department of Defense issues and international trade. She is regarded as one of the smartest people in the Senate.

- Aaron Fielding, 47, is a first-term Republican who just won a landslide victory in Louisiana. Married, with two teenaged children, he served earlier on the Baton Rouge School Board and then was elected to the Louisiana state legislature from one of Baton Rouge's poorer districts. He served 11 years at the state level, rising to the second highest position in his party's legislative caucus. Although known for his compassion for social issues, he is a fiscal conservative.

- Oscar Hernandez, 52, is known as the "wild card" Republican in the Senate. A father of four who recently went through a nasty divorce, Hernandez has been criticized in the media for his passion for gambling. He is a tough negotiator in committee, with a deep knowledge of Senate rules, which he uses to his advantage. This is his third term, but he has not yet staked a claim to any single set of issues and is seen as often more interested in the deal-making aspects of legislation than in the substance. His reelection is considered safe.

How might each of these senators see the BCOS factors in the proposed obesity legislation? Conversations, Google searches, and a review of their records might yield profiles like those described in Table 7.1.

Social marketers also know it is important to pay attention to *competition* for the federally funded school exercise curriculum proposal as perceived by Contemplators. In the case of legislators, there are several possibilities (Andreasen & Kotler, 2003):

- *Brand competition.* Alternative legislative proposals may allocate the money for buildings and equipment rather than people, and still others may prefer a staffing approach but want it to be funded by the states or local school systems rather than the federal government (i.e., an unfunded mandate).
- *Product competition.* Alternative legislative approaches to children's lack of exercise may not involve the schools. Some senators and their staffers may prefer to create grants for after-school programs at nonprofit organizations such as the YMCA or the Boys & Girls Clubs. Others may want to subsidize the creation of new municipal exercise facilities—preferably named after their senator.
- *Enterprise competition.* There may be proponents of exercise programs that do not involve federal legislation at all. Some may argue that it is a state or local school board issue and not the federal government's role. Others may say that we should leave interventions up to the nonprofit sector and interested funders such as the Robert Wood Johnson or W. K. Kellogg foundations. Others may propose that existing federal agencies such as the Centers for Disease Control and Prevention already have the mandate to act and the capacity to address the problem without the need for any new legislation (for example, the CDC's [2005] VERB program may be deemed adequate).

Table 7.1   BCOS Factors for Hypothetical Senators

BCOS Factor	Sally Brown	Aaron Fielding	Oscar Hernandez
Benefits	• The issue appeals to Hispanic voters who are important to her • The California governor supports the issue and would welcome new funding • Chance to diversify her legislative portfolio, which is seen as too narrow • Future opponent will have hard time challenging the law	• Knows friends with obese children; "feels their pain" • Extra funding will help strapped schools • Chance to raise his profile on a safe issue	• The issue appeals to his Hispanic voters • Extra funding will help strapped schools • Chance to negotiate with • Democrats Will reverse Dept. of Education neglect of his state in last session
Costs	• Not her issue—she risks looking uninformed • Her family is too old and grandchildren too young; supporting the bill challenges her credibility	• Might appear to be supporting federal impositions on states • Risks an outcome in which states or cities will have to bear unexpected costs • No experience at building coalitions; worries about alienating leaders	• Non-Hispanics attend private schools and see only burdens in the bill • Risks reminding constituents of divorce issues • Faces tough Republican caucus opposition, harming his negotiating record • Staff is opposed and will be upset if asked to work on the bill

BCOS Factor	Sally Brown	Aaron Fielding	Oscar Hernandez
Others	• The other California senator supports the bill • Chair of her foreign relations committee is an education champion • Unions worry that more physical education time will detract from basic skills education	• Unsure which Republican senators would be for or against the issue • Party whip has spoken against the bill • Republican president has not taken a position but is "education friendly" • A powerful Louisiana supporter favors the bill	• Two major New Mexico corporations have come out in support • Party whip has spoken against the bill • Republican president has not taken a position but is "education friendly"
Self-assurance issues	• Not sure where she can turn to get objective tutoring on the issue • Finding time may be a problem, as a major international trade bill is coming up at the same time	• Needs skills to build coalitions • Staff is inexperienced in drafting legislation	• Lacks quid pro quo for potential allies; already supports their issues • Needs better connections to state education activists who will want involvement

- *Generic competition.* There are always other pieces of legislation on other topics on the legislative horizon. Party leaders may be urging a focus on other issues for other constituencies.

These competitive options are set out in Table 7.2.

Given information about the BCOS factors and Competition, the social marketer will then need to make choices among our three hypothetical senators. It may be that the best choice initially is to concentrate on Senator Aaron Fielding. This is a "feel-good" issue for him, with little downside risk for a freshman senator. Some of the strategies and tactics that might be employed to move him to the Action stage in regard to federally funded school exercise

Table 7.2   Legislative Competition

Type of Competition	Competitors Your Bill Is Likely to Have	
Generic	Trade bill	Energy bill
Enterprise	Foundation sponsorship	State sponsorship
Product	Nonprofit grants	Public projects
Brand	Unfunded mandate	Equipment subsidies

programs would be as follows. (Before going on, you may want to take another look at the Aaron Fielding column in Table 7.1.)

Benefits. Discussions of the issue should include vivid stories of real children affected by the problem, preferably poor kids in Louisiana or, better yet, Baton Rouge. Success stories about exercise innovations that work can be highly impactful. Emotional approaches may be particularly effective with this senator. Estimates should be provided showing the projected funding gains for Louisiana school systems and compared with figures showing school deficiencies (which Fielding should already know). The social marketer should offer assistance in publicizing to constituents back home Senator Fielding's involvement in this issue and his leadership role—a major benefit to future campaigns.

Costs. Senators are always worried about federally imposed mandates on local jurisdictions. These concerns should be allayed by indicating that this proposal is not unfunded and that, if the challenge is simply left to the states, the rich states will get good programs and Louisiana may not get any. Concern about future unanticipated costs can be allayed by reporting success stories of programs in other states or other communities that did not have major unexpected costs. (However, one must be careful to be honest with this target audience. Senators are smart people who will appreciate honesty and candor. If their state has to bear some of the burden of implementation, this should be discussed up front.) Senator Fielding's concerns about alienating senate leadership—especially in his own party—should be addressed by providing a rundown on the stances of major party figures and by offering help in mitigating any negative political fallout.

Others. A list should be created of other senators who have indicated either support for the legislation or support for the broader enterprise category (federally funded exercise programs). Prior conversations with the party whip should have been undertaken to assess levels of support. Senator Fielding should be equipped with some "talking points" that will help him convince the party whip to support the legislation (or at least not oppose it). Fielding should be lobbied by other supporters of your legislative approach among the Republican Party leadership and members of the Senate Committee on Health, Education, Labor and Pensions. Statements from the White House that support more exercise initiatives, although not necessarily this specific legislation, should be reproduced. Visits or phone calls to Senator Fielding by powerful Louisiana supporters should be arranged when possible and should be continuous. Constituent call-ins, letter writing, and e-mails can be very helpful. There are a number of consultants available to help set up such a grassroots minicampaign.

Self-assurance. If the senator's staff does not have the time or expertise to craft specific legislation or amendments that Senator Fielding could offer, the social marketer could offer specific drafting help. If legislation already exists, the senator could be carefully tutored on its strengths and weaknesses. A road map could be drafted for the senator to use to build coalitions for the legislation in the Senate, particularly among those on key gatekeeper committees. Assistance with drafting will be particularly appreciated if it helps tutor Senator Fielding in skills to be used in future negotiations on other issues. In the process, it is also important to make the legislative process easy for *the senator's own staff.* They will be the ones who will do most of the serious analysis of the issue and advise the senator. Social marketers should not usurp their role: Staff should feel in control of the process.

COMPETITION

The social marketer will have a considerable challenge keeping abreast of competitive challenges, both public and behind-the-scenes. Competition concerning exercise programs may be less than it would be if the focus were on food policy interventions. In recent books, Marion Nestle (2002) and Brownell and Horgen (2004) make clear that the food industry is a formidable competitor. In the case of exercise, the senator will typically be very appreciative of monitoring data on competitors' planned actions because it can keep him from being blindsided by opposition. The social marketer should also provide rejoinders and relevant counterarguments to the senator and his staff.

Preparing and Acting

Getting the senator to "go public" on the issue and introduce the legislation should be relatively easy if the BCOS factors have been addressed. The social marketer may assist at this point by helping schedule floor time and preparing materials for the senator to use when circulating drafts for debate and enactment.

Maintenance

As the legislation moves forward, it will be important to closely monitor any changes in the BCOS factors or Competition that may affect the senator and retard progress as the issue moves through the cumbersome process of hearings, markup, and eventual enactment. The social marketer should be available to recruit potential expert witnesses to testify at committee hearings in support of the legislation (and in support of Senator Fielding). The social marketer should be alert for new sources of interpersonal influence (Others) that may appear on the scene as they get wind of the possible legislative move. During the Maintenance stage, the social marketer may want to spend time with staffers of other Senate offices, including those of the relevant committee chairs. It is not unknown for rival staffers in other offices to undermine an initiative to advance their own agendas.

Ethical Concern: Is Social Marketing to Legislators in the Public Interest?

How much attention should a social marketer pay to the senator's personal motivations and ambitions to achieve the ends the *social marketer* wants? The reader might ask: Isn't this manipulative? Doesn't this mean that social marketers are really trying to prompt behavior for the wrong reasons—for example, convincing the senator to support the legislation because it will advance that senator's career? Don't we want legislators to simply act in the public interest? Wouldn't a focus on their private career motivations lead us down a slippery slope where social marketers have to offer golf tours and cases of champagne to get a social problem addressed? Isn't this why we get bribery and corruption, with unscrupulous lobbyists and big business bribing vulnerable legislators? Wouldn't social marketers be guilty of the sin mentioned in chapter 1—believing in the inherent goodness of the actions they are proposing but allowing many questionable tactics as justifiable in the cause of "doing good"?

These are important questions. It would be nice to think that all legislators act solely in the pubic interest. Undoubtedly the majority of legislators believe they are doing so, although they sometimes misread the public interest and sometimes are forced to choose between competing public interests. Not every public interest can be served.

There are two arguments that, I believe, justify attention to the target audience's (in this case, the senator's) personal interests when seeking upstream solutions to social problems. First, it would be foolish to deny the reality that, in the main, people act to serve their own interests. A great deal of economic and psychological theory makes this clear. Free market economists since Adam

Smith have argued that this is a good thing—that if everyone pursues their own interests and there is full information about the options, we will end up with the greatest good for the greatest number. Of course, in reality, individuals often misinterpret information, listen to the wrong sources, and make dumb choices. Still, they are *trying* to act in their own self-interest.

Legislators are no different. They act to further their own interests. When they say they are "acting in the public interest," they are really saying to themselves, "acting in the public interest meets my personal motives to be altruistic and socially conscious—and, I hope, respected by others for this. I am good to others because that is the kind of person I want to be. It will make me feel good about myself."

I would argue that, if a legislator has a strong motivation to serve the public interest, the way to get him or her to support a piece of legislation is to emphasize, support, and reinforce how the legislation will serve this motivation. The social marketer should not talk as if "the pubic interest" is some abstract goal but should act as if pursuing this legislation *meets the legislator's own need to serve the public interest.*

The second argument is that it is the social marketer's duty to respond to the *reality* of the senator's needs and wants no matter how selfish and career focused they may be. Assuming that the social change being promoted is a desirable outcome for society, then the social marketer owes it to society to *listen* carefully to the target audience—not invent a nobler version of the target audience, the audience that one might want him to be. This intense focus on the target audience is what we social marketers are good at—it is one of the virtues we bring to the process.

If the greater good of the campaign does not justify attention to the more plebian needs of the senator, then I would argue that the social marketer has an ethical responsibility *not* to be involved.

SOLICITING ALLIES

Successful lobbying of a legislator is almost always a joint venture requiring many partners. Many forces will be needed if major change is to happen (see De Vita & Mosher-Williams, 2001). As an issue rises on the public and media agendas, there will always be a range of organizations that will be willing to help with the social marketer's campaign, either by directly lobbying themselves or in some other way. These groups or individuals can provide research data, contacts to explore, expertise for Senate hearings, or volunteers to conduct grassroots call-in or e-mail campaigns to influence legislators.

How does one secure the help of allies? The same social marketing models that apply to other behavioral challenges would apply to efforts to recruit allies. In his book on citizen lobbying, Donald deKeiffer (1997) writes exactly what a social marketer would say:

The first thing you should recognize about potential friends is that they rarely volunteer. . . . Organizations whose members are politically experienced will not join you for philosophical reasons: you will have to show them very specific ways your issue will benefit them. You will also have to remind them of promises they have made regarding their support. Underlying oaths of friendship carry little practical weight: you will have to spend as much time giving backbone transfusions to your allies as you do in the political trenches on Capitol Hill. (p. 19)

The Legislative Cycle

Social marketers are well advised wherever possible to work with seasoned lobbyists. They are especially helpful in guiding someone through the various steps of the typical legislative process. They will point out the rhythms and sets of rituals that determine the progress of any particular act or amendment. These can differ depending on whether one is developing new legislation or simply revising existing statutes. In either case, timing of social marketing interventions is often critical, and the best lobbyists are those who understand these processes well and who have the kinds of insight and contacts that allow fine-tuning of various campaign inputs.

For example, a critical task for controversial (or potentially expensive) legislation is simply to get it on the calendar of one or more relevant committees. All legislation at the U.S. federal level must first be considered by one or more committees that have some jurisdiction in the area.[1] Such "calendaring" will raise an issue's visibility for both committee members and their staffs (more likely the latter), who will be forced to become familiar with the issues and their nuances. Achieving this step often requires careful attention to the particular interests and ambitions of the committee chair or the ranking member from the minority party. Barring support from either of these, a piece of legislation will not be brought up for discussion (let alone voted on) unless a forceful committee member can be recruited to carry the charge.

The media can play an important role here, especially if they can (with the lobbyist's help) portray dramatic stories that highlight the need for action. Demonstrations, rallies, protests, or some other variety of what Daniel Boorstin (1992) calls "pseudo-events" can move an issue to the front burner. These events can force media coverage and create a sense among congresspeople that "something must be done." Polling research that shows high levels of public interest can reinforce the media coverage and provide a compelling positive benefit for the legislator who is considering offering support.

Once a piece of legislation is taken up by a committee, the next step in the legislative cycle is to draft or revise the prospective legislation. Here, the key people will be the committee's staff (not usually the staffs of individual committee members unless they have a special interest or expertise). This is the place where social marketers can have a very powerful impact. By helping the committee amass evidence (often from the social marketer's own studies), think through the issues, and arrive at the many decisions most legislation requires, the perceptive social marketer can influence the subtleties of proposed law.

It is here that the best lobbyists adopt an approach that social marketers would recommend. They recognize that the only way staffers—and eventually legislators—will listen to the lobbyist's opinions is if they think the lobbyist is positioning the help as (at least partially) *in the politician's or committee's interest*. Good lobbyists know that, over a long career, they will return again and again to the committee and talk with the senator and congresspeople about other issues and other legislation. If lobbyists are seen as simply advancing only their *own* interests and those of their client, they will be received warily and will find that their research data and views are treated with skepticism. They will be more welcome if they come across as smart, well-versed experts—albeit with a point of view and a client—and at the same time, people who recognize that, ultimately, the legislation must meet the legislators' own interests. The tenacious lobbyist who fights tooth and nail for his or her own position will inevitably be seen as "too partisan" and someone who has limited consideration for the legislators' interests. Such a lobbyist is not likely to be welcomed back. It is a mistake that an experienced social marketer would never make.

The final stages of the legislative cycle occur as a bill gets to the floor of the House or Senate. There, the bill may be subject to amendments (sometimes having nothing to do with the focus of the bill) and a final up or down vote. Very often, bills passed in the two houses of congress will differ, requiring that the two versions go to a joint conference committee (unique to each situation) for resolution. The agreed-on compromise then goes back to the two bodies. Once passed, the legislation goes to the White House for the president's signature.

It is inevitable that, on important topics, legislation will be tinkered with at many stages of the cycle, particularly because compromises need to be made. The social marketer needs to make sure that the target senator does not waver in important ways. He or she is at the Maintenance stage; this means that the savvy lobbyist must spend time reinforcing the congressperson's actions and continue contacts both during and after each stage of the legislative process. This is critically important. Nothing will make the congressperson more reluctant to continue to support your initiatives than if he or she feels "used," and nothing will signal this better than the lobbyist or social marketer's disappearance the day after any vote—especially one in which the congressperson acceded to the lobbyist's position in some fashion.

STAFFERS

A critical role lobbyists play is that of expert. The legislative branch of the federal government considers thousands of bills, too many for any one congressperson or staffer to comprehend and manage. The challenge is nicely described in a *Washington Post* article:

> At the dawn of 2005, legislation by Rep. Ralph Regula (R-Ohio) to cede the nation's capital back to Maryland faces certain death, along with a pitch by Rep. John Conyers Jr. (D-Mich.) to make Election Day a holiday for federal employees. If these and the thousands of other ideas proposed each year by members of Congress went the distance, Rep. Barney Frank (D-Mass.) would stop the federal government from interfering with the right of states to allow the medicinal use of marijuana. And Rep. Dennis J. Kucinich (D-Ohio) would establish a Department of Peace. Calendars would recognize National Transparency Day, National Weatherization Day, National Asbestos Awareness Day and, importantly for equine lovers and Rep. Jack Kingston (R-Ga.), National Day of the Horse. They are destined for the same fate: They will expire at midnight Dec. 31. . . . Since Jan. 1, 2003, 10,472 bills and resolutions were introduced—6,842 in the House and 3,630 in the Senate. By Nov. 1, only 122 Senate bills and 292 House bills, or 4 percent, had become law. (Maffei, 2004)

Given the staggering number of bills that appear each session, staffers simply have no time to understand them all and therefore are appreciative of the lobbyist who can help educate them—without seeming to educate them to have a particular, narrow point of view. Social marketers should pay particular attention to the benefits a staffer might seek. Donald deKeiffer (1997) suggests four basic motivations.

1. Protecting the congressperson. The staffer's challenge is to minimize embarrassment or potential criticism and to make sure the congressperson is adequately briefed should he or she be required to venture an opinion or vote.

2. Promoting the congressperson. Reelection is important to both staff and legislators. The voices of constituents can play a major role here.

3. Being smart about the issue. Staffers have to deal with all of the legislation that comes up, and they appreciate any help they can get in understanding and sorting out each issue. Larger congressional offices—for example, those largely funded out of the congressperson's own budget, such as in the case of Senator Ted Kennedy—can afford to have specialists, usually called legislative assistants (for specific issues), but this is rare. Most staffers get help from the Congressional Research Service but will value the kind of briefing paper that a lobbyist can provide, especially when it is *short, straightforward, accurate,* and *honest.*

4. Being respected. Staffers are typically young, less than 35 years old, and relatively inexperienced. Too often, they are ignored or treated poorly. A lobbyist with a social marketing mind set will naturally respond to this need and not be condescending.

DeKeiffer (1997) offers 10 commandments for the effective lobbyist, shown in the box.

TEN COMMANDMENTS FROM *THE CITIZEN'S GUIDE TO LOBBYING CONGRESS*

1. Know your facts and be accurate in expressing them.

2. Know your opposition.

3. Correct errors immediately.

4. Plan, coordinate, and follow up with each contact.

5. Avoid zealotry.

6. Cultivate your allies; make sure they do their part.

7. Know the legislative process.

8. Be frugal with your money.

9. Grow a thick skin.

10. Win.

Approaching Bureaucrats

Laws are not effective if they are not implemented, or if they are implemented wrongly or halfheartedly. For many legislative initiatives, there will be some agency or office that is responsible for managing or implementing the programs included. These individuals "on the ground" can support a program or sabotage it.

The approach to potential administrators is not unlike that which would be adopted if they were the primary focus of the campaign and not just secondary players. By definition, they will be in the Contemplation stage—it is their job to deal with the legislation. Thus, to get a desired behavioral response, a social marketer would haul out the BCOS framework and look for *benefits* for the bureaucrat in implementing the legislation, *costs* to minimize, *allies* to recruit or enemies to deflect (Others), and *self-assurance* issues that may need attention if the bureaucrat and his or her colleagues are to believe they can carry out the efforts implied by the legislation.

A reasonable expectation is that bureaucrats will have, at minimum, several recognizable benefits and costs they would deem important. One important benefit would be career enhancement in some fashion. A bureaucrat might consider this a benefit if the legislation leads to a larger budget, more staff, or more "face time" with superiors. The legislation might be embraced if the bureaucrat could learn important new skills or if it yielded new contacts that would pay off in the longer run in other efforts. Although this may seem to reinforce the stereotype, it is important for the social marketer to remember that most bureaucrats believe they are *already* overworked. The risk is that perceived workload costs may appear to the bureaucrat to trump any benefits the social marketer might propose.

Bureaucrats may also worry about the impact on their resources. Will the proposal result in a net addition to the bureaucrat's budget, personnel, or facilities? Will new people have to be hired? Must there be coordination with other agencies—for example, parallel state agencies? If new people are brought in, a perceived cost may be potential negative effects on the organizational culture. If the initiative introduces new individuals or new partnerships that operate from different values, this can be especially threatening.

The influence of others can be brought to bear here. The desire to maintain favorable relations with the lawmaker will often be a potent motivator. The chance to work with new colleagues or new agencies may be attractive, especially if the new contacts are ones from whom the bureaucrat can learn or from which some prestige benefits may rub off.

Finally, there will be issues of self-assurance for the bureaucrat. Many of the costs suggested here may diminish if the bureaucrat can be helped with the various steps needed to implement the new legislation. Offering successful and adaptable models from previous applications—for example, from other states or other countries—can be both instructive and reassuring. The provision of short-term "coaches" who can help the bureaucrat through the new activity can also diminish the concern. Finally, provision of grant monies for capacity building may provide a buffer against bureaucrats' worries that they or their staff will not be able to perform as expected or as the bureaucrats would like to see demonstrated.

SOCIAL CHANGE THROUGH EXISTING LEGISLATION

Bureaucrats can often bring about structural changes without new legislation. In the matter of obesity, the Food and Drug Administration (FDA) and the Federal Trade Commission (FTC) have significant potential to influence how food products are labeled and advertised. As issues gain prominence on the public and political agendas, these agencies are likely to become involved. For example, in July 2003, the FDA used its existing authority to announce that it would require food processors to design their food product labels to carry information on the amount of trans fatty acids they contain. It is estimated that the average American consumes 35 grams of "bad fat" per day and that he or she is unlikely to be aware of the fact that seemingly "good" products such as Kellogg's Crackling Oat Bran cereal and Nabisco Wheat Thins have "bad fats" (16 crackers equals 3.5 grams of bad fat) (Abboud, 2003).

It is interesting to speculate whether this administrative move will pressure restaurants to also include this information. Private lawsuits may need to play a role in getting action from government agencies. Walter Willett, the chairman of the Department of Nutrition at the Harvard School of Public Health, noted: "The big gap is fast food and casual restaurants. If people eat foods high in trans fat and there is no warning label and then they have a heart attack at some point, there has to be legal liability." Dr. Willett points out that, unlike saturated fats, which are natural parts of many foods, trans fats must be added. This creates a potential liability much like the cigarette industry faced over cigarette additives (Burros, 2003, p. 1).

The Food and Drug Administration also announced in 2003 a loosening of the restrictions on the health claims that food producers (including makers of dietary supplements) can give consumers. In the past, health claims had to be backed by both solid research and scientific consensus. However, FDA commissioner Mark McLellan noted: "There's good competition now in the marketplace on price and taste and ease of preparation, but the number one area of competition should be the health consequences of a food product" (Kaufman, 2003, p. A1).

Note

1   Legislation to establish the Department of Homeland Security went through several committees because it touched on so many legislative domains—defense, foreign affairs, housing and urban development, the judiciary, and others.

8

Structural Change: Recruiting Business Allies

What do AT&T Wireless, Greyhound bus lines, Safeway, and DKNY Jeans have in common? The answer is that they were all corporate partners in the Office of National Drug Control Policy's national antidrug campaign from 1997 to 2002. The campaign worked very hard to get corporations to use their own resources to reach target audiences in diverse settings and, wherever possible, to associate the antidrug program with "cool" brands that were highly popular with the teens who were the campaign's principal target.

AT&T funded the development and production of a guidebook for the creation of community antidrug murals. Greyhound posted campaign materials in their bus stops and on their Web page. Safeway put PSAs on their private label milk cartons and ran radio and video PSAs in many of their stores. DKNY Jeans spent more than a million dollars on cobranded celebrity calendars for teenage girls and conducted in-store events on drug issues. These well-known companies were joined by others who made campaign materials available through their own channels. United Air Lines ran videos on 120,000 flights; Borders Books distributed parenting brochures in 1100 stores; and Capital One included campaign materials in 40 million customer credit card statements.

Much of the campaign's success in securing these partnerships was in being flexible enough to tailor involvements to match companies' strategic interests—not having a few proposals that had to

> be "sold" to potential partners. Campaign leaders also found that careful management of the relationship was critical, as was the presence of a dedicated social enterprise team in the corporation (Frazier & Gagné, 2004).

C learly, major upstream social change requires the involvement of a great many organizations and individuals. In the previous chapter, we considered the role of legislators and bureaucrats in bringing about structural change. However, legislation and enforcement are essentially coercive tools. They are most necessary when people are opposed or reluctant to act. As a means of making change, coercive strategies are potentially flawed (Andreasen, 1984b). Too often, those affected resent being made to undertake change and often look for loopholes or other ways to avoid acting as we would like. In this chapter, we turn to positive motivations that will encourage potential allies to make structural changes to promote the social good.

In the case of childhood obesity, the range of possible allies is not unlike what one would find in many other areas of social change. The possibilities are outlined in Table 8.1.

In this chapter, we shall focus on business—including the media—as potential allies. (The media business is considered in more detail in the next chapter.) Businesses can be important sources of ideas and resources for bringing about social change. They can make change happen—or at least be possible—within their own domains, and they can help others. Fortunately, the climate today is ripe for more business involvement beyond the marketplace. There is considerable enthusiasm these days in boardrooms for more corporate "social entrepreneurship"—ventures that take companies beyond the marketplace. The Enron and Arthur Anderson scandals have made the corporate world see the need for collective image enhancement. Corporations have seen other positive payoffs from direct social initiatives (Weeden, 1998). In this chapter, we shall look at how social marketing mind sets and frameworks can maximize the frequency and value of these kinds of contributions, to the benefit of both the corporations and society.

Businesses as Allies

The private sector is very often cast in the role of the villain when it comes to social welfare and social change. In the view of many, especially those on the left side of the political spectrum, it is the business community's smokestacks and oil

Table 8.1   Potential Allies in the Fight Against Childhood Obesity

Sector	Industry	Organizations	Potential Role
Business	Transportation	Service providers	Create bike paths, bike rentals
		Product manufacturers	Design bikes for more target audiences
	Building design		Incorporate more stairs, exercise possibilities
	Physical activity	Service providers	Reduce prices, broaden clientele
		Product manufacturers	Create products for seniors, children
	Food	Service providers	Reduce portions, add healthy options, label offerings
		Product manufacturers	Create healthier products, improve labeling
		Retailers	Promote healthier eating, add healthier takeout
	Entertainment	Television, radio stations	Portray characters eating better, exercising
		Movie makers	Portray characters eating better, exercising
	Information technology	Game makers	Design games with physical activities
		Internet providers	Provide pop-ups urging activity
	Media	Print, television, radio news	Raise issues, publicize solutions
	Retail	Shopping malls	Allow after-hours walking, include exercise areas
	Property owners		Convert space to exercise facilities

(Continued)

Table 8.1 (Continued)

Sector	Industry	Organizations	Potential Role
	All employers		Provide more exercise opportunities, better meals and snacks
	Health care	Hospitals, nursing homes	Provide nutrition, exercise treatment
		Physicians, nurses	Address obesity issues, promote fit policyholders
	Insurance		Cover exercise and diet programs, lower rates for fitness
Government	Recreation	Parks, playgrounds	Offer more organized activities
	Education	School boards, administrators	Teach energy balance, change menus, add exercise, sports
		Medical, nursing schools	Teach nutrition, exercise options
Nonprofits	Advocates		Push for change
	Foundations		Fund programs and innovations
	Youth organizations		Emphasize exercise and nutrition behaviors

spills that cause the most serious environmental pollution. Gas-guzzling automobiles make us dependent on foreign oil. Callous export practices cripple nascent industries in poor countries. Major retailers support sweatshops. Global branding is homogenizing cultures around the world and imposing American values on nations that are losing their own rich traditions (Johansson, 2004; Ritzer, 2004). Also, of course (so the rhetoric goes), McDonald's and KFC target children and contribute dramatically to the obesity epidemic.

It is certainly true that there are thoughtless—even malevolent—corporations, and that there are CEOs with few scruples and an unhealthy fixation on the bottom line. Too many corporate decisions are made to benefit stockholders or other narrow corporate constituencies, to the exclusion of other interests. On the other hand, critics should recognize that the seeming indifference of many businesses and their leaders to broad issues of social welfare is what they believe is required of them as a matter of corporate ethics. In their judgment, *they are not supposed to intervene to create social change.* Some management scholars and economists such as Milton Friedman argue that society expects only one role for corporations: creating successful enterprises that create products, jobs, and economic growth (Allen, 1992; Friedman, 1970; Friedman & Friedman, 1990; Smith, 1997). These authors argue that corporations are not created and given important legal protections by societies so that they can figure out what social changes are needed. Executives, of course, can offer personal opinions as individual citizens about what social changes are needed and how to achieve them. However, their companies do not have the right or, in fact, any particular competencies to bring about such changes. Social change is more properly the role of government and nonprofit organizations.

A corporation with this perspective might *appear* to be undertaking programs to improve social welfare, as when Marriott and Lockheed became involved in government welfare-to-work programs, but conservative corporations would argue that these ventures are merely imaginative ways to use their core competencies to increase revenues and profits. Conservative corporations are not inattentive to social concerns—they certainly endeavor to obey the laws in the countries in which they operate and seek to provide decent environments for their communities, decent work conditions for their employees, and safe products and services for their customers. They do not, however, intend to become what Kotler and Lee (2005) call "corporate social entrepreneurs." Their role is to serve their stockholders. If the stockholders favor a particular social change, the stockholders themselves, as individuals, can take action. They can invest their corporate dividends in social programs, can volunteer their own time, and can urge others to do likewise.

Sometimes these corporations look like they are moving beyond stockholder interests. They donate to charities, especially in the communities and countries in which they do business. They engage in cause-related marketing by sponsoring races and book distributions. They support the arts. They take an active interest in "good government." However, given their belief that their only proper role is to advance stockholder interests, all of these activities can be seen as merely serving those interests. For example, supporting local charities increases the pool of labor wanting to work in the community by reducing poverty and urban blight, taking care of the homeless and the elderly, and otherwise improving the physical and social environment. Such social involvements by executives also build community goodwill that can have later concrete payoffs. A company that is viewed favorably by local city officials or a country's minister of trade may be more likely to receive favorable treatment than its competitors.

Conservative corporations represent one end of what Greg Dees (1996) calls the "Social Enterprise Spectrum." At the other end, there are corporations and CEOs that can be labeled "communitarian" (Etzioni, 1995). These leaders argue that the basic social charter given to corporations by a society implies significant obligations not unlike those of any other member of that society. State charters give stockholders, boards, and management special liability protections to encourage business investment that will ultimately benefit the broader society. As a consequence, it is argued that corporations owe a special obligation to meet that society's broader needs. Aaron Feuerstein, CEO of Malden Mills, is a classic communitarian. After his factory burned down in December 1995, he continued to pay his 3000 workers with full benefits for 3 months. Feuerstein simply said that he owed it to his workers and to the community. As a 1996 commentary put it:

> Feuerstein did not throw his money away. It was not largesse. It was a well reasoned and sound *leadership* decision to *invest* millions in Malden Mills' most critical asset, its workers. The contrast between this CEO and the currently celebrated CEOs making 30, 60 or 100 million dollars a year by eliminating jobs and moving plants is simply astounding. How much are you willing to wager that every company that closed a plant in recent years to boost stock prices has a vision statement with words like . . . *we value and respect our employees as our most important asset?* How many of the laid off employees do you suppose believe that? (Boulay, 1996)

Firms such as Malden Mills are "stakeholder centered," not stockholder centered (Donaldson & Preston, 1995). They believe they can and ought to take actions that are not solely in the stockholders' interests because "it is the right thing to do." Corporations must be good citizens, just as people must be good citizens. This means, among other things, helping others when they need it. Such actions may put some strain on the corporate bottom line, but communitarian leaders would argue that their ethical compass *requires* them to do so.

STRATEGIC PHILANTHROPY AND CAUSE MARKETING

Corporate social involvement underwent a major shift in the 1980s and 1990s (Smith, 1994). Prior to that time, corporate social involvement typically amounted to charitable giving and employee (and management) volunteering. Corporations were good citizens "giving back" to their communities. This all changed in the early 1980s, when American Express created the first-ever cause-related marketing effort. This venture dramatically changed the relationship between corporations and society. As I and my coauthor described this in a nonprofit textbook:

> Cause-related marketing started in 1982 when Jerry C. Welsh, then chief of worldwide marketing for American Express Company, agreed to make a 5 cent donation to the arts in San Francisco every time someone used an American Express card and $2 every time American Express got a new member. In three months, the

campaign raised $108,000. The approach gained national attention when American Express tried it on a country-wide basis. In 1983, AmEx agreed to set aside 1 cent for every card transaction and $1 for each new card issued during the last quarter of 1983 to support the renovation of Ellis Island and the Statue of Liberty. The program was a great success. American Express reported sales increases of 28 percent over the same period a year earlier with a total of $1.8 million eventually donated to the renovation project. Since that first national event, cause-related marketing has grown dramatically. Cone Communications estimates that by 2000, cause marketing had grown into a $2 billion set of enterprises. (Andreasen & Kotler, 2003, p. 247; see also Wall, 1994)

The new approach recognizes that social ventures need not just be give-aways; they can make direct contributions to a corporation's core strategies—they can have bottom-line effects. Social ventures can generate sales, change corporate positioning for customers and the investment community, reduce employee turnover, and make government concessions easier to achieve (Weeden, 1998). Segawa and Segal (2000) described the change in thinking:

> Almost anywhere you look you can find evidence of stepped-up business-social interaction. . . . This phenomenon may seem to some to be a passing fad. But we see in these exchanges a new paradigm for business and the social sector, one that eliminates barriers between the sectors while preserving their core missions. This new paradigm pairs visionary companies that see how the social context in which they operate affects their bottom lines with a new breed of social entrepreneurs who understood how business principles can enable them to fulfill their social missions more effectively. (p. 3)

There is growing (although still controversial) evidence linking a concern for social interests with increased stockholder payoffs. Margolis and Walsh (2001, 2003) conducted a meta-analysis of studies over 30 years that sought to link financial performance to some measure of social performance. They found a positive relationship in 42 of 80 studies (53%). Social performance led to better financial performance. However, the results were not unequivocal. They also found a reverse causation in 19 studies, giving rise to the argument that a concern for society may come about only *after* good financial performance allows it to happen.

The potential for social marketing alliances is significant. Kurt Aschermann of the Boys & Girls Clubs of America has said that if his organization has to get funding for its programs from the corporate charitable giving department, the amounts will be modest. However, if he can find a way in one of his presentations to tie his programs to corporate marketing objectives or other strategic issues, he will find, "you're talking about millions of dollars, not thousands!" (Aschermann, 2001). This thinking has led the Boys & Girls Clubs to develop $60 million ventures with Coca-Cola and a $100 million partnership with Microsoft (Drumwright, 1996; Rangan, Karim, & Sandberg, 1990).

BUILDING CORPORATE ALLIANCES

How does one go about securing the assistance of corporations in bringing about social change? How would a social marketer apply the various frameworks discussed in this book to achieving this goal?

Defining the Behavior

Business allies can play one of three roles in social change programs. First, they can *stop being competitors* for the downstream behaviors—that is, they can stop promoting unhealthy eating, smoking, too-thin female bodies, and so on. Food companies can remove high-sugar products from school vending machines or eliminate advertising and other promotions urging kids to "supersize" their portions. TV stations can stop urging couch potatoes to sit still for the next several TV shows.

Second, business allies can *directly participate* in behavior change programs. Companies can get their employees exercising and eating better by creating fitness contests or offering bonuses and prizes for workers meeting certain healthy living goals. They can also support the Ad Council. Food marketers can create specially packaged kids' meals that are highly nutritious. Advertisers and producers can include messages in their child-oriented video games or TV programs urging kids to "take a play break" from time to time. Movies and TV shows can portray characters eating better and making more efforts to exercise regularly. Insurance companies can introduce reduced rates for individuals with BMIs below a certain level or charge higher premiums for those who are obese.

Third, business allies can *facilitate* desirable changes by making good behavior easier. Corporations can install exercise rooms in their office buildings or factories, provide more nutritious cafeteria fare, give staff time off to exercise, and subsidize health club memberships. Food manufacturers, supermarket chains, and restaurants can provide detailed and easy-to-understand nutrition information on menu items and food products. They can subsidize and participate in school-based nutrition education and exercise programs. Insurance companies can offer reimbursements for weight reduction programs and prescriptions—even surgery—for the seriously obese.

Kotler and Lee (2005) provide a dramatic example of the potential for corporate involvement in actually creating change. Diane Deitz, North American marketing director for Procter & Gamble's Crest toothpaste brands, saw an opportunity to address a serious social problem in a way that would also benefit her own bottom line. Deitz had read a surgeon general's report describing the high rate of oral disease in America, especially among the poor. The report indicated that cavity rates were twice as high among the poor and that poor children missed 51 million hours of school each year because of dental problems. Working with the Boys & Girls Clubs and the World Health Organization, Crest developed a "Healthy Smiles 2010" program. Since 2001, Crest has

- Invested $1 million to create "cavity-free zones" in 3300 local Boys & Girls Clubs
- Developed curricula for younger kids and teens on oral hygiene taught in 2640 clubs
- Donated toothpaste and toothbrushes to club members and families
- Helped poor families find low-cost, local dental care
- Funded the construction of five full-service dental clinics in club buildings in New York City, Los Angeles, Chicago, Houston, and Cincinnati (Procter & Gamble's home city)

Procter & Gamble also made sure that its good work had corporate payoffs. They introduced millions of Boys & Girls Clubs kids and their families to Crest products. They advertised their social involvement to the general public. The overall effect was to increase brand preference. According to Kotler and Lee,

> Among consumers who are aware of the program, the company's market research shows an increase in purchase intent. And Crest has already achieved what [Crest brand manager Bryan] McCleary describes as an "incremental" increase in sales through a partnership with Walgreens, in which in-store signs advertised Crest's work with the Boys & Girls Clubs (2005, p. 22)

Target Audience

Once the social marketer determines what he or she wishes the private sector to do, the next challenge is to identify targets of opportunity. One place to begin looking is in companies that others have identified as being very socially responsible. Various business magazines rank such companies from time to time, and several mutual fund organizations, such as Calvert and Domini,[1] maintain portfolios of such companies. Calvert Group (2005) identifies five characteristics of firms high on its social responsibility index:

- *Environmental efficiency and awareness.* Increased potential for cost savings in energy, water, land, and raw materials; reduced cleanup costs; decreased chance for legal liabilities; improved public image and community relations
- *Workforce diversity.* Enhanced global competitive edge, resulting from a greater range of skills and perspectives; greater ability to attract and retain talented employees from a broad-based labor pool; reduced likelihood of equal employment opportunity lawsuits and negative publicity
- *Product safety and quality.* Decreased chance for product liability lawsuits (e.g., tobacco); greater satisfaction and loyalty

- *Innovative personnel policies.* Increased productivity, reduced employee turnover and absenteeism through flextime and job sharing, enhanced recruitment efforts, higher employee morale
- *Positive corporate citizenship.* Enhanced community relations and local recruiting efforts; improved public image

Calvert identifies as socially responsible several firms that might be expected to have a potential interest in addressing childhood obesity issues, including Colgate Palmolive, General Mills, Heinz, Hershey's, Kellogg, Whole Foods, Walgreens, and J. M. Smucker.

Another possible target list is found in the United Nations Global Compact (2005), which focuses on human rights, labor practices, and the environment and now has about 1000 corporate signatories. The publication *Business Ethics* also assembles an annual 100 best corporate citizens list ("*Business Ethics* 100," 2005). Other guides to socially responsible companies are available from the Social Investment Forum (2005).

A second approach to finding potential allies is to identify corporations that have philosophies that suggest a major social concern. Such statements can then be used to develop corporate proposals that speak to the corporation's strategic needs. Here are examples of the statements of two firms, McDonald's and Kraft Foods, that are the source of many of the current nutrition concerns:

- At McDonald's, responsibility means striving to do what is right, being a good neighbor in the community, and integrating social and environmental priorities into our restaurants and our relationships with suppliers and business partners. It also means communicating about our efforts to address social and environment issues that matter to our customers and other stakeholders.

  Corporate responsibility is part of our heritage, dating back to our founder Ray Kroc. It is also an integral part of our business strategy. Our customers' trust is a precious asset and one we strive to preserve and build every day. We know we must have that trust to achieve our vision of being "our customers' favorite place and way to eat."

  We work hard to understand the complex issues that confront our industry and how we can make a significant difference. As you will see, we invest in a commitment to industry leadership. And, on this Web site and in our Corporate Responsibility Reports, we share what we are doing and seek feedback. (McDonald's Corporation, 2005)

- Kraft recognizes the importance of healthy living. Over the years, the products we offer have provided a wide range of nutritional choices. We've been a source of useful nutrition and fitness information. And we've funded public education and lifestyle intervention programs.

  As a company, we want to sustain the growth of our business in a responsible way. We want the sale of our products and our commercial success to support Kraft's corporate vision of helping people around the world eat and live better.

> To live up to this vision, we have taken a number of steps. We have established healthy living principles to guide our activities. We have strengthened our policies and practices in the areas of product nutrition, marketing, labeling and health claims. We are introducing new products and improving existing products to give consumers more choices to address their health and wellness needs. We are stepping up our efforts to provide useful nutrition and fitness information through our websites, recipes and publications. We are advocating constructive changes in related public policies. And we are increasing our financial support for education and intervention programs. (Kraft Foods, 2005)

By contrast, in August 2004, neither KFC nor Burger King had any relevant statement or social promise on their Web sites. Like other organizations, these two companies list traditional charitable activities. For example, KFC donates to the United Negro College Fund, offers awards to meritorious seniors nominated by kids, and has a charity devoted to improving child care.

If one wishes to focus on the exercise and activity side of what the National Cancer Institute calls the "energy balance" problem, there are other options. One could seek out firms in the exercise industry, such as Nike, that blend activism with a clear, compelling company payoff. If the focus of the campaign is to be school-based initiatives, one could find firms with educational programs focusing on exercise. An obvious candidate in the latter regard is Scholastic Inc. Scholastic provides literacy and other educational materials for children and schools and has a long tradition of social responsibility. On its Web site, it notes: "For more than 80 years, Scholastic has recognized the importance of working with public, private, and non-profit organizations that share its mission and goals to improve the well being of children" (Scholastic Inc., 2005). Such an organization might participate in creating educational materials for any broad-scale program concerning childhood nutrition and exercise. It is particularly well equipped to use social marketing, as it has experience applying such approaches to campaigns such as the U.S. Census 2000 project (Andreasen, 2002).

A final, somewhat perverse strategy for identifying potentially cooperative firms is to pay attention to negative corporate publicity, especially as it applies to childhood nutrition and physical activity. An important motivator for many firms to become more sensitive to society's concerns is when that society (for example, through the media or aggressive lawyers) becomes upset about corporate practices. *USA Today* reported in 2003 that "McDonald's is feeling the pressure. [In April,] McDonald's named its first-ever corporate vice president of healthy lifestyles" (Horovitz, 2003, p. 1a). The company's CEO was quoted in the same article as saying, "If healthy lifestyles are becoming more important to our customers, we want to play a role." The latter statement is, of course, reflective of sound marketing principles—give the customer what he or she wants.

A company that seems to be an early leader here is Kraft Foods. Because Kraft is part of the Altria Group Inc., which includes Philip Morris, undoubtedly, Kraft executives know firsthand from the "smoking wars" the potential dangers of not addressing consumer concerns about corporate responsibility for a social problem. As noted in their corporate responsibility statement (provided earlier), Kraft's efforts here are broad ranging, composed of more than just the few tentative initiatives that other firms seem to be undertaking. Other examples are found in Richard Earle's (2000) book on advertising, advertising agencies, and the Advertising Council's involvement in social change programs. Sue Adkins (1999) portrays a range of initiatives in the UK; and Hamish Pringle and Marjorie Thompson (1999) offer examples of experiences within the Saatchi and Saatchi advertising agency. James Austin provides both numerous examples of business and nonprofit collaborations and an excellent framework for developing such collaborations. His work covers both the United States (Austin, 2000) and Latin America (Austin et al., 2004).

Using the Three Models to Secure Cooperation

Once one has identified a set of behaviors and a corporate target audience to be influenced, how does one mount a campaign to induce voluntary behavior in that audience? How can the Stages of Change and BCOS factors guide such an approach, and what is the role of Competition? In my experience over a wide range of corporate social initiatives (Andreasen, 1996), it is very likely that corporations will respond in one of four ways.

1. Some will reluctantly participate as a matter of damage control. Firms with sweatshop or environmental challenges will often participate in social initiatives to deflect attention, recoup lost reputation, or discourage more punitive or troublesome future attacks. These will be good targets for partnering with highly respected nonprofits or with government agencies. They are not likely to be in it for the long haul, however, especially once their image has rebounded.

2. Some will participate not because they believe in the issue or its direct value to the corporation but because it is a means to getting another benefit. For example, helping a nonprofit or a government agency today can build personal connections and goodwill that will pay off later when the corporation needs someone to vouch for it in a touchy situation, provide a favorable tariff reduction, or put in place infrastructure or a favorable regulation that will make business life easier.

3. Some will participate positively but consider it a one-time venture that is simply another tactic in a diverse array of initiatives designed to increase sales and profits. These are what Austin (2000) calls "transactional partnerships," not true integrated collaborations. A supermarket might have a

monthlong nutrition campaign to promote healthy eating and feature an array of healthful products. Such a promotion might be coordinated with suppliers and brand marketers, as well as a specific nonprofit program. The promotion will have a fixed time horizon and disappear as the chain moves on to other tactics-of-the-month.

4. Some—the ideal cases—will see the initiative as fitting in with their long-term corporate interests. They will see initial social ventures as learning experiences and seek ways to make the involvement grow (Austin, 2000).

The last group has two subcategories: firms that go it alone and firms that work with a defined partner or set of partners. There are many examples of the latter in the broad domain of cause-related marketing projects. Timberland has built lasting relationships with City Year. Bert's Bees (cosmetics) has long worked with The Nature Conservancy, and American Express for many years had a close partnership with the food programs of Share Our Strength (Shore, 1995). For large-scale programs, many corporations partner with the Advertising Council or major nonprofits such as the American Lung Association or Save the Children. The Advertising Council (2003) has already mounted an obesity prevention campaign described as follows:

> The Obesity Prevention campaign encourages families to make small dietary and physical activity changes, such as using stairs instead of the escalator, or replacing a Sunday drive with a Sunday walk. Viewers are encouraged to visit www .smallstep.gov to learn more about small steps they can take toward a healthier lifestyle.

In partnership with the DHHS and the Ad Council, Sesame Workshop, the nonprofit educational organization behind Sesame Street, has produced two public service advertising spots using the beloved Sesame Street characters Luis, Elmo, and Rosita to encourage parents to make healthier eating and physical activity part of their family's regular routine—and as early as possible in their children's lives. The Sesame ads, available in both English and Spanish, encourage viewers to visit http://www.smallstep.gov to learn more.

Much of the advertising in this campaign is created pro bono by the McCann Erickson advertising agency.

THE IMPORTANCE OF INDIVIDUALS

It is critical to remember a central premise of this book: namely, that it is *individuals* who make change happen. Corporate partnerships typically emerge because a specific individual, such as Diane Deitz at Crest, sees the value of a social initiative and gets the firm involved. These same individuals frequently shepherd collaborations through their early stages and help them grow into more elaborate partnerships down the road. These key players will often be ambitious executives, executives assigned to a project, or, best of all, individuals with a personal attachment to the issue. For decades, Wendy's was deeply involved in adoption issues because its late CEO Dave Thomas was himself an orphan.

Social marketing is all about getting these target individuals to act.

STAGES OF CHANGE

The search for target audiences through reputational listings, Web sites, or news reports should provide insight into where various corporations are in the Stages of Change. Those in the Precontemplation stage will be the ones that either follow a stockholder maximization philosophy or believe that a corporation's social role is simply to be ethical and engage in traditional philanthropy, like any member of a civil society. The best opportunities, of course, will reside with Contemplators. Some Contemplators will be in the early stages of thinking about collaborating—seeing a few benefits but not having thought much more about it. Others may be in Late Contemplation, having thought extensively about the possibilities but not having concluded that corporate social marketing is the route to use.

Companies in the Preparation and Action stage are those who have engaged in one or two short-term cause partnerships and may be ready to expand their involvement. Finally, there will be some companies in the Maintenance stage, such as Procter & Gamble: The corporation is already involved in various social partnerships and only needs to be encouraged to add new ventures to its portfolio.

THE BCOS FACTORS

For those companies in the Contemplation stage, the BCOS and Competition concepts can be useful guidelines for how one might move them forward to Preparation and Action and, eventually, Maintenance. Here, there are two sets of BCOS factors that are important. There are those that apply to the corporation and those that apply to the *individuals* who can make the alliance happen—and succeed. As I keep repeating, social actions take place because individuals do things. In the corporate world, target individuals might ask themselves:

- What might I get out of this?
- How might it affect my future career?
- What extra burden might I be taking on?
- What could go wrong?

Benefits to the Corporation

The critical challenge in seeking a corporate alliance is finding an answer to the question: How does this alliance fit the firm's strategic needs? The answers are sometimes obvious. Clearly, if a firm is under attack for its practices or otherwise has "reputational problems," an obvious benefit from participation in a social venture will be the chance to enhance the sullied image and rebound in the marketplace. Appealing to this benefit can, however, lead to prickly relationships and alliances that are likely to disappear once the corporate threat is eliminated or diminished.

Other, more positive benefits from a social cause partnership include the following:

1. Sales benefits: attracting new customers, reducing defections by old customers, encouraging either group to spend more

2. Human resources benefits: having access to a better pool of future hirees eager to work for a socially responsible organization, improving workplace morale, and reducing employee turnover

3. Positioning benefits: helping reposition an organization (e.g., from uncaring to caring) and providing a point of differentiation from competitors

4. Goodwill benefits: securing favorable feelings and positive attitudes on the part of government agencies, local politicians, and the media that can have future strategic benefits

In the obesity case, many firms may see the surgeon general's Call to Action on Obesity as an excellent chance to get out in front on an issue that is high on the public and political agendas. For those willing to quickly get out in front on this issue, there is what is called in the marketing literature the "first mover advantage." This doctrine asserts that firms that come out first in some evolving market can often build a position that, in many respects, is unassailable by subsequent me-too players. Thus, Avon got a first-mover advantage by being one of the earliest organizations to make a major commitment to the breast cancer problem. Avon became a dominant player in that domain, reeling in significant publicity and positive customer responses for its activities in this area. Breast cancer now boasts hundreds of corporate partnerships, and it is virtually impossible for any new entrant to make a distinct impression. Avon still maintains very high visibility.

The Avon story is highly relevant to the present discussion because it illustrates the long-term advantages of identifying companies that can see involvement in a social issue as fitting their most fundamental corporate strategic needs. Avon touts itself as "The Company for Women." Its customers are women, and its worldwide sales force of 3½ million independent representatives is all female. Breast cancer is thus a natural area for social involvement that would appeal to both customers and the sales force. Avon describes its program as follows:

> Knowing that breast cancer is the most commonly diagnosed cancer among women, the goal of the Avon Foundation Breast Cancer Crusade is to benefit all women through research, clinical care, education and support services. However, there is special emphasis on reaching medically underserved women, including low-income, elderly and minority women, and women without adequate health insurance. Reversing historical disparities in breast cancer care is a priority of the Avon Foundation Breast Cancer Crusade. (http://www.avoncompany.com/women/avoncrusade/background/overview.html)

The program continues to be one that has made Avon one of Fortune's "Most Admired Companies" for more than a decade.

Sales benefits are important in these cases. In two studies in 1993 and 1998, Cone Communications found that

- Eight in 10 Americans have a more positive image of companies that support a cause the respondents care about (84% in 1993, 83% in 1998).
- As in 1993, nearly two thirds of Americans (approximately 130 million consumers) report that they would be likely to switch brands (66% in 1993, 65% in 1998) or retailers (62%, 61%) to one associated with a good cause.
- In 1993, consumers said that when price and quality are equal, responsible business practices will make a difference in the brand choices of 31% of respondents. One in five, in fact, had already made such a choice in the previous 12 months.
- In 1993, 54% said that they would pay more for a product that supports a cause they care about (Cone, Inc., & Roper Starch Worldwide, Inc., 1999).

Cone and Roper (1999) also found that 90% of employees of companies supporting social causes "feel proud of their companies' values" and 88% "feel a strong sense of loyalty." The comparable figures for the companies surveyed that were *not* involved in causes were 66% and 68%, respectively.

A second example of the possibilities of multiple benefits to corporations from social involvement is Coca-Cola's long-term partnership with Boys & Girls Clubs of America. From Coca-Cola's standpoint, a key benefit is that Boys & Girls Clubs members are in the prime market for soft drinks. Opportunities for product promotion abound. However, the partnership had an important potential HR payoff because it provided a vehicle for employee volunteering all across America and increased cooperation between Coca-Cola and its many independent franchisees around the country. Coca-Cola has franchises in most Boys & Girls Clubs locations and was eager not only to sell more soft drinks to its prime market but also to find ways to bind the independent franchisee bottlers more closely to the company.

In the fast food industry, there is some evidence that a concentration on nutritious offerings can offer a clear basis for differentiation for smaller competitors. The Subway franchise chain has been very successful in positioning itself as the healthy fast food outlet. It particularly benefited from the story of Jared Fogle, who became a media favorite for losing 245 lbs by eating nothing but Subway sandwiches for almost a year on his self-designed diet program of careful eating and walking.

Subway has actively sought to take advantage of the current concern about childhood obesity. In 2004, it commissioned a study and found that, although 8 of 10 kids 5 to 12 years old knew someone who was very overweight, only 20% were worried about them. They seemed relatively unconcerned. For example, one in four overweight kids thought they were "about the right weight" and, although most know they should eat better, few did so (Subway, 2004). As a consequence of the study, Subway launched a national campaign called F.R.E.S.H. Steps (F.R.E.S.H. = feel responsible, energized, satisfied, and happy). The campaign features paid ads, school curricula, guidelines, and information on the Subway Web site. Subway franchises now offer a Kids' Pak with deli sandwiches and other branded products, such as Minute Maid 100% juice fruit punch, that are less unhealthful than the average fast food kid's meal.[2]

Benefits to Corporate Individuals

Partnerships are unlikely to work unless individuals see personal benefits from working in them. Among the possibilities I have discovered in my own work in this area are the following.

Alliances provide occasions for individuals to stretch their management and marketing skills by learning how these would work in new contexts. How does one adapt concepts such as *exchange* and *segmentation* and *positioning* to cases in which one is not selling goods and services? How does one position desirable behaviors when products or services are not involved and the audience does not pay any money (e.g., recycling)? How does one promote behaviors that have no obvious immediate rewards or that have rewards that come only after a long time (e.g., taking high blood pressure pills)? How do you promote childhood immunization when *nothing happens* to the child beyond the trauma of the injection? Stopping smoking means more years at the end of one's life 50 years hence. Marketing such concepts and behaviors is much more challenging than selling burgers or PlayStation3.

Working on social problems can be a rewarding break from a high-pressure work life. The opportunity to work with others committed to social change can be very rewarding to people who spend the majority of their lives peddling computer software or disposable diapers. For example, McKinsey & Co. has found that many of its consultants relish the chance to use their skills on nonprofit challenges that are often a far cry from the rest of their consulting careers.

Social ventures are a chance for individual collaboration and relationship building outside the traditional workplace. These connections can lead to other career payoffs in future, including job mobility.

Corporate social initiatives can look very impressive on an executive's year-end report of accomplishments, as well as on his or her resumé.

There are personal satisfactions in contributing to solutions for a social problem in which the improvements in social welfare can be dramatic.

There is chance for personal publicity ("raising my profile")—again with the potential for career advancement.

Costs

Both corporations and executives will be thinking about a number of potentially significant costs during the Contemplation stage. First, many social problems will constitute very difficult challenges, and the possibility is that the effort will not be successful. Jerry Lewis has spent more than 39 years and much personal capital raising money to find a cure for multiple dystrophy—but there is still no cure. A corporation or executive may worry about the potential wasted time and resources and even bad publicity from a failed effort.

Behavior change in obese children may be particularly challenging, because, although there may be a social demand for behavior change, there is typically no individual demand (Siegel & Doner, 1998). Certainly, consumers seem to be of mixed minds. A 2003 study by Multimedia Audience Research Systems found that 63% of fast food restaurant patrons were concerned about food quantity and 73% about the nutritional value of fast foods; 63% also thought that fast food contributes to weight and health problems *for society at large*. On the other hand, 13% "super-size" on most or all of their visits, and 54% purchase large combination meals at least some of the time (Sandelman & Associates, 2003).

A second critical cost that may enter into consideration is the risk to the corporation of losing customers if a social program requires changing their product and service offerings. For example, fast food restaurant chains have been very reluctant to make changes in their offerings or recipes because consumers rate taste as the most important feature they seek in a quick-service chain's offerings. Sandelman & Associates (2003) found that, among 12 attributes consumers considered as extremely or very important in choosing fast food outlets, "taste or flavor of food" was rated number one. By contrast, "availability of healthy/nutritious food" was ranked 11th, although it was still described as important by 60% of respondents.

This concern may partially account for the reluctance of McDonald's to change the oils it has used in frying. In 2002, with much publicity, McDonald's said it would switch from partly hydrogenated oil to one without trans fats, but by May 2004, the company had still not actually made the switch for its french fries. Its hesitation may have been a sound strategy. There is now evidence that trans fats are not any worse than other suspect cooking oils. Indeed, as Gina Kolata (2005) recently noted, the FDA, the DHHS, the National Heart, Lung and Blood Institute, and the National Academy of Sciences "have come to the same conclusion: Trans fats are on a par with saturated fats, like butter or lard. Both increase cholesterol levels and most people would be better off if they ate less of all of them. Period" (p. WK4).

Finally, a potential worry for corporations seeking repositioning benefits is that consumers may be suspicious of their motives. If the subject of the corporate alliance seems not at all related to the firm's core strategies, customers and the general public may cynically conclude that the company is just "doing it for the PR." The result may be a boomerang effect and a decline in image (Hoeffler & Keller, 2002; Sen & Bhattacharya, 2001).

For *individuals* considering involvement in promoting a social cause, important costs will be the time and frustration working on the project. This may mean taking time away from their "real" job and, for some, a detour in their upward job mobility. (It is why some hard-charging executives gripe about being asked to serve on nonprofit boards or otherwise volunteer.) There are other predictable frustrations.

The paperwork before, during, and after an alliance can be very intensive and time-consuming. Nonprofits have public or charity funding sources, and their funders are typically obsessive about having documentation to justify what is happening to their money and what outcomes were achieved. This is frustrating for an executive who just wants to have an impact and who prefers to pay attention mainly to bottom-line performance—as in the corporation.

Decision styles are often quite different (Stein, 2002). Corporate executives are accustomed to spirited debates about strategy and tactics. In the private sector, such discussions culminate in a final decision by someone in charge and rapid implementation. In the social sector, the process is much more collegial and time-consuming. There is often a perceived need to "touch base" with everyone even remotely affected and to make sure that no party's interests are trampled on by any final choices. This usually means innumerable meetings and a much longer time for consensus and decisions to be reached.

Personal motivations are often very different. In the private sector, executives are interested in power, upward mobility, and a reputation for leadership and decisiveness. Standards are well understood, and people are held closely accountable for performance. By contrast, people often join the government or the nonprofit sector to escape such a "rat race." This can mean (although not always) a reluctance to make hard choices and a reluctance to criticize below-par performance. This can be very frustrating for the private sector partner who seeks decisiveness and accountability.

Goals and time horizons will be different. Corporations plan for and then track results over short periods, but social projects often have very long-term objectives and few measurable interim benchmarks. Social sector organizations are often relatively content if they are staying "on mission," trusting that, in the long run, there will be big social effects (Moore, 2000).

Leadership styles will be different. Corporations have instrumental leaders (get-the-job-done people); nonprofit organizations more often have expressive leaders (people who can articulate and advance the mission and values). Communication tends to be top-down in the former and horizontal in the latter. For a short-term, private sector collaborator, horizontal communication can be hard to navigate and a very real anticipated cost (see, for example, Etzioni, 1995).

Social marketers can help minimize the influence of these various costs by helping train executives before they become involved in social ventures. They can also prepare nonprofits and government agencies to address potential corporate concerns if they want to bring corporations and their executives on board.

Others

Strength in numbers comes from having multiple partners in a project. As noted in an earlier chapter, corporations avoided involvement in the HIV/ AIDS issue for many years as too controversial. It was only when Reverend Franklin Graham and Jesse Helms spoke up that corporate executives got on board and, most significantly, formed a roundtable to advance the issue (i.e., to give each other cover).

Calls to action by prominent leaders can often bring about corporate involvement. President George W. Bush's call for aid in the Asian tsunami crisis of December 2004 (and his personal $10,000 contribution) was important in encouraging and reinforcing corporate and individual commitment to the problem. The subsequent involvement of Bill Clinton also kept it from being a "Republican thing." In the past, similar calls to action by Nelson Mandela or Bishop Desmond Tutu had powerful influences on corporate involvement in South Africa.

The Business Roundtable is taking up the challenge to build social alliances within the 160 companies they represent. They announced plans in 2005 to create a database that would catalog types of assistance that corporations could provide in future disasters, including donations, equipment, supplies, communications infrastructure, and so on. Business Roundtable members also plan to "contact relief organizations to establish ways they can coordinate with them in an emergency" (Wilhelm, 2005).

Participation in alliances with organizations with similar social objectives can provide both contacts and reinforcement. Thus getting an association such as Business for Social Responsibility behind a particular social change can be motivating for both members and nonmembers. Business for Social

Responsibility (2005) has been particularly vocal about such issues as cause-related marketing, off-shore sweatshops, business ethics, environmental impacts, and human rights.

It must also be recognized that other organizations and individuals can *inhibit* corporations from taking initiatives. Organizations in tight-knit industries may be reluctant to take solo actions that risk offending others in their industry who might retaliate or not cooperate in other ventures. Currently, several food industry groups are attempting to deflect criticism of the industry on the subject of obesity. Should one food-producing firm forcefully advertise the fact that their offerings do not have certain nasty ingredients that contribute to childhood obesity, this may be seen as "breaking ranks" and implicitly criticizing competitors. In subject areas in which the science is not totally clear (as in smoking), competitors may see the socially responsible firm as "going off the deep end" and being unfairly critical. Other marketers may also be upset if the renegade marketer seems to be undermining specific industry efforts to gain legislative and regulatory changes. An insurance company that allows claims for weight loss programs at no extra premium cost may be seen as antagonistic to colleagues and competitors who are attempting to hold the line and not offer costly new benefits.

Obviously, the challenge for social marketers is to marshal as many positive social pressures as they can and anticipate (and deflect) counterpressures from other individuals and firms.

Self-Assurance

Well-meaning corporations and individuals are not likely to join an alliance unless they can see their way clear to reaping the benefits. This is not to say that they need to know that the intervention will be successful—only that they can effectively contribute and reap the corporate and individual pay-offs they anticipate along the way. If simple actions are contemplated—for example, putting up notices in restaurants or adding a new benefit to an insurance policy—this is not likely to seem daunting. However, helping a community create a network of well-lit bike paths may prove more difficult. Firms or individuals who have had little experience dealing with local municipalities and zoning laws may find the challenge difficult. A road map and experienced partners may raise corporations' self-assurance—their feeling that they can actually get something done.

COMPETITION

Social marketers who wish to generate corporate alliances can expect competition from several sources. First, as suggested earlier, there will be industries, firms, associations, and their allies that will feel that the proposed interventions will negatively affect their own welfare. Marion Nestle (2002) makes the point in her book *Food Politics:*

> A message to eat less meat, dairy and processed foods is not going to be popular among the processors of such foods. . . . The message will not be popular with cattle ranchers, meat packers, dairy producers, or milk bottlers; oil seed growers, processors, or transporters; grain producers (most grain is used to feed cattle); makers of soft drinks, candy bars, and snack foods; owners of fast-food outlets and franchise restaurants; media corporations and advertising agencies; manufacturers and marketers of television sets and computers (where advertising takes place); and, eventually, drug and health care industries likely to lose business if people stay healthier longer. (p. 363)

Vested interests may also provide competition by raising the possibility that other important values will suffer if the initiative goes forward. Marion Nestle (2002) quotes Dr. Rhona Applebaum of the National Food Processors Association, who argues that we can only change the upstream environment in regard to eating

> if the federal government, in the role of "Big Brother," mandates what foods can and cannot be produced—which is not the role of the government in a free market economy. Controlling, limiting, and outright banning of products deemed "unfit" does not work, and history attests to the failure of such extremist measures. . . . [C]onsumers are in the driver's seat. . . . [Y]ou cannot force people to comply with the Dietary Guidelines and it is wrong to try. It is an unworkable, totalitarian approach that brings with it all the evils associated with such a philosophy. (p. 359)

Those opposing the intervention may also claim that the real culprit is elsewhere. One common tactic is for social change competitors to dispute the research evidence supporting action. For example, the U.S. Chamber of Commerce's Institute for Legal Reform commissioned a review of evidence and concluded that fast food restaurants are not responsible for increased obesity. Their researcher, Todd Buchholz, argued that the source of childhood obesity is really too much between-meal snacking and more sedentary lifestyles (U.S. Chamber of Commerce, 2003).

A similar approach of laying the blame elsewhere is taken by the Center on Global Food Issues, a unit of the conservative Hudson Institute. On their Web page, Dennis Avery (2003) writes: "American teen obesity has increased 10 percent in the last 20 years—but they're eating only one percent more calories. Unfortunately, they are also exercising 13 percent less. That's the verdict from federal data bases at the Centers for Disease Control and the U.S. Department of Agriculture, says Dr. Lisa Sutherland of the University of North Carolina. . . . [G]etting [food] corporations to change will not reduce the number of calories" (Avery, 2003).

Potential personal counterattacks may be a competitive deterrent for some executives who may wish to become involved. For example, the Center for Consumer Freedom (2005), an industry-funded group, refers to its various opponents in the nutrition battles as someone who "has never met a lawsuit he didn't like. . . . [and who] can always be counted on to sink as low as possible" (John Banzhaf); someone who "is more than willing to use junk science and sensationalism to scare Americans about the food they eat" (Michael Jacobsen, Executive Director of the Center for Science in the Public Interest); and "one of the country's most hysterical anti-food-industry fanatics" (Marion Nestle, chair of the Department of Nutrition and Food Studies at New York University).

Affected businesses and their associations often carry out competitive communications campaigns on controversial issues, of course. Thus the Sugar Council actively opposes any implication that sugar is a culprit in the obesity problem. Corporate supporters of the council may be reluctant to participate in any program that may imply otherwise.

MAINTENANCE OF ALLIANCES

It is beyond the purview of this book to offer detailed advice on how to move alliances from Preparation and Action to the Maintenance stage. Excellent guides are available in the work of Alice Korngold (2005), James Austin (2000; Austin et al., 2004), and others on how to develop and grow collaborations. Austin (2000) suggests that healthy alliances between corporations and social sector organizations and agencies typically move along a continuum from philanthropy to transaction-based collaborations to full-fledged integration (Maintenance). To reach Maintenance requires careful management of the partnership and constant seeking for ways to make it evolve into even richer interactions. Austin's (2000) "Seven C's of Collaboration" are summarized in Figure 8.1.

Business Responses to the Overweight and Obesity Challenge

As the overweight and obesity issue dramatically rises on the public, media, and political agendas, corporations are seeing both threats and opportunities. There are opportunities to discover new markets as consumers seek solutions to their weight problems and those of their children. Thus early 2005 saw the following products introduced on store shelves (Mayer, 2005):

- Goldfish Crackers with extra calcium
- Hershey syrup enriched with calcium

CONNECTION With Purpose and People. Alliances are successful when key individuals connect personally and emotionally with the alliance's social purpose and with each other.

CLARITY of Purpose. Collaborators need to be clear—preferably in writing—about the purpose of joint undertakings.

CONGRUENCY of Mission, Strategy, and Values. The closer the alignment between the two organizations' missions, strategies, and values, the greater the potential gains from collaboration.

CREATION of Value. High-performance collaborations are about mobilizing and combining multiple resources and capabilities to generate benefits for both parties and social value for society.

COMMUNICATION Between Partners. Even in the presence of good personal relations and emotional connections, strategic fit, and successful value creation, a partnership is without a solid foundation if it lacks an effective ongoing communication process.

CONTINUAL Learning. A partnership's evolution cannot be completely planned or entirely predicted, so partners should view alliances as learning laboratories and cultivate a discovery ethic that supports continual learning.

COMMITMENT to the Partnership. Sustainable alliances institutionalize their collaboration process. They weave incentives to collaborate into their individual systems and embed them in organizational culture. As insurance against the exit of key individuals, they ensure continuity by empowering all levels of the organization.

Figure 8.1   James Austin's Seven C's of Strategic Collaboration

SOURCE: Austin (2000). Reproduced with permission.

- Reduced-sugar Cocoa Puffs and Trix
- Oscar Mayer Lunchables with less fat and sodium

General Mills and Kraft are adding more whole wheat to crackers and cereals. Kellogg has introduced Tiger Power, a "whole-grain" cereal with more calcium, fiber, and protein. Fast food chains are offering kids fruit instead of french fries. Burger chains are adding more salads, and McDonald's has added a fruit and walnut salad to its menu. Milk is now offered in fancy bottles, and McDonald's says that its milk sales doubled in 2004. The big soft drink manufacturers are planning milk-based offerings that should help their school vending challenges: Swerve for Coca-Cola and Quaker Milk Chillers for Pepsi.

Perhaps more dramatic is the announcement by McDonald's that it will adopt an "energy balance" and "balanced lifestyles" theme for 2005 (MacArthur, 2005). The head of global marketing for McDonald's is quoted as saying: "People always talk about it in terms of childhood obesity. . . . It's about well-being—not just nutrition—for a healthy and happy life. That works great with our Happy Meal. How do we make a Happy Meal happier?" (MacArthur, 2005). The company plans to promote milk, yogurt, and fruit choices for kids and to create a Ronald McDonald video on energy balance. The video will go to more than 80 countries. (See also the corporate Web site at http://www .mcdonalds.com/usa/good/balanced_active_lifestyles.html.)

These actions are not without their critics. There are charges that sweetened milk is not the way to teach kids healthy eating and that many foods with less sugar still have the same number of calories. Margo Wootan of the Center for Science in the Public Interest argues that "fortified junk food is still junk food" (Mayer, 2005, p. A4). Others note that smart marketers are charging higher prices for more healthful alternatives.

Brian Wansink of Cornell University's Food and Brand Lab and Governor Mike Huckabee of Arkansas see the food industry's response to threats regarding obesity as evolving through three phases: denial, appeal to consumer sovereignty, and development of win-win opportunities. In a recent article, Wansink and Huckabee (2005) propose a number of positive options for the industry under what they label approaches to "de-marketing obesity." However, the responses of the industry to date speak well to the value of a combination of regulatory actions (or threatened actions), private litigation, and efforts by the industry to directly market better health.

Notes

1. For more about these organizations, visit their Web sites at http://www.calvert group.com and http://www.domini.com.

2. To view Subway's kids page, go to http://subway-kids.com.

9

Recruiting Allies in the Media and Health-Care Communities

Peter Mitchell of the Academy for Educational Development has played active roles in many social marketing campaigns, most prominently the Florida teen smoking initiative. He has thought a lot about how to get reporters to cover social marketing stories to advance campaigns and about the real world that reporters face.

> Obviously, reporters are human. They have opinions. They're all different. But if you think like a marketer and consider reporters a critical intermediary audience, you might find one common determinant of behavior—the desire to have a story splashed across the front page, picked up by the national wire, or featured as the lead item in a newscast. They need something that is new, something shocking, something they think readers might mention around the water cooler next day. . . . Reporters are trying to predict what people will talk about tomorrow or at least predict what their editors think people will talk about tomorrow. (Mitchell, 2002, p. 37)

Mitchell would say that this goes a long way toward explaining why the front page of most print media in mid-2005 is filled with stories about Michael Jackson and why the genocide in Darfur and the malaria problem in Africa are on page 32—if they're there at all.

I n this chapter, we turn to two other key sectors that have roles to play in social change issues that concern health care: the media and the organized health-care system. It is impossible to cover a wide selection of possible targets of social marketing efforts in these two sectors. The media comprise a very diverse set of organizations and individuals, ranging widely from movies and television to the Internet to print media and cell phones. Similarly, the health-care sector includes physicians and hospitals, pharmaceutical companies, laboratories, school nurses, and acupuncturists. I narrow the range here to focus on showing how social marketing concepts and tools can be used to induce key individuals to play upstream roles to increase motivation, opportunity, and ability among downstream audiences.

The Media

The media have many roles they can play in the agenda-setting process described in chapter 2. Among these roles are the following.

Discovering and publicizing the existence of a social problem. Investigative reporters are often the ones who first note rare but significant events deserving social attention. This was the case in the reemergence of the Ebola virus in the 1990s. Ebola was discovered in Zaire in 1976 but became the source of considerable public concern when a new outbreak occurred in Africa in the 1990s and the virus migrated in monkeys shipped to the United States. Major contributors to the public's apparent panic over this rare virus (beyond its obvious frightening effects) were the publication of Richard Preston's popular novel *The Hot Zone* and the later movie, *Outbreak*.

Raising the issue on the public agenda. As a social issue gains traction, the media can accelerate its rise by bringing the issue up on talk shows, publicizing conferences on the topic, recounting vivid stories of victims, reporting political pronouncements and debates, writing or publishing editorial comments, and conducting polls about how the public feels about the issue.

Outlining choices and helping choose possible courses of action. The media can help the public understand the options and suggest criteria for choosing among them. They can offer venues for advocates of alternative solutions and report think-tank studies of possible effects and problems.

Promoting solutions. Once there is some agreement about what is to be done, the media can (a) help induce Precontemplators to begin to consider the problem and possible action. These can be downstream targets who need to change their behavior or upstream participants, such as legislators or school principals, who have to make structural changes to facilitate action. (b) The media can help Contemplators think through the *benefits* and *costs* of taking action; for example, by providing case histories or interviews with early adopters of the new behavior. (c) The positive pressure of *others* can be brought to bear by media reporting of the increased prominence of the issue in recent polls, publicizing of success stories, and allowance of time and space to political leaders and celebrities who will promote desired actions. (d) The media can fight the negative pressure of *others* who oppose action through editorials or retransmission of the positions of supporters. (e) Those at the Preparation and Action stage can be assisted through publication of how-to information and provision of role-playing examples (for example, on television shows or movies). (f) The media can provide reinforcement for those in Maintenance by (again) reporting success stories, publicizing favorable statistical trends, and printing editorials endorsing good behavior.

Helping monitor interventions. By reporting both statistics and anecdotes on social progress, the media can offer social marketers and the general public insight into what is or is not working. Large media organizations can use their resources to conduct interviews and their own polls on how issues are progressing. They can conduct specific investigations of specific programs. They can publicize malfeasance where it exists and keep the pressure on managers and watchdogs until changes are made.

THE MEDIA'S ROLE IN PRACTICE

A good example of the role the media can play early in the social change process for childhood obesity is an article in the *Washington Post Magazine* in March 2003 by Peter Perl, "The Incredible Shrinking Duyers." Like many similar articles now appearing in popular media, Perl's piece helps a public now at Stage 4 of the agenda-setting process—outlining the choices. Perl's goal was to illustrate the obesity challenge, describe the options one family chose to address it, and point out the difficulties of achieving lasting solutions. He says in his introduction: "Overeating and under-exercising have become a way of life. That made the Duyer family all too typical—until they decided to launch a full-scale attack on fat."

The article then proceeded to humanize both the dilemma for the family and their struggles to take action. The author begins by describing a visit by 15-year-old Emma Duyer and her overweight mother and father to the Clopper's Mill Village Center for their weekly weigh-in at Weight Watchers. After suggesting that the problem might be partly related to a "genetic tendency toward the same big bulky body type," their plight is described as "too many years of unhealthy eating, too many late-night pizzas, too many all-you-can-eat french fry binges, too much of everything—except exercise."

The author then quotes experts and puts the social change issue in a broader context. He quotes James Hill, an obesity researcher at the University of Colorado:

"You can't blame obese people, but you can't totally excuse them either." ...
Though exercising willpower is important, it is ultimately futile for most people,
Hill says, given America's toxic nutritional environment—awash in high fructose
corn syrup, palm oil and other high-fat or high-calorie additives, in everything
from soda to cereal. "This environment is so difficult, it's hard to make good
choices even if you have good willpower," says Hill.

The story follows the Duyer family over several months and describes in
detail the complex dynamics within the family, particularly the mother's difficult decisions about how much to push her daughter to change. By the end of
5 months, we learn that the mother has lost 35 pounds and the father 24, but
the daughter has dropped less than 10 and has missed two Weight Watchers
meetings. The mother reflects: "I guess maybe Emma has to decide when it's
her time to really do something. Maybe I just gotta let it ride, and maybe I just
have to let go for now."

Applying Social Marketing to the Media

MEDIA TARGETS

There are many ways in which the media can be partitioned as the social
marketer considers who might be targeted and attempts to understand how
they might be influenced. A useful typology is to begin by distinguishing
between content creators and content transmitters. The former would include
Hollywood studios and their writers, magazine writers, photographers, blog
writers, and newspaper reporters. Content transmitters include the Internet;
various magazines, newspapers, and newsletters; TV and radio networks; and
billboard and poster providers. In the 21st century, we should also probably
include telephone companies, which now transmit text, pictures, and videos
over cell phones. All of these represent individual organizations with
approachable executives who can be asked for help. In the case of the Internet,
of course, there is no owner who can be influenced to help. However, organizations such as AOL, Microsoft, and Mozilla provide connectivity, and the
owners of various Web pages can provide pipelines for various kinds of content prepared by the Web site owners and others.

A second dimension in which to partition the media is by role. There are
media that primarily produce information and news, that report what is going
on.[1] These obviously include newspapers; magazines such as *Time, Business
Week,* and *U.S. News and World Report;* newsletters; TV and radio news operations; telecommunications organizations; and an array of Web sites. Then there
are media that seek to educate, comment, and influence. These include numerous TV and radio talk shows, general and specialized magazines and journals

such as *Foreign Policy* and the *New Yorker,* and the nonfiction sector of the book publishing industry. Finally, there are those media that seek to entertain but that, in the process, can educate and influence target audiences by what they transmit. Here, one would include the TV networks, movie studios, the comic book industry, producers of fiction in magazines and books, and makers of video games.

INFLUENCING MEDIA BEHAVIOR

Obviously each target audience has its own peculiarities, and experienced marketers soon learn which ones are most likely to respond to campaign efforts to secure their cooperation. Such insights often are accompanied by awareness of what themes and approaches are most likely to get the best response. To see how a social marketer might use the tools described in earlier chapters to approach the challenge, we will take a simple example: getting a TV news director to cover some event that will advance a specific social change campaign. Our three models, the Stages of Change, BCOS, and Competition, are all relevant here.

Stages of Change

The distribution of media targets across the Stages of Change will obviously depend on where the issue is on the media agenda. Most will be in Precontemplation when an issue is emerging, and a significant segment will be in Maintenance when alternative choices of action are being debated.

A typical target news director will be someone in Contemplation. Here, the social marketer's challenge is to discover those who have expressed some interest in the topic area in the past or who have covered similar issues. Assuming a specific news director is identified, the social marketer then needs to think about how the BCOS factors might be brought to bear to secure coverage. Public relations experts whose principal job is to understand and influence the media spend considerable time gathering such information through "listening" occasions in informal meetings or at conferences, or through simple observation of the news director's past choices.

The BCOS Model

Although each TV station will have its idiosyncrasies, there are some general BCOS elements that are likely to be considered by the typical news director.

Benefits. The first place to start is with the goals and ambitions of the news director and the media outlet. Does the news director simply want to provide the most up-to-date information, or does she or he want to be a leader in supporting social change? What does the director believe the viewers want to see and hear about? Does this director have personal ambitions that cause her or him to look for stories that could have national "play"? Does she or he seem to like contact with experts or celebrities? Does the director seem interested in data-rich stories or stories with lots of warm and fuzzy personal dimensions? Are there dimensions of the social change issue that would be especially appealing—for example, the impact on kids or on Hispanic households?

The important feature to keep in mind here is to focus on the target audience's needs and wants. It is often the case that promoters of social change are so focused on their own particular issue that this is all they talk about when approaching someone like our hypothetical news director. They tell the news director how important the social change issue is and how much the campaign needs to have the story covered. However, the critical message should be not how coverage will benefit the campaign but how much it will benefit the news director and the media outlet.

The news director will undoubtedly also consider who is actually going to cover the story. Here, the director may think about how she or he can motivate key reporters to take on the issue. Some reporters will love data, others the human interest. Some may want to become experts in the topic area and use it as the basis for a series of reports (and possible career advancement).

Costs. For the news director and reporter, key costs will be the anticipated time to put the story together, the expenses involved for travel, camera crews, editing, and the like, and the mental cost of having to get up to speed on a new social concern. There are sometimes potential reputational risks if the issue is at all controversial. News directors and reporters may fear that a complex issue will bore their viewers. They may see the issue as "all facts and rhetoric," with no human interest side. Clearly, the social marketer's challenge is to reduce or eliminate these costs. Social marketers can help defray expenses or suggest human interest angles and agree to set up interviews. At the same time, they need to be candid about any controversial issues so that the news director will develop *trust* in the social marketer and his or her organization. As any media person will tell you, nothing will turn off a reporter or a news director to future cooperation like learning that a social marketer has withheld crucial information or otherwise deceived a potential ally.

Others. Certainly, the competitive media environment often offers opportunities to bring competitive pressures to bear. Offering exclusive coverage—not offered to rivals—can be an important consideration in getting media support. Media people like to be first to report on an issue and to show its ramifications and personal cost. They like "scoops" and to be seen as leaders. If exclusive coverage is not forthcoming, the social marketer can subtly mention that rival outlets are getting on top of the issue as a means of employing a bandwagon approach; that is, indicating to the potential media ally that "important others" are actively covering the issue. Depending on the context, interpersonal pressure can also be exerted by a celebrity or political figure urging the news director to cover the issue. A call from Michael J. Fox talking about the urgent need for research on multiple sclerosis can often galvanize coverage—even more so if he shows up for an interview or provides a personalized videotape.

Self-Assurance. It will be important to make coverage as easy as possible for the media organization. It is one thing to get news directors interested in a story. It is another to actually get them to act, if they feel that they really cannot bring it off. It may be that they see a daunting challenge trying to get their arms around a complex new issue. Clearly, extensive briefing materials can reduce this concern. They may not know the sources they will need to contact to fill out their stories. Again, a contact list can be very valuable. There are typically issues of timing. TV outlets have news cycles and need to feel that the story can be produced to meet their deadlines. If it is a live event that needs covering, advance materials should be made available in easily digested form. The social marketer should make sure that the station's reporters get VIP treatment at the event and that the coverage process is as smooth and quick as possible. For example, planners can set aside designated parking areas for the TV crew, have interviewees ready precisely on schedule and well prepped, and have a packet of follow-up information and future contact information ready to go at the conclusion of the event. Visual backdrops will be important and need to be in place. For some news directors and reporters, it may even be helpful to offer rough drafts of copy material prepared for the outlet to adapt. Prepackaged sound bites can be made available as video news releases for the outlet to use as needed. Finally, providing positive reinforcement after the coverage can go a long way toward increasing the reporter's self-assurance regarding future stories.

Competition

Media people have limited time and—possibly—attention spans. Papers and magazines have only so many pages; TV and radio stations have only so many available minutes for coverage. They are undoubtedly being approached (if not bombarded) with pleas from other social marketers to *please* cover their event. It is important to understand news directors' competitive alternatives and be sympathetic to the pressures they are under. One must understand what else they might do with their time, equipment, and talent. Is the main competition other social change issues, or is it newsworthy topics in other areas? What might seem appealing about these competitors, and how can your issue seem to offer *superior benefits?* How will competitors be appealing? Will they offer to make coverage easier than you will, provide better celebrities, or offer more to reduce or share coverage costs? Whatever they do, it is important to suggest that you will implicitly meet or beat their offer. Overall, it is important to remember that if you are better at being customer focused rather than organization focused (e.g., emphasizing why your challenge is *greater*), you should win out more often in the competitive media environment.

Tim Russert of NBC News's *Meet the Press* has provided an insider's look at how a savvy staffer uses these ideas to improve relations with the press. For several years, Russert was responsible for communications for Senator Daniel Patrick Moynihan. Here's how he describes his approach:

> I enjoyed dealing with the press. Reporters have a job to do, and when you're straight with them and accessible, they tend to give you the benefit of the doubt. I worked hard to understand the legislative issues well enough to explain them to reporters, and sometimes I'd ask our legislative point man to write out key provisions of a bill as if he were sending a letter to his father. Whenever possible, I gave reporters other information that might be useful to their story, even if it had nothing to do with Moynihan. *I tried to see things from their perspective*, and a few times, when a reporter [wasn't] able to reach a source, I would provide the person's phone number. (Russert, 2004, p. 260; italics added)

The Entertainment Media

News programs, magazine articles, and Web logs (blogs) can all alert the public and legislators to the importance of an issue and to the need for action. However, we also learn a good deal about our world and what is desirable behavior from informal sources—watching our parents, talking with friends, and being exposed to movies and television. Social marketers in a number of areas have made use of entertainment media over the years as a vehicle for advancing social change (Rogers, Aikat, Chang, Poppe, & Sopory, 1989; Singhal & Rogers, 1999). By weaving messages into the scripts of radio dramas, movies, songs, and TV shows, social marketers have found they can educate target audiences about the importance of an issue and model desired behaviors. By showing celebrities and archetypal figures (village leaders, health officials) carrying out the desired behavior, they can influence social norms. Finally, where the entertainment is ongoing, as in soap operas or talk shows, messages can be repeated and reinforced. Variations can be introduced.

The use of such vehicles for advancing social change has several advantages. For example, entertainment media often have much broader audience reach. In many of the poorest countries around the world, radio has been a powerful force for social change, particularly where the citizenry has low literacy or limited access to other sources of information. Local community stations with limited transmission power but no censorship have proven critical in bringing about political revolutions, especially in Latin America (Gumucio, 2001). In India, Southeast Asia, and South Africa, radio and television soap operas have been a major part of social marketing campaigns.

Many of these approaches are described on the highly valuable Web site for the Communication Initiative (2005). A typical campaign is the "Heart and Soul" program in East Africa:

> Initiated in 2002 by the United Nations (UN) in Kenya in collaboration with all 24 UN agencies based in Nairobi, this multimedia communications strategy is centred on a prime-time television and radio soap opera called "Heart & Soul." Scripted, directed, acted, and produced by Kenyan talents in the film and television industry, the series explores social and development issues evoked by five key themes: HIV/AIDS, environment and natural disaster management, governance and human rights, poverty reduction, and gender issues. These issues, as well as the ordinary joys and trials of everyday life in Africa, are highlighted through focus on the rich "Meli" family and the poor "Karani" family. Heart & Soul's audience, which is potentially 50 to 75 million people across Africa, are the urban and rural, youth and adult population in Kenya and other Eastern Africa countries.

Live theater also has a long history of sparking social change. In Asia, puppet shows bring social messages to street-corner audiences. In the United States in the last century, music was an important vehicle for social change. Spirituals, songs about union solidarity, and, more recently, popular protest songs have all carried messages and influenced social norms. Low-cost video cameras have increased the potential role for this medium in effecting social change, as seen in some of the political uprisings in former socialist republics.

Finally, the Internet and computers generally are now proving to be a powerful medium for people to use to influence each other. Blogs get across ideas and opinions from "ordinary people." Web sites of social marketing campaigns provide opportunities for visitors to be entertained as they learn important information about desirable social behaviors. The Office of National Drug Control Policy has one Web site for kids called Freevibe (http://www.freevibe .com) where they can go to learn facts, play games, hear from celebrities, and learn the thoughts and experiences of other kids like themselves. The program maintains separate sites for parents and educators in six languages (http:// www.theantidrug.com).

MASS ENTERTAINMENT VEHICLES

Forty years ago, organizations promoting seat belt usage noted that actors in TV dramas—including law enforcement officers—were getting into their cars and not donning their seat belts. When the oversight was brought to the attention of producers and writers, the change was relatively quickly made, providing an infinite number of audience exposures to the "seat belt message." Today a great many major social change campaigns have specific staff members dedicated to enticing major networks, cable companies, and movie studios to incorporate campaign issues and themes in their regular programs. A vigorous user of this approach is the National Campaign to Prevent Teen Pregnancy (2002), which describes its accomplishments as follows:

> Through our Media Task Force, the National Campaign has developed partnerships with over 70 major media leaders and now works with every major television broadcast network and with many of the top cable networks most popular with teens and their parents. The National Campaign helps media leaders—including *Teen People* magazine, The WB Network, and Fox Broadcasting—weave prevention messages into the content of their work. National Campaign messages have appeared in television programs and magazines seen by over 275 million people.

The campaign faces a difficult challenge—getting programs, movies, and sitcoms to show actors using condoms. This could involve characters discussing who has the condom, showing a condom package in someone's hand, or having a camera "notice" a condom on a nightstand. An example of this approach is a February 2, 2003, episode of *Becker* in which actor Ted Danson urged a sexually active 15-year-old boy to use condoms. On a UPN sitcom, *Half and Half,* the character Mona says to Spencer: "You had sex without a condom? That is possibly the stupidest thing you have ever done." Research has shown that such portrayals can have an important effect. A study in *Pediatrics* found an influence on teens after the airing of an episode of *Friends* in which Rachel became pregnant when Ross's condom was not effective. A few weeks after the episode, 65% of teenagers surveyed remembered the incident and 10% had conversations with an adult about condom safety (Collins, Elliott, Berry, Kanouse, & Hunter, 2003).

Social marketers are aware, however, that when the media contemplate carrying out such behaviors, a cost they will consider will be negative reaction if the issue is controversial (e.g., condoms). Opposition to the media's role in social change frequently comes from (competitive) conservative groups, who, in this case, believe that promoting condoms is equivalent to promoting illicit sex. Brent Bozell (2003), of the Media Research Center, complained:

> Is this true health education or condom promotion? . . . [W]hat Viacom and Kaiser are promoting is not "safer sex." It's promoting a sexually "liberated" viewpoint that at best is controversial and is not established science. . . . If the Knights of Columbus came to Viacom proposing a joint project to promote the joys of virginity or a patriotic message in time of war, you know the reaction. The Hollywood crowd would wail in protest over this propagandistic abuse of artistic products. But that's not the case when the message fits Hollywood like a glove—or a condom.

Despite these competitive challenges, many believe the potential for positive effects in areas such as family planning are significant. In 1990, Judith Senderowitz noted a major shift:

> The fall of 1987 was the breakthrough season. US television saw young people discussing family planning with their parents and with each other. . . . Parents do not usually want to talk to their children about birth control, and schools are not usually willing to go that far in sex education courses. Young people, then, look to TV for information and role models. . . . [Y]oung people borrow from TV scripts or programs and act them out in their personal lives. . . . We are at the point where TV, movies, and other media are ready to become allies with us. We no longer have to knock on their doors day after day, year after year to make them listen. Now, they are seeking us out because they are interested in communicating social needs, social development and social change, and because social ideas can be entertaining and profitable. (p. 16)

Of course, two of the most vivid recent examples of the power of entertainment media as a source of social influence are Michael Moore's movie *Bowling for Columbine* and Mel Gibson's *The Passion of the Christ*. The first-mentioned movie raised a number of issues related to gun control around the world. Gibson's movie generated significant discussion of religious issues as well as—probably unintentionally issues of anti-Semitism. The director, a fundamentalist Roman Catholic, used the release of the film as an opportunity to generate debate about Christianity and its origins. Both moviemakers had little difficulty getting on talk shows and newscasts to take up their issues—providing excellent examples of how social issues can rapidly climb the public and media agendas because of specific events and charismatic spokespeople.

Health-Care Practitioners

A great many of the social problems to which social marketing has been applied in the last 40 years have been in the health-care field. There has been downstream focus on family planning, safe sex, smoking, exercise, diet, prenatal care, disease prevention (flu, polio), child health, and so on (Andreasen, 1995; Donovan & Henley, 2003; Hornik, 2001; Kotler, Roberto, & Lee, 2002). Many of these campaigns have included upstream elements, seeking supportive behaviors from a wide range of health professionals, technicians, specialists, health-care workers, medical educators, and administrators in the health-care system. More upstream focus by social marketers in future campaigns can be expected.

TARGET AUDIENCES

The broad target audiences for any upstream social marketing campaign in health care can include

- Frontline patient-contact people, including physicians, nurses, office staff, hospital staff, school nurses, psychologists
- People to whom patients are referred, including nutritionists, exercise therapists, pharmacists
- Public health educators, including national, state, and local health agencies and nonprofit health organizations, such as the American Cancer Society and the American Heart Association
- Medical school educators: teachers, curriculum designers, accrediting groups

These broad target groupings can often be more finely segmented for special attention. For example, among physicians, one might distinguish among primary care physicians in sole practices; primary care physicians in group practices; hospital-based primary care physicians; pediatricians (in each of the same settings); emergency room physicians (often acting as primary care physicians for the poor); specialists affected by an intervention issue, further divided into those whose practices involve significant impacts (e.g., cardiologists, psychologists, psychiatrists) and those for whom the impacts are less severe (e.g., dermatologists, podiatrists); specialists not immediately affected (e.g., neurologists); physician managers in group practices or hospitals; physicians with access to the media; and heads of government public health programs (Cassady, Culp, & Watnik, 2002).

Then, to further complicate matters, one could divide some or all of these categories by the type of patient served. Some practices may contain significant representations of patients who are elderly or female or Hispanic or Vietnamese; others may comprise primarily white, middle class patients. The approaches to the health-care professionals could then be divided a different way, according to the Stages of Change in which the patients are found.

BEHAVIORS

To explore the possible behavioral alternatives, let us again spotlight the childhood obesity issue and choose a relatively straightforward target: a primary care family physician in a group practice serving a mix of white male and female adults and children. In this scenario, the physician typically will see multiple members of the same family but will also have many patients whose spouses or children see other doctors—or who do not see a physician at all. What behaviors might a program wish to target? In the case of childhood obesity, we might want the physician to routinely do the following:

1. Intervene with obese juvenile patients to get them started on actions to attain a safe weight

2. Inquire of obese adult patients whether their children are also obese and, if so, intervene to get these (nonpatient) children started on weight reduction—and at the same time get the adult to take similar proactive steps

3. Monitor past overweight and obese juvenile patients or adults who are already taking steps to reduce weight and provide praise to ensure they stay with an effective program

4. Refer patients, where relevant, to specialists such as nutritionists or exercise therapists to assist in, or take primary responsibility for, an exercise or diet regimen

5. Provide supportive materials (brochures, videos, Web addresses) to affected patients and make them available in the physician's office for others who may know of a child with an obesity problem

6. Where necessary or desirable, delegate to other office staff members some of the elements of the intervention (e.g., following up with patients or parent with reinforcing telephone calls or e-mail messages, praising visiting patients who seem to be making progress)

7. Ensure that obese office staff members are addressing their own weight problems

8. Urge colleagues in the group practice to become involved in similar interventions

9. Document successes and failures to help build a database of best practices to share with others in the health profession

10. Urge other parts of the medical system to provide more help and infrastructure to make the physician's job easier

11. Give talks to schools and civic groups on the dangers of childhood obesity

12. Enroll in education courses or attend seminars on the latest lessons and approaches to the childhood obesity problem

USING THE MODELS

My purpose here is not to propose specific strategies and tactics for influencing these behaviors. Rather, as in earlier chapters, it is to show how the various social marketing frameworks might be applied to develop such a campaign. To this end, let's consider how to get primary care physicians to intervene with overweight and obese juveniles to get them on a program of exercise and weight reduction. The reader might ask: Why wouldn't a physician confronted by an overweight child at the doctor's office do something about it? Why would any physician be in Precontemplation?

Precontemplation

There are two probable reasons for physicians to be in the Precontemplation stage with respect to this behavior. First, given their complex careers, perhaps their age, and the kinds of patients they typically serve, they may be unaware of the scope of the childhood obesity problem and the medical and social implications it entails. Second, it is more likely that, although the physician is aware of the problem, he or she has decided it is not a priority. Possible reasons for this reticence include the following.

- A great many physicians think of themselves as in the "curing business." They believe that their major responsibilities are to detect and treat serious immediate problems. They do not see themselves as public health workers who need to add prevention to their busy work schedules. A physician may be willing to treat any consequences of childhood obesity but unwilling to get involved in prevention.
- Physicians may see an obese child as "going through a phase" and therefore needing little attention. The child will grow out of it. Physicians need only offer a brief admonition or a pamphlet but should do little else.
- Physicians may see the child's obesity as a behavioral problem and not a medical one; therefore it is someone else's challenge.
- Physicians may believe that there are no "proven" best practices, and any effort is thus likely to be futile.

The challenge for moving such physicians to the Contemplation stage will undoubtedly require efforts by the medical establishment (the American Medical Association, various practice groups, universities) to push this issue up the physician's agenda and, in particular, get physicians to recognize the long-term implications for their patients. The availability of a set of accepted best practices may be the key to removing their blinders.

Contemplation

Physicians are more likely to be in the Contemplation stage. As we have seen, this is where the BCOS factors become critical. The first challenge is to discover the benefits of an intervention that would be important *to the physician*. Obviously, there will be benefits to the obese children and their families and to society as a whole if the physician acts. These can be worth mentioning, but the social marketer must keep in mind that it is the *physician* who has to be influenced and so it is *that physician's* potential benefits that need to be emphasized. Among the *benefits* a physician might consider valuable are the potential future reduction in patient load if the obese child comes less often in future and with fewer serious problems or if there are other health-care workers or specialists to whom the patient can be referred, greater remuneration from insurance companies for prevention efforts, feeling that one is at the forefront in combating a major new social problem and has the chance to publish results from innovative interventions, reaping second-order benefits from improvements in the eating and exercise behavior of *parents* of obese children who are also patients, achieving synergies and saving time by treating an entire obese family simultaneously, and having the opportunity to differentiate one's practice and perhaps bring in new patients.

The physician will balance these and other personal benefits against personal *costs,* which could include the following: performing services that are not compensated by insurance or not adequately compensated; having to tell the child or parents facts and implications that may be taken as personal criticism of the child's appearance and character; expecting poor patient cooperation; speculating that, if the physician were to address the problem, he or she would become dragged into complex family dynamics, lifestyle issues, and other factors that are outside the physician's capabilities to address; expecting that interventions will not be a one-time action but will "trap" the physician into a long series of return visits and further (perhaps uncompensated) attempts at intervention (unlike giving pills for a rash); anticipating a lack of cooperation by other key parties such as parents, peers, school administrators, and so on; and fearing that, if the physician takes on this prevention challenge, it will lead to new pressures to take on other (time-consuming) prevention activities.

The influence of interpersonal influences by *others* on physician behavior is very critical and has a very long history (Rogers, 1995). These influences could turn out to be positive or negative, as follows:

+ Learning that peers (including others in the physician's own practice) consider this a major problem and are exploring innovative interventions

+ Learning that community organizations will be pleased if the doctor takes on this challenge and perhaps will issue awards or other tokens of appreciation

+ Learning that other opinion leaders (e.g., American Medical Association speakers, professors at continuing education seminars) are urging greater efforts to deal with the childhood obesity problem

+ Learning that schools, park districts, major health-care nonprofits, and foundations are addressing the issue and giving it high priority (and are willing to provide materials, videos, and so forth)

− Learning that peers consider this a problem for which there is no "magic bullet" and argue that a physician should not waste time on it unless there are immediate medical consequences

− Learning that peers think that the problem exists because *families* today lack proper discipline and sensible lifestyles and that this is neither the fault or the responsibility of the medical profession

− Pressure from caregivers to "not be so mean to the child"

Finally, there may be important issues of *self-assurance.* If physicians believe that they cannot really have an impact on the child, they are unlikely to move to the Action stage, even on a trial basis. As we have noted, they may simply believe that there are no best practices in this area and are at a loss as to what to do. They may be daunted by the environmental competition—the fast food advertising, the peers urging fattening drinks and snacks, the families who see "healthy appetites" as a sign they are good providers, the video game marketers who are promoting more hours at the computer console, and so on. Physicians may also feel that they cannot do the job themselves. They may recognize that others have to act to change behaviors involving home and school meal patterns, TV watching, hours spent playing computer games, and exercise. Schools have to take action. Fast food outlets have to be less forceful in enticing kids to "super-size."

Finally, physicians may think that they really are not trained in psychology or group dynamics, and those are the skills one needs here. Physicians may feel that, although they are good at recognizing symptoms, ferreting out causes, and prescribing pills for recovery, they lack the interpersonal skills necessary to effectively intervene with an obese child. They may feel the topic has many potentially negative psychological connotations for the child and so must be approached very delicately. Physicians may also feel that they have no training in "family dynamics," and these skills may be important. Unless they acquire some modicum of these skills, they may simply not act.

These considerations point to two dimensions of self-assurance. First, target audiences need a sense that the physician knows *how* to carry out an effective intervention. Then there is what is sometimes called "outcome efficacy" (Bandura, 1977): the sense that, if the physician intervenes, the action will actually lead to the desired outcome—a permanently thinner child. Finally, there is the problem of recidivism. The physician may feel that, even if he or she can achieve some initial successes, the experiences of dieters worldwide would lead one to expect that the child will someday come back just as heavy or more so. So, why bother?

Action

Suppose, however, physicians have (perhaps reluctantly) concluded that they ought to take action. However, they just have not quite gotten around to getting started. What might be the problem here?

This is a point at which the third major model I use becomes important: Competition. Two common types of competition are the status quo and competing new behaviors. In the first instance, the physician may have a successful practice, have a good success rate for interventions, and be meeting patients' expressed immediate needs. To these physicians, the social marketer is suggesting that this routine be upset, that the physician learn new skills, that he or she take on cases that have high recidivism rates and can drag out for a very long time. To start with, the patient may not even feel "unhealthy." Better for the physician to "take a pass" on the obesity problem (it is not an immediate risk anyway) and go for the cases where a proven intervention is available, or relatively easily discovered, and the treatment program is predictable and finite. This is the status quo option.

A second kind of competition is offered by alternative new behaviors. Physicians, just like many others who are the targets of social marketing programs, are bombarded with alternative new things to do. Drug companies have new drugs. The medical journals, medical schools, and medical associations constantly propose new treatment protocols. The Department of Health and Human Services, the American Cancer Society, and the American Heart Association want the physician to focus more on *their* issues. Beyond the office, the physician may be under pressure to provide new pro bono care, sit on some community board, or help coach his or her daughter's soccer team. All of these alternative behaviors may offer packages of benefits and costs, social pressures, and assurance issues that may be competitive with (or superior to) those offered by a child obesity intervention. They represent competitive challenges the social marketer needs to address.

Maintenance

There may be a tendency for a social marketer to ignore physicians in the Maintenance stage, given the much greater challenge of motivating Contemplators to act. Further research on those in Maintenance should ask the following questions:

1. Is the physician convinced that this is a good action or set of actions to be undertaken, or is there a risk that the physician will fall back to the Contemplation or even Precontemplation stage? Does the physician need reinforcement and support?

2. If the physician is satisfied, would he or she be willing to (a) speak to other physicians to help apply social or professional pressure; (b) publish results in medical journals or more popular venues to encourage others to act; (c) appear on panels or give speeches at conferences of peers; (d) guest lecture at medical schools, promoting efforts to deal with the childhood obesity problem and passing along treatment lessons learned; or (e) participate in public relations efforts in conjunction with the campaign—for example, going on television or radio talk shows, appearing in a campaign video, or facilitating interviews with formerly obese patients and their families?

Campaign Strategy

Suppose for the moment that a social marketing campaign aimed at getting physicians to intervene more often with obese children has done the research suggested in the preceding paragraphs that would help them understand approximately how many physicians are estimated to be at each of the Stages of Change and what their demographic and professional characteristics are, what the key BCOS factors are at each stage, and what competitive forces affect physicians at each stage.

It is possible that the preliminary research may detect different clusters of BCOS factors within a given stage. Each would potentially merit a different approach. For example, Contemplators who do not see enough benefits may be different from those who see many benefits but high costs, and both of these are different from those who seem to be held back by social pressures marshaled against the new approach. There may also be a fourth group that feels it lacks the necessary skills. Each could merit separate interventions.

However, campaigns with limited budgets cannot do all things for all targets. Thus, as when addressing any target audience upstream or down, judgments must be made about which target audiences to select and which behaviors to address. Where budgets permit, some type of quantitative study of the target universe may be highly desirable. Typically, one of the major unknowns at the exploratory stages of any campaign will be simply how many physicians fit each segment profile and how many obese children these physicians are likely to treat. Further estimates will need to be made of the costs and probable success of addressing each segment. These and similar factors will help the campaign planners ascertain the potential numbers of obese kids who could be affected by the campaign, perhaps weighted by their "social value." This would be weighed against the challenges of reaching the target physicians, and decisions would be made as to which segments to address now and which to address later. These sequencing decisions should also take into account the kinds of interpersonal influences that Gladwell (2000) and Rogers (1995) have studied. Achieving early success with mavens, connectors, or salesmen may be more critical to long-term success than a broad attempt to mass market the desired behavior.

Note

1. Of course, they also offer editorials, opinion pieces, and the option for reader feedback.

PART IV

Conclusions

10

Repositioning Social Marketing for the 21st Century

The central argument of this book is that social marketing is a significantly underappreciated approach to social change, especially in upstream contexts. In some ways, this is an understandable product of its origins in family planning and health care. Because it has proven effective in influencing the behaviors of mothers, smokers, and those with high blood pressure, it has come to be seen by many as only a downstream approach. Downstream approaches target those who exhibit a problem behavior or are at risk of adopting one. To the field's significant credit, social marketers have developed over the years a powerful array of frameworks, concepts, and tools to bring about effective downstream interventions. Chapter 4 outlined the set of concepts and tools I have learned to use in consulting work and teaching.

As I made clear in chapters 1 and 2, however, social problems need to be addressed in much more complex ways than simply achieving downstream change. As we have seen, a society achieves major social change through a predictable chronological sequence of steps from the point at which a problem is initially detected through the point at which major permanent change has occurred and social welfare has been markedly enhanced. Historically, social marketing has only come into play at the point at which possible solutions have been advanced and, further, only with respect to those solutions that focus on individuals and their problem behaviors.

This narrow perspective does a disservice to both social marketers and social welfare. We have much more to contribute at many more stages, and I believe society has much to gain if we do so.

What Is Needed?[1]

As I have written in several places (e.g., Andreasen, 2002, 2004b), the major challenge before social marketers is to systematically carry out what private sector marketers refer to as "repositioning" of the field. If social marketing is considered a promotion of behavioral change, then it suffers from having the wrong image or being perceived incorrectly. It is not that it is seen as bad or evil or even ineffective—although some argue that, in the past, social marketers have diverted resources from better upstream approaches. It is only that social marketing is typically seen as useful for cases of individual problem behaviors. Agencies and their executives who might make greater use of social marketing approaches in upstream venues are simply not doing so. Foundations and commercial firms who might fund or otherwise support broader applications do not see the wisdom of such an approach. Thus the future of the field is unnecessarily restricted.

Concerns about social marketing's future are not new. Back in 1996, a "summit" of social marketing leaders was convened by Porter Novelli to address the field's future. In 1998, a conference at the Robert Wood Johnson Foundation recommended the establishment of a "center for integrated social marketing." Both events led to the founding of the Social Marketing Institute in 1999,[2] which began its activities by systematically identifying significant potential barriers to growth for the field. In a series of more than 300 personal interviews, 100 field questionnaires, and two focus groups,[3] institute researchers identified four major problem areas that still apply today.

1. There is a lack of appreciation of social marketing at top management levels. Social marketing has achieved significant acceptance among practitioners at the operations level of implementing organizations and within the consulting community to whom these practitioners turn for help. However, both groups lament the fact that senior executives of too many nonprofit organizations and major government agencies are unaware either of social marketing or of its potential for organizing and implementing major social change programs. Because of this lack of appreciation, promising campaigns often are unable to use social marketing approaches or, when they do, find themselves inadequately funded or their recommendations not thoroughly implemented.

2. The field has poor "brand positioning." Social marketing as an approach to social change lacks clarity and is seen by key influential people as having a number of undesirable traits. First, the field's image is fuzzy, because there are too many definitions of social marketing being used, and these definitions conflict in major and minor ways. Second, social marketing is not adequately differentiated from its competition, especially in ways that would be in its favor.

Third, social marketing is perceived to have attributes that are unattractive to important target audiences: most prominently, the perception that it is manipulative and not "community based." The latter is a trait that is particularly important to many agencies and foundations involved in international development (Gray-Felder & Deane, 1999).

3. There is inadequate documentation of and publicity for successes. Any social change approach gains favor to the extent that it can document its effectiveness and, particularly, its superiority to alternatives. Further, such documentation must be followed by adequate publicity that in large part makes clear that it is social marketing that has made the difference. Although successes clearly and widely exist (Alcaly & Bell, 2000; Carroll, Craypo, & Samuels, 2000; Chapman, Astatke, & Ashburn, 2005; Donovan & Henley, 2003), these are not widely known or appreciated—and there are not enough of them.

4. Social marketing lacks academic stature. A measure of the legitimacy for a field is the extent to which it (a) is taught on a regular basis at major universities, (b) leads to specific career options (and so merits formal learning), (c) is supported by a significant base of conceptual and theoretical material, and (d) is an accepted area of research study that increases the field's conceptual and theoretical base and sometimes makes contributions to other fields to which it is related. Social marketing is taught only rarely as a full academic course, more often as one or two class sessions in a marketing, communications, or public health course. There is no place where one can get a formal degree in the field, or even a specialization. On the other hand, the field is slowly developing a significant foundation of conceptual and theoretical underpinnings, as reflected by the growing number of solid studies appearing in such venues as the *Journal of Public Policy & Marketing*, the *Social Marketing Quarterly*, and the *Journal of Marketing*, among others.

These factors point to where social marketers need to concentrate to advance the field. A different way to frame the challenge is to see the problem as the one central to this book—and to social marketing: namely, *changing behavior*. How do we induce people who can significantly benefit from using social marketing approaches to begin to do so? How can we apply our own tools to this challenge? For example, how might we adapt the six-step social marketing process described earlier, and the Stages of Change, BCOS, and Competition frameworks, to develop a program of action that would lead to the desired behavior changes?

The six-step *process* would suggest that we start by defining the behaviors we want and the target audiences. Let us assume that the behavior is using social marketing anywhere it is relevant and the target audience for this exercise is, very generally, anyone in a position to use social marketing or to authorize or fund someone else to do so. The next step is to "listen" to potential target audience members to ascertain the stage at which they are at the moment. Undoubtedly, too many—especially those upstream—are in the Precontemplation stage: They are not thinking about using social marketing. It is possible that they are unaware of it, except vaguely, or, alternatively, they are aware of it but believe that it is inappropriate for the challenge they face or too expensive for the budget they have. If the social issue is just beginning to be recognized, they may assume that social marketing is only appropriate later in the agenda-setting process.

Others may be in the Contemplation stage: They are familiar with social marketing and vaguely aware that it may have value for nontraditional behavioral contexts but choose other approaches and tools. In dealing with such individuals, we need to understand where they are with respect to the BCOS and Competition factors. Several possibilities come to mind:

- *Benefits:* They do not believe that social marketing can produce the kind and scale of program effects they want.
- *Costs:* They find that social marketing lacks documented success stories in new uses. It presents high risk. Further, social marketing is seen as manipulative and does not properly accord target audiences participatory rights in interventions directed at them.
- *Others:* Coworkers, subordinates, funders, and peers may be unsympathetic or actively opposed to the approach.
- *Self-Assurance:* Contemplators may believe that social marketing will require them to learn new vocabulary and new procedures, to identify and hire new consultants and advisers, and, inevitably, to "market" the approach to other stakeholders, including their boss.
- *Competition:* They are comfortable with the old frameworks they have been using—diffusion theory, health promotion models, community mobilization approaches, political science, or media advocacy. The traditional approaches do not require new learning; they have a literature and (presumably) a research base of successes; they represent known—or at least predictable—risks of failure.

It is possible that there are some members of the target audiences who are at the Action stage: They have tried social marketing but have not yet committed to making it a consistent part of their behavior change arsenal. This could be because their experience was not or did not seem to be positive, or because they did not receive sufficient reinforcement. Finally, a minority may be in the Maintenance stage and simply need more reinforcement so as not to regress—particularly if they sense that many others are not following in their pioneering footsteps.

How, then, might some champion for social marketing (e.g., the Social Marketing Institute) proceed to reposition the brand and increase its adoption in a wider range of applications? Here there is a chicken-and-egg challenge.

Which comes first: documented success that encourages future applications or applications that allow future documentation? Both approaches deserve attention.

CREATING APPLICATIONS

To induce more applications, focus needs to be on Precontemplators and Contemplators who are clearly the majority. For Precontemplators, part of the challenge will be creating awareness. This will require the creation and promulgation of both hypothetical (as in this book) and real applications in as many domains as possible. In addition, a significant amount of infrastructure will have to be put in place to provide appropriate support—lists of consultants, Web sites with resources, plenty of articles and books, and (preferably) off-the-shelf concepts and tools that can be applied immediately both upstream and downstream. For Contemplators, several additional steps are suggested by the BCOS model.

Promote Benefits. This will be easier when greater amounts of documented evidence of success become available. In the meantime, marketers might take a number of possible actions. They might reinforce the fundamental principle of this book; namely, that social change is *all about the behavior.* What has worked for downstream targets can work for upstream targets such as community leaders, the media, legislators, private sector marketers, health-care workers, and the like. Marketers might suggest that adoption of a social marketing approach will put the user on the cutting edge of social change, or point out the benefits of *learning a single approach* that can be applied in areas previously requiring that one learn how to mobilize communities, influence the media, lobby, and build business alliances. Where possible, marketers might recast available case studies as examples of sound social marketing in upstream contexts. For example, Benjamin Herzberg of the World Bank and I recently recast a legislative change project in Bosnia-Herzegovina in social marketing frameworks (Andreasen & Herzberg, 2005).

Reduce Costs. Marketers can reduce perceived risks by the accumulation of successful case histories and the provision of time-tested, idiot-proof methodologies. They can also emphasize that, despite what is often said, social marketing need not be expensive—it is more a way of thinking about and approaching behavioral challenges, not a way of spending money. It is not about advertising campaigns.

Bring Social Influence to Bear. Marketers can publicize early adopters of social marketing approaches in new contexts, especially those leading social change, such as AARP, the Centers for Disease Control and Prevention, and Health Canada.

Increase Self-Assurance. An appreciation of the step-by-step methodologies described in this book will increase a target audience member's belief that a social marketing approach is not that difficult to comprehend and adopt. Its *mental portability* is, in my view, a very strong selling point.

With respect to this last point, two highly significant leaps forward in the diffusion of social marketing were the funding of an organization called the Turning Point Collaborative and the creation of a CD/ROM called *CDCynergy— Social Marketing Edition* in 2004.

Turning Point was founded in 1997, with funding from the W. K. Kellogg and Robert Wood Johnson Foundations. It has a particular focus on public health but has made a special effort to promote social marketing as a way to address public health problems. It has sought to address several of the four challenges outlined earlier and has done much to assemble materials that will advance social marketing adoptions.

It has produced four very useful monographs available for downloading at its Web site (http://www.turningpointprogram.org/Pages/socialmkt.html): *The Basics of Social Marketing, The Manager's Guide to Social Marketing,* an 80-page summary titled *Social Marketing and Public Health: Lessons From the Field,* and the *Social Marketing Resource Guide.* Perhaps even more helpful is the *CDCynergy* disk, available through Turning Point, which is described as follows:

> *CDCynergy—Social Marketing Edition* is a multimedia CD-ROM tutorial and planning guide for applying social marketing systematically to public health programs. . . . [It] can help public health professionals to analyze health problems and to plan, implement, and evaluate social marketing programs to address those problems. Designed as an interactive training and decision support tool, the CD-ROM contains case studies, commentary from experts in the field of social marketing and tutorials for each stage of effective program development. . . . The product is intended for the individual with some knowledge of social marketing and moderate familiarity with computer technology. It will assist the public health professional to take a step-by-step approach to developing and implementing a social marketing program. Users will learn how to: Define the public health problem being addressed, Conduct market research to better define target audience, Craft a marketing strategy, Plan the interventions, Plan program monitoring and evaluation, Implement and evaluate the intervention.

The *CDCynergy* disk is available at minimal cost from Turning Point, which also carries out a number of training sessions using it in the states where it operates.

FIGHTING COMPETITION

In the past, social marketing has had a history of ruffling establishment feathers. In the field's earliest days, we upset private sector marketers and scholars by suggesting that marketing applied to topics beyond the traditional economic marketplace (Luck, 1969). Later, in the 1980s, we apparently upset those trained in health education or health promotion, who felt that marketing offered nothing beyond what these scholars and practitioners were already doing. In the 1990s, many writers criticized the field for being too narrow in focusing on downstream targets and thereby distorting research and public policy priorities. They argued that attention to structural and environmental changes would lead to longer lasting—and more powerful—social impacts.

A major goal of this book is, in fact, addressing this last form of competition. I propose that the upstream-downstream debate is really moot. Social marketing is simply an approach to behavior change applicable wherever social change agencies choose to intervene. Therefore, we need to reframe the battle (as discussed in chapter 2), although in moving upstream, social marketing will leave itself open to new competitive challengers. We are likely to find opposition from community mobilization experts, media mavens, and political theorists and activists, who will argue that they know more about how to achieve upstream behavior change than we do. Further, they may offer the arguments that (a) social marketing is new and untested and (b) social marketers are generalists in behavior change, whereas they are specialists in their own domain.

To help frame our thinking about these competitive challenges, I have suggested that social marketing faces competition at five levels, which I have labeled *generic, intervention-level, subject-market, product,* and *brand competition* (Andreasen, 2002).

Generic Competition

At the *generic* level, social marketing shares the challenge faced by all systematic approaches to creating change: namely, that it competes with lethargy and habit. There are many programs, organizations, and people who do not believe (as does social marketing) in the need for an orderly, organized approach to bringing about change. These are the managers who disdain philosophies of management and think that good leaders just need to be enthusiastic, innovative, give praise, and point optimistically toward a brighter future. Although not unknown in the private sector, such managers are more typical in the nonprofit world, where charisma and motivational talent often carry the day in the early years of an institution's life.

Social marketing would surely benefit from any increase in the number of managers adopting any kind of planful approach to social change, but promoting such generic change is beyond the capacity of such a small, emerging field.

Intervention-Level Competition

This is the level of competition that has been the major focus of this book. The relevant literature suggests that there are three societal levels at which strategists consider interventions to bring about dramatic social change. First, there are those who believe that it is downstream *individuals* who ultimately must behave differently if major social problems such as drunk driving, teen smoking, or the spread of AIDS are to be reduced or eliminated. This class of interventions focuses on individual change and is practiced by many social workers, educators, and psychologists, as well as social marketers. This has been social marketing's traditional niche.

Second, there are those who believe that, particularly for *major* social changes, it is *whole communities* that must be the focus of interventions (see, for example, Farquhar et al., 1985). They argue that social norms, interpersonal influence, diffusion processes, and local leadership are powerful determinants of how social problems are addressed. The motivation for change must ultimately come from the community, and thus the community must play a major role in the design, implementation, and evaluation of programs. They believe that the transformation of community norms and values and the invocation of interpersonal influence will sweep individuals along and, further, that the creation of relevant community institutions along the way will ensure the sustainability of programs, something often missing in individual-based initiatives. Advocates of intervention approaches at this societal level include social workers, community mobilizers, anthropologists, and sociologists (e.g., Gray-Felder & Deane, 1999).

The third approach to social problem solving was discussed earlier in this book. It is offered by those who believe that social change is too often materially constrained by social structures (e.g., socially constructed laws, institutions, available technology, and public policies). Thus, this group argues, people die in highway crashes because speed limits are too high and not rigorously enforced, roads are poorly designed, and car makers lack sufficient incentives to make their cars safer. These structuralists argue that urging individuals to slow down and wear seat belts will have only a small impact, whereas real change will occur if laws are changed, roads redesigned, and automakers given regulations or incentives to build safer vehicles. Adherents to this third approach focus on media advocacy, policy change, the use of the courts, and lawmaking to achieve social ends (Wallack, 1990).

Social marketers can argue that each of these levels requires individuals to do things. Communities are abstractions—things happen in communities because people make things happen. Structural change comes about when lawmakers, automakers, and others act. In each case, social marketing is appropriate.

Subject-Market Competition

Social problems tend to be partitioned by their subject matter. There are health-care issues, environmental issues, and issues of crime, social welfare, the arts, and so on, each with its own subareas and specialties. Each subject has its own set of experts, journals, conferences, and federal and state administrators. Foundations often specialize by subject area, and individuals choose careers within these areas. Foundations compete with each other for government budgets, for talent, for foundation priorities and dollars, for volunteers, for media attention, and, ultimately, for a high place on "the public agenda." They often do not poach on other subject domains.

Much of social marketing work to date has been in the area of health care. As we have suggested earlier in the book, however, it has much to contribute in other domains, including environmental protection, crime, and abuse—even international relations.

Product Competition

Within each intervention level and subject matter area, there exist broad classes of intervention tools that I would label "products." Kotler and Roberto (1989) propose five types of major change strategies (products), including social marketing. The other four are technology, economics, politics and law, and education. Rothschild (1999) classifies the alternatives into three categories: education, marketing, and the law. All these authors believe that the role for marketers is one that is primarily useful at the individual intervention level and involves the crafting of programs using well-tested commercial concepts and tools to induce voluntary personal change—as opposed to, say, passing laws to *force* action or creating educational programs *hoping* people will act.

These authors would agree that, to the extent that funders and program managers believe that influencing *voluntary* individual social change is a superior product, social marketing as a field will dramatically grow. However, there is the risk that this growth would be merely in its traditional *downstream* domain.

Brand Competition

The final level of competition faced by social marketers is within the category of voluntary personal change approaches; what I label *brand competition*. Social marketing is only one of many sets of concepts and tools that organizations can use to bring about voluntary individual change. Although it is true that social marketers borrow liberally from these alternative approaches, as others borrow from it (Hill, 2001), it differs in the basic set of premises from which its interventions are developed. Among the alternative approaches to (principally downstream) behavior change are

1. The health belief model (Rosenstock, 1990), which emphasizes communicating information about risks and the benefits of action so as to change the knowledge, attitudes, and intentions of target individuals

2. Stages of Change approaches (Prochaska & DiClemente, 1983), which emphasize tailoring interventions to the stage at which one finds the target audience along the road to high-involvement behavior change

3. Social learning theory (Bandura, 1977), which, among other features, emphasizes building up the target audience's sense of self-assurance—its belief that individuals can actually make the behavior happen (for applications, see Perry et al., 1990, and Perry et al., (1988)

4. The precaution adoption approach (Weinstein, 1988), which combines elements of the social learning and health belief theories

5. Behavioral reinforcement theory (Bickel & Vuchinich, 2000; Rothschild, 1999), which emphasizes the manipulation of rewards and punishments in the environment surrounding desirable and undesirable behaviors

6. The PRECEDE-PROCEED model (Green & Kreuter, 1991; Howat, Jones, Hall, Cross, & Stevenson, 1997), which emphasizes extensive evaluation of the behavioral and social environment as an essential precursor for effective programs

7. Enter-educate programs, which combine educational messages with entertainment to change behaviors (Singhal & Rogers, 1999)

Again, social marketing will grow to the extent it wins this "brand competition." In my view, a major differential advantage we have is the universality and portability of the approach (as I have tried to argue in this volume).

COMPETITION VERSUS COMPETITORS

The competitive challenge is further complicated by the fact that observers may confuse competition among *approaches* with competition among *enterprises* in the area of social change. There are many enterprises—commercial, governmental, and nonprofit—that design, implement, and monitor social change programs. These include international agencies such as the World Bank; federal and state agencies such as the Centers for Disease Control and Prevention; private firms such as Porter Novelli, Golin/Harris, and Equals3; large nonprofit consultants such as the Academy for Educational Development; university centers such as Johns Hopkins' Population Information Program; and major foundations such as the W. K. Kellogg Foundation, the Robert Wood Johnson Foundation, and the Rockefeller Foundation, all of which promote various forms of social change.

These organizations differ from each other in the approach or approaches they emphasize. Some, such as Johns Hopkins' Center for Communications, have emphasized education in an entertainment context; others are more eclectic. What is confusing to potential adopters is that many organizations claim, at least in part, to have social marketing skills or to be "social marketing specialists," but in fact, these organizations are guided more by approaches that are not really social marketing or that incorporate only some elements of social marketing. This muddies the competitive waters, making it difficult for outsiders (i.e., potential adopters of social marketing) to understand what they might be getting if they hire a company that says it will be approaching a problem from a social marketing framework. It is difficult for critical gatekeepers and funders, such as heads of federal agencies or foundation program officers, to distinguish between what an enterprise does that can be properly considered social marketing and other tools and approaches that it may bring to a particular challenge but that are not social marketing.

Knowledge Development and Social Marketing: A Thought Exercise

If we accept the argument that social marketing is in competition with other approaches to social change, then the pressing question is: How does it go about competing? Let me propose a "thought exercise." Suppose social marketing was an organized collective of like-minded individuals and institutions that wanted the field to be a more effective competitor. Each contributor to this organization would have something to gain if the field were more successful and made greater inroads both downstream and upstream. Still, all contributors need to develop their own competitive capabilities to bring about the desired result.

How do firms in the private sector develop competitive strengths and differentiate themselves from others to become more successful? In the private sector, the latest thinking is to recognize that competitive advantage does not lie in factories and brands but in a firm's *intellectual capital*. That is, *the only solid base for long-term market power is one's knowledge*. The principal challenge for the social marketing field, therefore, ought to be building its intellectual capital. In my view, the most critical component of this intellectual capital lies in knowing how to influence behavior.[4]

This intellectual capital can be *explicit* or *tacit*. Explicit information is independent of the people and organizations that generated it. It is the kind of information contained in research data and reports, and it can be digitized and stored. Tacit knowledge, on the other hand, is person specific and not subject to codification. It is the accumulated wisdom *lodged in individuals*. It is, for example, the intuitive knowledge of an experienced social marketer who has studied data about a potential target audience, remembered past interactions with it or with similar audiences, applied something like the BCOS model to the challenge, and then turned these insights into an impactful intervention that achieved desired behavior change goals. It is these tacit insights that are the mark of the successful lobbyist, media relations consultant, and experienced social marketer.

How, then, should our hypothetical organization accumulate and manage knowledge so that the social marketing approach will be both more powerful and more easily diffused to new uses?

The field clearly needs to develop an explicit knowledge base that is accessible to everyone in the field and those who wish to enter it. There are many challenges.

A first challenge is to develop more consistent labeling (coding) of knowledge elements. This means that the field needs to agree on terminology. There is a tendency in many social marketing organizations to use their own jargon for their own practices. Sometimes this is simply a matter of custom; sometimes it is an attempt to develop points of differentiation for a particular organization. These terms are not always accessible to others. Perhaps the most common confusion is in the meaning of the term *social marketing* itself. Although there does seem to be some coalescing in the field concerning a definition centering on behavioral influence, I still find many referring to "behavior change." The latter may be acceptable if everyone knows that it includes interventions aimed at retaining *existing* behaviors. Diffusion will be harmed by confusion about what is being diffused. Clearly, I prefer a definition targeting behavioral *influence*, not behavior change.

A second challenge is to develop common standards for measuring various aspects of social marketing performance. It would be very helpful if the field could develop norms for these. In the early 1980s, an attempt was made to develop advertising norms under the Health Message Testing Service (Andreasen & Kotler, 2003, p. 480). One extensive study by the service concluded that effective PSAs had the following characteristics: (a) They emphasized both the health problem and the solution, (b) they used a person typical of the target audience when presenting a testimonial, (c) they visualized a reward from practicing the recommended healthful behavior, (d) they communicated the psychological benefits of practicing the healthful behavior, (e) they used an approach other than humor, (f) they demonstrated the healthful behavior (if possible), and (g) they used a high or moderate emotional appeal.

Unfortunately, the system was allowed to disappear. However, there remain many domains in which a centralized pool of accumulated norms can be developed. For example, we can develop norms for response rates for various kinds of direct mailings to various audiences, marketing budget levels needed to achieve specific communication or behavior change goals, Web site hit rates for various sizes of banner ads, comparative click-through rates from various combinations of actions and Web placements, and typical fees charged for the use of a social brand by a private sector organization.

A third challenge is making information widely accessible to the social marketing field. Fortunately, there are a number of prototypes for providing this kind of information. For example, the following Web sites provide various tools for communications interventions:

- Science Panel on Interactive Communication and Health: http://www.health .gov/scipich
- The Communication Initiative: http://www.comminit.com
- American Communication Association (links to many communications sites): http://www.americancomm.org/
- University of Iowa Department of Communications Studies (links to communications resources): http://www.uiowa.edu/~commstud/resources/
- Purdue University Coalition for Health Communication (searchable database): http://www.healthcommunication.net/Online_Resources.html
- Centers for Disease Control and Prevention Agency for Toxic Substances and Disease Registry (risk information): http://www.atsdr.cdc.gov/HEC/primer.html
- Centers for Disease Control and Prevention Office of Communication (HealthCommKey): http://www.cdc.gov/od/oc/hcomm
- National Cancer Institute (communication research): http://cancercontrol .cancer.gov/cancer_resources.html
- Health Canada, Environment Canada, and associated groups: http://www.tools ofchange.com
- National Youth Anti-Drug Media Campaign: http://www.mediacampaign.org

For the field to expand, it must also develop improved mechanisms for sharing *tacit* knowledge. Indeed, much social marketing knowledge today is tacit rather than explicit. The field must find ways for the knowledge of practitioners to be available to other practitioners and would-be practitioners. We need to create and perpetuate what are referred to as "communities of practice" that regularly engage in sharing and learning, based on common interests (Lesser & Storck, 2001). Obviously, social marketing competitors may not be willing to share all of their proprietary tacit (or even some explicit) knowledge. However, we are fortunate that the field appears to be very open to knowledge sharing at this point in its history.

Vehicles that can increase tacit knowledge sharing include the following.

Listservers are extremely valuable conduits for tacit knowledge. The social marketing listserver at Georgetown University (soc-mktg@listproc.georgetown .edu) has proven to be such a vehicle. Started in the early 1990s, the listserver now has over 1200 participants. It is used for other purposes as well, but a principal function is allowing individuals around the world to identify and contact others who can share tacit knowledge. A typical inquiry might be something like: "We are starting a program seeking to influence unwed pregnant teenagers in Peru to get good prenatal care. Is there anyone on the listserver who has experience that would help us?"

Another valuable vehicle common to many disciplines and professions is regular *conferences*. One can distinguish among several formats.

Annual conferences within the discipline. These are predictable occasions at which individuals come ostensibly to learn the latest concepts and tools but also to meet face-to-face with old and new colleagues who can share tacit knowledge that is difficult to set down in report documents or even within e-mail messages. At this writing, there are two regular conferences for social marketing professionals. The Social Marketing Institute organizes the *Innovations in Social Marketing* conference. This is an invitation-only event that brings together leaders in the field to discuss ways in which the frontiers of the field can be advanced. Also, the University of South Florida and BestStart Social Marketing have for some time sponsored the *Social Marketing and Public Health Conference* in Florida each June. This event attracts both leaders in the field and beginners seeking to learn about it for the first time. The conference is typically preceded by training workshops on specific concepts and tools.

Special workshops on specific topics. There are several varieties of these. (a) Workshops or miniconferences are sometimes convened to address new social problems. As I write, there is a proliferation of meetings, conferences, workshops, and similar initiatives on the subject of obesity. (b) Workshops that focus on specific concepts and tools exist for broad topics such as cause partnerships, but specialized workshops are needed on subjects such as the use of the Internet in social marketing or the challenges of securing assistance from TV and movie producers.

Cross-Disciplinary Workshops. One of the inevitable but unfortunate concomitants of disciplinary growth is the creation of intellectual silos and silos of practice. Individuals in a given field share tacit and other knowledge only with members of their own clan. They have their own conferences and their own journals. Great insights and expanded intellectual horizons can often be achieved, however, when one moves beyond these silos. In the mid-1990s, after a chance encounter with two high-level nonprofit marketers who apparently had never met (but should have), I convened the first-ever workshop bringing together senior marketing managers from the very largest nonprofit organizations. Participants were thrilled to have the chance to share learnings with people like themselves from outside their silo. As one participant said: "I always meet with 'the disease people'—I did not realize how restrictive this was!"

At the present moment, what would be most valuable is *conferences and workshops across upstream and downstream interventions.* Social marketers need to find ways to meet with advocacy and media specialists, experts in organizational change, lobbyists, and community mobilizers. The tacit expertise of these disciplines ought to materially enrich social marketing's capabilities. Indirectly, such events will help bring social marketers "to the table" and encourage conventional fields to consider them as also having useful concepts and tools with which to effect social change.

The Role of Academia

Universities and colleges can play a major role in advancing the growth of knowledge in and the repositioning of social marketing. Among the steps that can be taken are the following.

Increase the frequency with which social marketing is formally taught. At minimum, more courses in related fields ought to include social marketing assignments and content. These include courses in marketing, public health, and communications. As the field grows in stature and is frequently used upstream, social marketing could be included in courses in public policy, political science, social work, and community organization.

At the next level would be specific *courses* in social marketing. These are now very rarely found but would logically find homes in public health programs and marketing departments of business schools (as do the courses I teach). The level after that would involve giving students the option to major in social marketing or have it designated as an area of concentration. This is probably now a possibility in a few schools of public health, but not in business schools.

Assuming social marketing continues to grow in stature, one might imagine the development of specific degree programs in social marketing. A less satisfactory alternative to this would be so-called certificate programs in social marketing. These have less stature in most universities, are more often attended by practitioners than by simple learners, and are often seen by universities only as moneymakers. However, they are often desirable for practitioners.

Create more and better teaching materials. For example, textbooks: There are now at least three books that can be the basis for courses in social marketing. These would be my own *Marketing Social Change*; Kotler, Roberto, and Lee's *Social Marketing*; and Donovan & Henley's *Social Marketing* (and I am hopeful that the present book would prove to be a useful addition). Readings books: The first *Innovations in Social Marketing* conference produced a useful readings book by Goldberg, Fishbein, and Middlestadt in 1997. However, nothing has appeared since. Chapters in traditional textbooks: Social marketing is now a chapter (not surprisingly) in my own text, *Strategic Marketing for Nonprofit Organizations* (with Philip Kotler). It is also included in a widely used collection of original chapters for public health edited by Glanz, Lewis, and Rimer, *Health Behavior and Health Education*. Supplementary teaching materials: Videotapes and collateral material are ideal for enlivening class sessions (as are guest speakers). Some are available from the Web sites of specific programs, such as the federal antidrug campaign (http://www .mediacampaign.org). The *CDCynergy* disk has many examples, and a workbook on social marketing has been produced Nedra Weinreich (1999). Cases: The universities of Western Ontario, Harvard, and Stanford all make available an array of published cases, teaching notes, and related materials focusing on traditional business school topics. There are, however, few cases that are directly valuable for social marketing.

Ultimately, for any field to develop stature in the academic firmament, it must develop *extensive scholarship*. This is a daunting challenge. There are few incentives for scholars to make social marketing a career. In my own field of marketing, it makes no sense for a junior scholar to specialize in social marketing. There are three reasons for this. First, career advancement comes about primarily through publication in the so-called top-tier journals in the basic discipline of marketing. These journals look for major contributions to the advancement of science and knowledge in their fields. I have argued elsewhere that the general domain of social marketing is fertile ground for new knowledge in basic areas (Andreasen, 1993). However, a junior scholar must focus on the basic research issue, not on social marketing.

The second impediment is, for the same reasons, that there are no teaching jobs in social marketing. Department chairs in business schools do not go looking for people with social marketing teaching capabilities (although this may be different in schools of public health). Third, social marketing does not guarantee a sustained stream of research funding for scholars. Again, there may be exceptions in public health that may hold the best prospect for building a respectable base of intellectual capital.

The challenge is not insurmountable. For progress to be made, we would need (a) journals. The field has had its own journal, the *Social Marketing Quarterly*, for more than a decade. However, the journal still seeks greater academic stature and a broader range of articles testing concepts and theories. At this point, it serves a major role in spreading tacit knowledge as, for example, in reporting the proceedings of the Innovations in Social Marketing Conference and in the regular column produced by Bill Smith of the Academy for Educational Development. (b) Special issues or special sections of mainstream journals: To date, there have been two social marketing issues of the *Journal of Public Policy and Marketing* and one in *Marketing Theory*. More are desirable. (c) Impactful single journal articles in top-tier mainstream journals: This is not impossible. Michael Rothschild's article, published in the summer 1999 issue of the top-tier *Journal of Marketing*, is very frequently cited.

Centers for social marketing need to be founded. Many universities are eager to have such centers developed. The Institute for Social Marketing, now at the University of Sterling in Scotland, is a good example of what can be done. Centers can serve many functions, such as differentiating a university or a specific department in a cluttered academic environment. They can be vehicles for soliciting donations from wealthy individuals and sympathetic commercial and nonprofit organizations. They can offer certificate programs that will generate significant revenue for the university and for the center itself. Depending on university regulations, they can carry on contract research, as is done in the UK. With imagination, centers can also serve to advance knowledge development in our field by supporting case development, providing homes for scholars or practitioners seeking a base during their sabbatical, providing research grants or funds for released time for teacher-scholars, conducting fieldwide studies (as opposed to campaign-related research), and providing a site and logistics for the various kinds of conferences described earlier.

The Case for Superiority

It is my hope that this volume has made the case for positioning social marketing in domains beyond those in which it is traditionally found. If nothing else, it offers fresh ways of thinking about influencing behavior in communities, the media, Congress, business boardrooms, and doctor's offices. We need not be shy about our power and accomplishments. To the extent that social marketing meets competitive challenges, I believe we can bravely position social marketing as superior along the following dimensions.

Breadth of use. Social marketing has the potential to affect *every* dimension of a social problem that involves influencing the behavior of individuals. This means that we have much to offer in many intellectual and practical domains that were thought to be the exclusive purview of other technologies and theories. Specialists in community mobilization, communications, and lobbying are valuable resources for social change organizations but primarily, if not exclusively, *in their own domains.* Community mobilizers cannot reasonably claim to be helpful in influencing legislators (except indirectly), nor can political scientists be particularly helpful in influencing media or potential corporate partners.

Private sector resources. Social marketing is intentionally derivative of private sector marketing practice. We draw our concepts and tools from it, and sometimes we give back good ideas. Private sector marketers have wide experience in all of the upstream domains in which we wish to be involved—media, community involvement, partnering, and advocacy. They recognize that the corporate challenge is to influence all sorts of individuals—not just potential customers. Social marketers are ideally positioned to draw on these private sector ideas and tools. Also, we do not have the visceral antipathy that many who use other technologies have toward commercial marketers and marketing concepts (Johansson, 2004).

A growing history of successes. Although our documentation needs considerable improvement, we do have a significant record of big successes in areas that involve important upstream and downstream components. This would certainly be true in cases of tobacco use, high blood pressure, family planning, and HIV/AIDS (Chapman et al, 2005).

Private sector resources is the area in which I believe we have the strongest claim. It is also an area in which we have much work to do. We need to get better at transferring the explicit and tacit knowledge of private sector marketing professionals to our domain (Andreasen, Goodstein, & Wilson, 2005). This means encouraging them to join us at conferences, such as the Innovations in Social Marketing annual conference or the American Marketing Association annual nonprofit marketing conference. These are occasions in which they can both tell us what they know and think about ways in which their tacic and explicit knowledge can advance our field.

Some Concluding Ethical Issues

Before closing, it is important to take this discussion back to its roots. We began by saying that social marketing has an undiscovered potential to have a major impact outside its traditional downstream "home turf." These are grand ambitions and, as we have noted in this chapter, will probably face some opposition. Some of the hostility will simply be in the nature of "turf protection" by others who argue that (a) they are the experts in their own domain (advocacy, community mobilization, media relations) and (b) we properly (?) are only relevant downstream.

However, these critics can make at least one charge that bears exploring: namely, that social marketing is, at its base, manipulative, no matter where it is used. Although those in media relations or politics might not find this prospect troubling, others will be more concerned. Let me address the issue by drawing on the work of a colleague, George Brenkert (2002).

It is the stated purpose of social marketing interventions and of social marketers to improve social welfare. We say we do this by improving the lives of individuals or of the broader society of which they are a part, through carefully designed interventions both downstream and upstream. Professor Brenkert raises the crucial question: What is meant by "improving social welfare"? Although social marketers claim to be transferring private sector marketing concepts to the social sector, a crucial attribute of the private sector is ignored. In the private sector, as Adam Smith would argue, the Invisible

Hand of the marketplace ensures that the goods and services offered are those that consumers will pay enough for to support the profit-making enterprises that supply them. Thus, in theory, we get a private sector marketplace that generally meets consumers' needs and wants. Unwanted products and services disappear from the market, and wanted products and services thrive. Within the constraints of product and service costs, consumer welfare is maximized by the market system.

However, in the world of social welfare transactions, there is no equivalent mechanism that ensures that members of a society will have their collective welfare maximized. The conundrum arises from the notion that social marketers, just like private sector marketers, fundamentally seek to influence behavior. *Who chooses which behaviors to influence?* In the private sector, consumers express their preferences by putting up legal tender to complete transactions for enterprise offerings. The dollar metric allows us to calibrate the value consumers place on various goods and services. In the domain of social welfare, there is no similar metric.

Social marketers and those who hire them are typically the ones who decide (a) whose welfare is to be improved and (b) what behaviors will constitute improvement. Thus we say that smoking is bad and that smokers and non-smokers alike would be better off if everyone around the world did not smoke *ever*. What of the impoverished smoker in Southeast Asia who says, "I do not want this aspect of my welfare improved. The few cigarettes I have each day constitute the one affordable pleasure I get in my bleak and oppressive life. They reduce the terrible tensions I suffer and distract me from the sense of hopelessness I feel almost every minute." Would it not be manipulative to attempt to change this person's behavior? Certainly, he is not demanding change.

A social marketer might argue that this smoker is more or less free to accept or reject the behavior change we market. Surely, we could argue, this absolves social marketers of responsibility—but no; it simply sidesteps the issue. What is the choice mechanism whereby campaigns are launched? There are no market signals. Individuals very often do not know that their behavior involves a social problem. Surveys to measure the state of the public agenda are fraught with potential biases and errors (Yankelovich, 1991). In the private sector, we do not *make* customers buy widgets so that the widget workers will have a decent wage and Widgetville will have better parks and fire protection. Still, this seems to be what we do when we try to influence social problems.

Brenkert would argue that target audiences would not be swayed by arguments that "we know best." When it comes to spending money, it is realistic to think that target audiences have a reasonably well-defined preference structure for products and services—or at least economists would have us believe this is the case. Is it reasonable to analogize that they also have a good sense of either what they themselves would want in terms of greater welfare or what welfare would accrue to society from various social marketing outcomes? In my view, this is not reasonable, in part because most individuals do not think in these terms—certainly not in terms of the relationship between their actions and general social welfare.

If this is granted, then the decision as to what campaigns ought to be mounted eventually falls to the sponsors and the implementers of such campaigns. The sponsors decide broadly what social welfare issues are worth pursuing (e.g., less river pollution), and implementers decide who needs to do what (e.g., farmers need to use smaller quantities of chemical pesticides and minimize their runoff). However, the farmers have little or no say in the selection of this goal and probably do not want to change their behavior. What if society is lukewarm about the issue or ranks other issues higher? Should the sponsor still pursue this option? Should a social marketer participate? One can argue that any sponsor with adequate funds and a representative board of directors can somehow intuit the degree to which society values certain interventions that might improve welfare.

This is not controversial where there is broad consensus that addressing a given social problem is socially desirable. Brenkert (2002) notes that most of the issues dealt with by social marketers to date are the easy ones. Few people will argue against campaigns to reduce obesity or child abuse. What of cases where there are conflicting views about whether society will be better off? The Vatican opposes family planning, but social marketers have promoted it for years. Some groups wish that doctors would stop giving abortions; others want them not to change their behavior. Which campaign maximizes social welfare?

What is the social justification for social campaigns? Who or what mechanism gives social change agents—that is, social marketers—the right to pursue some course of action? Suppose a group with funds decides that there are "too many" Lutherans and short people in Minnesota and the state would be better off if these people were moved to Wisconsin or elsewhere. The sponsor then mounts an aggressive campaign to "market" this behavior—getting the target audience to move to Wisconsin. Should society permit such campaigns? They are not illegal. Do our free speech guarantees extend to any social marketing campaign that can get funds? Should social marketing experts and consultants rent themselves out for such efforts? Some social marketers might argue that they are merely "technicians"—give them a behavior and they will help you craft powerful campaigns to achieve the desired behavioral results (I have sometimes said this myself).

Perhaps the moral issue for social marketers is merely a personal one. Perhaps the answer lies in each person's conscience. All potential social marketers must ask themselves: What are the campaigns with which I am willing to be associated? Which ones are *really* for the good of society? Should this simply be a matter of personal judgment or personal freedom to act, or ought there to be general standards?

Brenkert (2002) argues that we cannot leave these decisions to self-appointed social change agents. One solution might be to defer to foundation boards and consultants, elected legislatures, or a "universal code," such as the United Nations statement of universal human rights. However, elected bodies and boards can be corrupt, and so—Brenkert says—"social marketers must develop the criteria and standards for individual and social welfare that such bodies must use" (p. 18). His own position is that "such criteria and standards should result from inviting people to become part of a process of change to enhance their welfare" (p. 18). Presumably he would argue that no socially controversial social marketing campaign should proceed without the participation in some form of the target audiences.

I would therefore propose the following steps to use in carrying out an evaluation of the ethics of any social marketing campaign, particularly one in upstream contexts:

1. A conscientious effort should be undertaken to ascertain the wishes and preferences of target audiences, whether through personal interviews, referenda, talks with opinion leaders, or other wide-ranging and unbiased approaches.

2. If the social welfare objective sought by the campaign is widely supported and there is not likely to be any significant group arguing that the behavioral objectives would yield a *decrease* in social welfare, then the campaign is ethically justified.

3. If there is at least one significant group opposing (or highly likely to oppose) the proposed intervention or if there are disparate impacts from a proposed campaign (e.g., marketers will be hurt, consumers will benefit), then the social marketer should first turn to alternative external standards in the following order: (a) universal standards of right and wrong, such as those contained in the United Nations Universal Declaration of Human Rights (http://www.hrweb.org/legal/udhr.html); (b) codes of ethics of professions to be employed (e.g., see the American Marketing Association's "Ethical Norms and Values for Marketers" at http://www.marketingpower.com/content435.php); or (c) established codes of ethics of the marketer's own organization (if they exist).

4. If the proposed campaign passes the preceding tests, then the social marketer must carefully assess the welfare impacts (positive and negative) of various interventions on various target groups and attempt to calculate (albeit this will of necessity be partly subjective) the overall welfare effects of alternative choices. The more serious the impacts, the more important it is that the best expertise be brought to bear on such calculations.

Finally, it should always be the case that every social marketer should have his or her own personal standard of what he or she would participate in. Conscientious objection to a proposed campaign is always the right and noble pathway, however dire the monetary and career consequences.

As social marketing makes its way tentatively into new upstream domains involving new kinds of players, new kinds of target audiences, and new kinds of behaviors, it must address these challenges to develop and apply clear ethical standards, both for campaign objectives and for the tactics employed within them. New terrain always brings new challenges, and I am hopeful that ethical discussions are part of our approach to those challenges.

This is certainly essential if social marketing is to move to the next level in both the practical and academic worlds.

Notes

1. This and other sections that follow are adapted from Andreasen (2002).

2. Further information about the institute is available at http://www.social-marketing.org.

3. Significant roles in this research effort were played by Karen Gutierrez, Lynn Doner, Andrew Larson, Terry Baugh, and Sally Bloomberg.

4. One might argue that such intellectual capital is also crucial in the private sector.

References

Abboud, L. (2003, July 10). The truth about trans fats: Coming to a label near you. *Wall Street Journal*, pp. D1, D3.

Adkins, S. (1999). *Cause related marketing: Who cares wins.* Oxford, UK: Butterworth-Heinemann.

Advertising Council. (2003). Obesity prevention. Retrieved August 18, 2005, from http://www.adcouncil.com/campaigns/healthy_lifestyles/

Agatston, A. (2003). *The South Beach diet: The delicious, doctor-designed, foolproof plan for fast and healthy weight loss.* New York: Rodale Books.

Aguilera, E., Migoya, D., & Sherry, A. (2003, June 15). AFA board ignored assaults: Often-absent legislators, execs praised academy amid sex charges. *Denver Post*, p. A-01. Retrieved August 23, 2005, from http://nl.newsbank.com/nlsearch/we/Archives?p_product=DP&p_theme=dp&p_action=search&p_maxdocs=200&s_dispstring=AFA%20Board%20Ignored%20Assaults%20AND%20date(2003)&p_field_date-0=YMD_date&p_params_date-0=date:B,E&p_text_date-0=2003&p_field_advanced_0=&p_text_advanced-0=("AFA%20Board%20Ignored%20Assaults")&p_perpage=10&p_sort=YMD_date:D&xcal_useweights=no

Alcaly, R., & Bell, R. (2000). *Promoting nutrition and physical activity through social marketing: Current practices and recommendations.* Sacramento: University of California Davis Center for Advanced Studies in Nutrition and Social Marketing.

Allen, W. T. (1992). Our schizoid conception of the business corporation. *Cardozo Law Review, 14,* 261-282.

American Heart Association. (2005a). Facts about women and cardiovascular diseases. Retrieved August 23, 2005, from http://www.americanheart.org/presenter.jhtml?identifier=2876

American Heart Association. (2005b). *Heart disease and stroke statistics—2005 update.* Retrieved August 23, 2005, from http://www.americanheart.org/downloadable/heart/1105390918119HDSStats2005Update.pdf

American Heart Association. (2005c, February 1). Women's heart risk underestimated by doctors, resulting in less preventive care than in men. Retrieved May 5, 2005, from http://www.americanheart.org/presenter.jhtml?identifier=3028550

American Legacy Foundation [Home page]. (2004). Retrieved August 6, 2005, from http://www.americanlegacy.org/americanlegacy/skins/alf/home.aspx

Amos, A., Gray, D., Currie, C., & Elton, R. (1997). Healthy or druggy? Self-image, ideal image and smoking behaviour among young people. *Social Science Medicine, 45*(6), 847-858.

Anderson, J., & Boyd, J. (1979). *Confessions of a muckraker.* New York: Random House.

Andreasen, A. R. (1975). *The disadvantaged consumer.* New York: Free Press.

Andreasen, A. R. (1982). Nonprofits: Check your attention to customers. *Harvard Business Review, 60*(3), 105-110.

Andreasen, A. R. (1983, July-August). Cost conscious marketing research. *Harvard Business Review, 61*(4), 74-77.

Andreasen, A. R. (1984a, December). Life status changes and changes in consumer preferences and satisfaction. *Journal of Consumer Research, 11,* 784-794.

Andreasen, A. R. (1984b). A power potential approach to middleman strategies in social marketing. *European Journal of Marketing, 18*(4), 56-71.

Andreasen, A. R. (1993). Presidential address: A social marketing research agenda for consumer behavior researchers. *Advances in Consumer Research, 20,* 1-5.

Andreasen, A. R. (1994). Social marketing: Definition and domain. *Journal of Public Policy & Marketing, 13*(1), 108-114.

Andreasen, A. R. (1995). *Marketing social change.* San Francisco: Jossey-Bass.

Andreasen, A. R. (1996, November-December). Profits for nonprofits: Find a corporate partner. *Harvard Business Review, 74*(6), 47-59.

Andreasen, A. R. (Ed.). (2001). *Ethics in social marketing.* Washington, DC: Georgetown University Press.

Andreasen, A. R. (2002, Spring). Marketing social marketing in the social change marketplace. *Journal of Public Policy & Marketing, 21*(1), 3-13.

Andreasen, A. R. (2003). Life trajectory of social marketing. *Marketing Theory, 3*(3), 293-303.

Andreasen, A. R. (2004a). A social marketing approach to changing mental health practices directed at youth and adolescents. *Health Marketing Quarterly, 21*(4), 51-75.

Andreasen, A. R. (2004b, April 20). Social marketing: Upstream and earlier. Paper presented at the Innovations in Social Marketing Conference, Austin, TX.

Andreasen, A. R., & Drumwright, M. (2001). Alliances and ethics in social marketing. In A. R. Andreasen (Ed.), *Ethics in social marketing* (pp. 95-124). Washington, DC: Georgetown University Press.

Andreasen, A. R., Goodstein, R., & Wilson, J. (2005, Summer). Transferring marketing knowledge to the nonprofit sector. *California Management Review, 47*(4), 46-67.

Andreasen, A. R., & Herzberg, B. (2005). Social marketing applied to economic development. *Social Marketing Quarterly, 11*(2), 3-17.

Andreasen, A. R., & Kotler, P. (2003). *Strategic marketing for nonprofit organizations* (6th ed.). Upper Saddle River, NJ: Prentice Hall.

Aschermann, K. (2001, June 26). How charities benefit by promoting their brand. *Chronicle of Philanthropy, 13*(9). Retrieved August 26, 2005, from http://philanthropy .com/premium/articles/v13/i19/19004002.htm

Atkins, R. C. (2001). *Dr. Atkins' new diet revolution.* New York: Avon Books.

Austin, J. (2000). *The collaboration challenge.* San Francisco: Jossey-Bass.

Austin, J., Ezequiel, R., Berger, G., Fischer, R. M., Gutiérrez, R., Koljatic, M., et al. (2004). *Social partnering in Latin America: Lessons drawn from collaborations of businesses and civil society organizations.* Cambridge, MA: David Rockefeller Center for Latin American Studies, Harvard University.

Avery, D. (2003). Can lawsuits make our kids thin? Retrieved August 18, 2005, from the Hudson Institute Center for Global Food Issues Web site: http://www.cgfi.org/ materials/articles/2003/may_27_03.htm

Avon Foundation. (2005). Crusade mission and background. Retrieved August 29, 2005, from the Avon Web site: http://www.avoncompany.com/women/avoncrusade/background/overview.html

Backer, T. E., & Rogers, E. M. (Eds.). (1993). *Organizational aspects of health communication campaigns: What works?* Newbury Park, CA: Sage.

Backer, T. E., Rogers, E. M., & Sopory, P. (1992). *Designing health communications campaigns: What works?* Newbury Park, CA: Sage.

Bandura, A. (1977). Self-efficacy: Toward a unifying theory of behavior change. *Psychological Review, 84,* 191-215.

Bandura, A. (1986). *Social foundation of thought and action.* Englewood Cliffs, NJ: Prentice Hall.

Bandura, A. (Ed.). (1995). *Self-efficacy in changing societies.* Cambridge, UK: Cambridge University Press.

Banzhaf, J. F., III. (2003, June 19). Letter sent to Burger King, KFC, McDonald's, Taco Bell, and Wendy's fast food restaurant corporations to put them on legal notice that new research about the addictive effects of fattening food may require the corporations to post a health warning or other appropriate informational notice to avoid possible legal liability for failing to make this disclosure. Retrieved August 8, 2005, from the Professor John F. Banzhaf III Web site: http://banzhaf.net/docs/ ffltr.html

Banzhaf, J. F., III. (2004). Professor John F. Banzhaf III [Home page]. Retrieved August 25, 2005, from http://banzhaf.net/

Barlow, S. E., & Dietz, W. H. (1998, September). Obesity evaluation and treatment: Expert committee recommendations. *Pediatrics, 102*(3), 626.

Bartels, R. (1974). The identity crisis in marketing. *Journal of Marketing, 38,* 73-76.

Berkowitz, D., & Adams, D. B. (1990). Agenda-building and information subsidy in local television news. *Journalism Quarterly, 67,* 723-731.

Bickel, W. K., & Vuchinich, R. E. (Eds.). (2000). *Reframing health behavior change with behavioral economies.* Mahwah, NJ: Lawrence Erlbaum.

Blair stakes credibility on end of crisis. (2000, September 12). Retrieved September 2, 2005, from the BBC News Web site: http://news.bbc.co.uk/1/hi/uk_politics/922250.stm

Bolton, L. E., Cohen, J. B., & Bloom, P. N. (in press). The marketing of "get out of jail free" cards. *Journal of Public Policy and Marketing.*

Boorstin, D. J. (1992). *The image: A guide to pseudo-events in America.* New York: Vintage Books.

Boulay, A. (1996, October). Malden Mills: A study in leadership. *Quality Monitor Newsletter.* Retrieved August 17, 2005, from the Organizational Productivity Institute Web site: http://www.opi-inc.com/malden.htm

Bozell, L. B., III. (2003, February 14). AIDS education . . . or condom promotion? Retrieved September 1, 2005, from the Media Research Center Web site: http://www.mediaresearch.org/BozellColumns/entertainmentcolumn/2003/co l20030214.asp

Bradley, B., Jansen, P., & Silverman, L. (2003, May). The nonprofit sector's $100 billion opportunity. *Harvard Business Review, 81*(5), 94-103.

Brenkert, G. G. (2002). Ethical challenges of social marketing. *Journal of Public Policy and Marketing, 21*(1), 14-25.

Brookings Institution. (2003, June 25). About Brookings. Retrieved August 9, 2005, from http://www.brookings.edu/index/aboutresearch.htm

Brownell, K. D., & Horgen, K. B. (2004). *Food fight: The inside story of the food industry, America's obesity crisis, and what we can do about it.* Chicago: Contemporary Books.

Burke, T. (1996). *Lifebuoy men, Lux women.* Durham, NC: Duke University Press.

Burros, M. (2003, July 10). F.D.A. announces label requirement for artery-clogger. *New York Times,* p. 1.

Business Ethics 100 best corporate citizens 2005. (2005, Spring). Retrieved August 17, 2005, from the *Business Ethics* Online Web site: http://www.business-ethics.com/whats_new/100_best_corporate_citizens_chart_2005.pdf

Business for Social Responsibility [Home page]. (2005). Retrieved August 18, 2005, from http://www.bsr.org/

Caldeira, G. A., Hojnacki, M., & Wright, J. R. (2000). The lobbying activities of organized interests in federal judicial nominations. *Journal of Politics, 62*(1), 51-69.

Calvert Group, Ltd. (2005). Social analysis criteria. Retrieved August 30, 2005, from the Calvert Online Web site: http://www.calvertgroup.com/sri_647.html

Campos, P. (2004). *The obesity myth: Why America's obsession with weight is hazardous to your health.* New York: Gotham Books.

Caplovitz, D. (1963). *The poor pay more: Consumer practices of low income consumers.* New York: Free Press of Glencoe.

Carroll, A., Craypo, L., & Samuels, S. (2000). *Evaluating nutrition and physical activity social marketing campaigns: A review of the literature for use in community campaigns.* Sacramento: Center for Advanced Studies in Nutrition and Social Marketing, University of California, Davis.

Carson, R. (1962). *Silent spring.* Boston: Houghton Mifflin.

Cassady, D., Culp, J., & Watnik, M. (2002). Using social marketing to promote a healthy diet and physical activity: The need for training public health professionals. *Social Marketing Quarterly, 8*(4), 53-62.

Celsi, R. L., & Olson, J. C. (1988, September). The role of involvement in attention and comprehension processes. *Journal of Consumer Research, 15,* 210-224.

Center for Consumer Freedom. (2002, June 4). CSPI and Brownell: Two Twinkies in one package. Retrieved August 26, 2005, from http://www.consumerfreedom.com/news_detail.cfm/headline/1441

Center for Consumer Freedom. (2005). Key players. Retrieved August 29, 2005, from the ActivistCash.com Web site: http://www.activistcash.com/index_keyplayers.cfm

Centers for Disease Control and Prevention. (2000). *Healthy people 2010.* Washington, DC: U. S. Department of Health and Human Services.

Centers for Disease Control and Prevention. (2005, February 7). Verb campaign overview. Retrieved August 8, 2005, from http://www.cdc.gov/youthcampaign/overview.htm

Chambré, S. (1999). Civil society and the intervention of social policy: State, society and citizenship in the fight against AIDS [U.S. Civil Society Project]. Washington, DC: Georgetown University Center for the Study of Voluntary Organizations and Services.

Chapman, S., Astatke, H., & Ashburn, K. (2005). The performance of social marketing interventions in developing countries: A systematic review (Working paper). Washington, DC: Population Services International.

Citro, C. F., & Michael, R. J. (Eds.). (1995). *Measuring poverty: A new approach.* Washington, DC: National Academy Press.

CNN. (2005, April 20). Study: Obesity death risk overstated: New calculation: Obesity now no. 7 among causes of death. Retrieved May 6, 2005, from http://www.cnn.com/2005/HEALTH/diet.fitness/04/20/obesity.deaths.ap

Coffman, J. (2002). *Public communication evaluation: An environmental scan of challenges, criticisms, practice, and opportunities.* Cambridge, MA: Harvard Family Research Project.

Cohen, B. C. (1963). *The press and foreign policy.* Princeton, NJ: Princeton University Press.

Cohen, G. A. (2000). *Karl Marx's theory of history.* Princeton, NJ: Princeton University Press.

Collins, R. L., Elliott, M. N., Berry, S. H., Kanouse, D. E., & Hunter, S. B. (2003, November). Entertainment television as a healthy sex educator: The impact of condom-efficacy information in an episode of *Friends. Pediatrics, 112,* 1115-1121.

Communication Initiative [Home page]. (1995). Retrieved August 5, 2005, from http://www.comminit.com

Communication Initiative. (2005, June 3). Programme experiences: Heart & Soul—a soap opera for Africa—East Africa. Retrieved August 19, 2005, from http://www.comminit.com/experiences/pdskdv122002/experiences-1062.html

Cone, Inc., & Roper Starch Worldwide, Inc. (1999). *1999 Cone/Roper cause related trends report: The evolution of cause branding.* Boston: Author.

Critser, G. (2003). *Fat land: How Americans became the fattest people in the world.* Boston: Houghton Mifflin.

Cuca, R., & Pierce, C. (1977). *Experiences in family planning: Lessons from the developing world.* Baltimore, MD: Johns Hopkins University Press.

David, S. (2004). Assessing the impact of the national youth anti-drug media campaign. *Social Marketing Quarterly, 10*(2), 43-54.

Davidson, D. L., & Goodpaster, K. (1983). Managing product safety: The Ford Pinto [Harvard Business School Case #383-129]. Cambridge, MA: Harvard Business School Publishers.

Dees, J. G. (1996). *The social enterprise spectrum: Philanthropy to commerce.* Cambridge, MA: Harvard Business School.

Deininger, K., & Squire, L. (n.d.). *Measuring income inequality: A new database.* Retrieved July 29, 2005, from the World Bank Group Economic Growth Research Web site: http://www.worldbank.org/research/growth/dddeisqu.htm

deKeiffer, D. (1997). *The citizen's guide to lobbying Congress.* Chicago: Chicago Review Press.

Denniston, R. (2004). Planning, implementing, and managing an unprecedented government-funded prevention communications initiative. *Social Marketing Quarterly, 10*(2), 6-12.

Department of Health, Social Services, and Public Safety. (2000, April 3). Minister welcomes launch of UK food standards agency [Press release]. Retrieved August 9, 2005, from http://www.nics.gov.uk/press/hss/000403b-hss.htm

De Tocqueville, A. (2001). *Democracy in America.* New York: Signet Books.

De Vita, C. J., & Mosher-Williams, R. (2001). *Who speaks for America's children? The role of child advocates in public policy.* Washington, DC: Urban Institute Press.

Donaldson, T., & Preston, L. (1995). The stakeholder theory of the corporation: Concepts, evidence and implications. *Academy of Management Review, 20*(1), 65-91.

Donovan, R. J. (1999). Targeting male perpetrators of intimate partner violence: Western Australia's freedom from fear campaign. In C. B. Weinberg &

R.J.B. Ritchiee (Eds.), *Fifth innovations in social marketing conference* [CD-ROM]. Vancouver, BC: University of British Columbia.

Donovan, R. J., & Henley, N. (2003). *Social marketing: Principles and practice.* Melbourne, Australia: IP Communications.

Donovan, R. J., & Owen, N. (1994). Social marketing and mass interventions. In R. K. Dishmane (Ed.), *Advances in exercise adherence* (2nd ed.). Champaign, IL: Human Kinetics Books.

Downs, A. (1972, Summer). Up and down with ecology: The issue attention cycle. *Public Interest, 28*, 38-50.

Drumwright, M. E. (1996, October). Company advertising with a social dimension: The role of noneconomic criteria. *Journal of Marketing, 60*, 71-88.

Earle, R. (2000). *The art of cause marketing.* Chicago: NTC Business Books.

Edwards, R. W., Jumper-Thurman, P., Pleasted, B. A., Oetting, E. R., & Swanson, L. (2000). Community readiness: Research to practice. *Journal of Community Psychology, 28*(3), 291-307.

Elliott, B. J. (1991). *A re-examination of the social marketing concept.* Sydney, Australia: Elliott & Shanahan Research.

Etzioni, A. (1991). *A responsive society: Collected essays on guiding deliberate social change.* San Francisco: Jossey-Bass.

Etzioni, A. (Ed.). (1995). *New communitarian thinking: Persons, virtues, institutions and communities.* Charlottesville: University of Virginia Press.

Ewald, W. B. (1984). *Who killed Joe McCarthy?* New York: Simon & Schuster.

Farquhar, J. W., Fortmann, S. P., Maccoby, N., Haskell, W. L., Williams, P. T., Flora, J. A., et al. (1985, August). The Stanford five-city project: Design and methods. *American Journal of Epidemiology, 122*(2), 323-334.

Fine, S. (1981). *The marketing of ideas and social issues.* New York: Praeger.

Fine, S. (Ed.). (1990). *Social marketing: Promoting the causes of public and nonprofit agencies.* Boston: Allyn & Bacon.

Flora, J., Maccoby, N., & Farquhar, J. (1991). Communications campaigns to prevent cardio-vascular disease. In R. Rice & C. Atkin (Eds.), *Public communications campaigns* (pp. 233-252). Newbury Park, CA: Sage.

Fraser, C., & Restrepo-Estrada, S. (1998). *Communicating for development: Human change for survival.* London: I. B. Tauris.

Frazier, H., & Gagné, M. (2004). Corporate outreach: Opportunities and challenges. *Social Marketing Quarterly, 10*(2), 62-66.

Friedman, M. (1970, September 13). The social responsibility of business is to increase its profits. *New York Times Magazine,* pp. 32-33, 122, 124, 126.

Friedman, M., & Friedman, R. (1990). *Free to choose.* Orlando, FL: Harcourt Brace.

Gamson, W. A. (1975). *The strategy of social protest.* Homewood, IL: Dorsey.

Gerbner, G., Gross, L., Morgan, M., & Signorelli, N. (1980). The "mainstreaming" of America: Violence profile No. II. *Journal of Communication, 30*, 10-29.

Gidding, S., Rudolph, S., Leibel, L., Daniels, S., Rosenbaum, M., Van Horn, L., et al. (1996). Understanding obesity in youth. *Circulation, 94*, 3383-3387.

Gladwell, M. (2000). *The tipping point: How little things can make a big difference.* Boston: Little, Brown.

Glantz, S. A., & Balbach, E. D. (2000). *Tobacco war: Inside the California battles.* Berkeley: University of California Press.

Glantz, S. A., Barnes, D. E., Bero, L., Hanauer, P., & Slade, J. (1996). Looking through the keyhole at the tobacco industry: The Brown and Williamson documents. *Journal of the American Medical Association, 274*, 219-224.

Glantz, S. A., Slade, J., Bero, L., Hanauer, P., & Barnes, D. E. (1996). *The cigarette papers.* Berkeley: University of California Press.

Glanz, K., Lewis, F. M., & Rimer, B. K. (Eds.). (1999). *Health behavior and health education* (2nd ed.). San Francisco: Jossey-Bass.

Glassner, B. (1999). *The culture of fear.* New York: Basic Books.

Goldberg, M. E. (1995). Social marketing: Are we fiddling while Rome burns? *Journal of Consumer Psychology, 4*(4), 347-370.

Goldberg, M., Fishbein, M., & Middlestadt, S. (Eds.). (1997). *Social marketing: Theoretical and practical perspectives* (pp. 111-120). Mahwah, NJ: Lawrence Erlbaum.

Goldberg, M. E., Sandikci, O., & Litvack, D. (1997). Reducing the level of violence in hockey. In M. E. Goldberg, M. Fishbein, & S. Middlestadt (Eds.), *Social marketing: Theoretical and practical perspectives.* Mahwah, NJ: Lawrence Erlbaum.

Goldstein, K. M. (1999). *Interest groups, lobbying, and participation in America.* Cambridge, UK: Cambridge University Press.

Goodnough, A. (2003, June 25). Schools cut down on fat and sweets in menus. *New York Times.* Retrieved August 26, 2005, from http://www.nytimes.com/2003/06/25/nyregion/25NUTR.html

Government unit "urges fat tax." (2004, February 19). Retrieved August 16, 2005, from the BBC News Web site: http://news.bbc.co.uk/1/hi/health/3502053.stm

Granovetter, M. (1978). Threshold models of collective behavior. *American Journal of Sociology, 83*, 1420-1443.

Grant, R. (2003, March). Heart disease: A woman's biggest health threat. *HealthScout News.*

Gray-Felder, D., & Deane, J. (1999). *Communication for social change: A position paper and conference report.* New York: Rockefeller Foundation.

Green, L. W., & Kreuter, M. W. (1991). *Health promotion planning: An educational and environmental approach.* Mountain View, CA: Mayfield.

Greene, B. (2002). *Get with the program.* New York: Simon & Schuster.

Gumucio, D. A. (2001). *Making waves: Stories of participatory communication for social change: A report to the Rockefeller Foundation.* New York: Rockefeller Foundation.

Handy, C. (1988). *Understanding voluntary organizations.* London: Penguin Books.

Harrison, K., & Marske, A. L. (2005). Nutritional content of foods advertised during the television programs children watch most. *American Journal of Public Health, 95*, 1568-1574.

Harrison, L. (2003, January 13). The rich-poor gap: If Brazil can address it, the U.S. can and should. *Christian Science Monitor, 95*(33), 9.

Harvey, P. D. (1999). *Let every child be wanted: How social marketing is revolutionizing contraceptive use around the world.* Westport, CT: Auburn House.

Hastert, D. (2003, March 10). Suing your way to better health is not the answer. Retrieved August 26, 2005, from http://speaker.house.gov/library/health/040310 foodpersresponse.shtml

Hastings, G., & Donovan, R. J. (2002). International initiatives: Introduction and overview. *Social Marketing Quarterly, 8*(1), 2-4.

Hastings, G., & Haywood, A. (1991). Social marketing and communication health promotion. *Health Promotion International, 6*(2), 135-145.

Hastings, G., & Haywood, A. (1994). Social marketing: A critical response. *Health Promotion International, 69*(1), 59-63.

Hastings, G. B., Macfayden, L., & Anderson, S. (2000). Whose behavior is it anyway? *Social Marketing Quarterly, 6*(2), 46-58.

Heise, L., Ellsberg, M., & Gottemoller, M. (1999, December). Ending violence against women [Population Reports No. L11]. Baltimore, MD: Johns Hopkins University School of Public Health.

Heritage Foundation. (2005). About the Heritage Foundation. Retrieved August 9, 2005, from http://www.heritage.org/about/

Higham, S., & Horwitz, S. (2001, March 8). D.C. failed to investigate child sex abuse reports. *Washington Post,* p. A01. Retrieved Spetember 1, 2005, from http://www.washington post.com/ac2/wp-dyn?pagename=article&contentId=A37911-2001Mar7&not Found=true

Hill, R. (2001). The marketing concept and health promotion: A survey and analysis of recent "health promotion" literature. *Social Marketing Quarterly, 7*(1), 29-53.

Hirschman, E. (1991). Secular mortality and the dark side of consumer behavior [Presidential address]. In M. R. Solomon & R. Holman (Eds.), *Advances in consumer research* (Vol. 17). Provo, UT: Association for Consumer Research.

Hodgson, G. (2000). *The gentleman from New York: Daniel Patrick Moynihan: A biography.* Boston: Houghton Mifflin.

Hoeffler, S., & Keller, K. L. (2002). Building brand equity through corporate societal marketing. *Journal of Public Policy and Marketing, 21*(1), 78-89.

Hornik, R. (Ed.). (2001). *Public health communication: Evidence for behavior change.* Mahwah, NJ: Lawrence Erlbaum.

Hornik, R., McDivitt, J., Zimicki, S., Yoder, P. S., Contreras-Budge, E., McDowell, J., et al. (2002). Communication in support of child survival: Evidence and explanations from eight countries. In R. Hornik (Ed.), *Public health communication: Evidence for behavior change* (pp. 219-248). Mahwah, NJ: Lawrence Erlbaum.

Horovitz, Bruce. (2003, July 1). Under fire, food giants switch to healthier fare. *USA Today,* pp. 1a-2a.

Howat, P., Jones, S., Hall, M., Cross, D., & Stevenson, M. (1997). The PRECEDE-PROCEED model: Application to planning a child pedestrian injury prevention program. *Injury Prevention, 3*(4), 282-287.

Huddleston, C. T., & Perlowski, H. (2003, November 6). *Employers beware: Obese workers suffer discrimination on the job, lawsuits likely* [Press release]. Retrieved August 27, 2005, from the Arnall, Golden, Gregory Web site: http://www.agg.com/Contents/NewsArticleDetail.aspx?ID=775

Interview: Frank Luntz. (2004, November 9). *Frontline.* Retrieved August 29, 2005, from the PBS Web site: http://www.pbs.org/wgbh/pages/frontline/shows/persuaders/interviews/luntz.html

Johansson, J. K. (2004). *In your face: How American marketing excess fuels anti-Americanism.* New York: Financial Times Prentice Hall.

Johnson, J. (1989). Horror stories and the construction of child abuse. In J. Best (Ed.), *Images and issues: Typifying contemporary social problems* (pp. 5-19). New York: De Gruyter.

Jones, G., Steketee, R., Black, R. E., Bhutta, Z. A., Morris, S. S., & the Bellagio Child Survival Group. (2003, July 5). How many child deaths can we prevent this year? *Lancet, 326*(9377), 65-71.

Jordan, M. (2004, March 4). Nestle markets baby formula to Hispanic mothers in U.S. *Wall Street Journal*, B1.

Katz, E. (1957). The two-step flow of communications: An up-to-date report on an hypothesis. *Public Opinion Quarterly, 21*, 61-68.

Kaufman, M. (2003, July 11). FDA eases rules on touting food as healthful. *New York Times*, pp. A1, A7.

Kersh, R., & Morone, J. (2002). How the personal becomes political: Prohibitions, public health and obesity. *American Political Development, 16*, 162-175.

Kolata, G. (2005, August 14). The panic du jour: Trans fats in food. *New York Times*, p. WK4.

Kollman, K. (1998). *Outside lobbying*. Princeton, NJ: Princeton University Press.

Korngold, A. (2005). *Leveraging good will: Strengthening nonprofits by engaging businesses*. San Francisco: Jossey-Bass.

Kotler, P. (1972, April). A generic concept of marketing. *Journal of Marketing, 36*, 46-54.

Kotler, P., & Lee, N. (2005). *Corporate social responsibility*. Hoboken, NJ: John Wiley.

Kotler, P., & Levy, S. J. (1969). Broadening the concept of marketing. *Journal of Marketing, 33*, 10-15.

Kotler, P., & Roberto, E. (1989). *Social marketing: Strategies for changing public behavior*. New York: Free Press.

Kotler, P., Roberto, E., & Lee, N. (2002). *Social marketing: Strategies for changing public behavior*. Thousand Oaks, CA: Sage.

Kotler, P., & Zaltman, G. (1971). Social marketing: An approach to planned social change. *Journal of Marketing, 35*, 3-12.

Kraft Foods. (2005). Nutrition, health and wellness: Our commitment to nutrition, health and wellness. Retrieved August 29, 2005, from http://www.kraft.com/responsibility/nhw.aspx

Lang, G. E., & Lang, K. (1983). *The battle for public opinion: The president, the press and the polls during Watergate*. New York: Columbia University Press.

Lawrence, M. (2003). *Using domestic law in the fight against obesity: An introductory guide for the Pacific*. Retrieved August 10, 2004, from the World Health Organization Web site: http://www.wpro.who.int/NR/rdonlyres/5B6A2364-E2B6-42DF-9F68-BA508EB49159/0/using_domestic_law.pdf

Lazer, W., & Kelley, E. K. (Eds.). (1973). *Social marketing: Perspectives and viewpoints*. Homewood, IL: Richard D. Irwin.

Lefebvre, R. C., Lasater, T. M., Carleton, R. A., & Peterson, G. (1987). Theory and delivery of health programming in the community: The Pawtucket heart health program. *Preventive Medicine, 16*, 80-95.

Lesser, E. L., & Storck, J. (2001). Communities of practice and organizational performance. *IBM Systems Journal, 40*(4), 831-841.

Letts, C. W., Ryan, W. P., & Grossman, A. S. (1999). *High performance nonprofit organizations: Managing upstream for greater impact*. New York: John Wiley.

Luck, D. J. (1969). Social marketing: Confusion compounded. *Journal of Marketing, 38*, 70-72.

MacArthur, K. (2005, January 10). McD's '05 strategy hinges on balance. *Advertising Age*, p. 6.

MacInnis, D. J., Moorman, C., & Jaworski, B. (1991, October). Enhancing and measuring consumers' motivation, opportunity, and ability to process brand information from ads. *Journal of Marketing, 55*, 32-53.

Macionis, J. J. (2002). *Social problems*. Upper Saddle River, NJ: Prentice-Hall.

MacKinnon, C. (1987). *Feminism unmodified: Discourses of life and the law.* Boston: Harvard University Press.

Maffei, G. (2004, November 26). Futility is the norm among bills introduced in Congress. *Washington Post,* p. A37.

Magnuson, W. G., & Carper, J. (1968). *The dark side of the marketplace: The plight of the American consumer.* Englewood Cliffs, NJ: Prentice-Hall.

Maibach, E. W., & Cotton, D. (1995). Moving people to behavior change: A staged social cognitive approach to message design. In E. Maibach & R. L. Parrott (Eds.), *Designing health messages* (pp. 41-64). Thousand Oaks, CA: Sage.

Mainstream Marketing Services, Inc., TMG Marketing, Inc., and American Teleservices Association v. Federal Trade Commission, No. 03-1429, 2003 U.S. Dist. Colo. Retrieved August 9, 2005, from http://64.233.179.104/search?q=cache:V0bJ 8Hu54sJ: www. ataconnect.org/ataconnect.org-asp//documents/ATAFOIACrossSJAppendixA. pdf+%2B%22september+29%22+%2Bregistry+%2Btelemarket*+%2Bftc+%2Bc ongress+%2Blaw&hl=en

Manoff, R. K. (1985). *Social marketing.* New York: Praeger.

Margolis, J. D., & Walsh, J. P. (2001). *People and profits?* Mahwah, NJ: Lawrence Erlbaum.

Margolis, J. D., & Walsh, J. P. (2003). Misery loves companies: Rethinking social initiatives by business. *Administrative Science Quarterly, 48,* 265-305.

Mayer, C. E. (2005, January 10). Putting a healthy spin on processed foods. *Washington Post,* pp. A1, A4.

McAdam, D. (1986). Recruitment of high-risk activism: The case of Freedom Summer. *American Journal of Sociology, 92*(1), 64-90.

McAdam, D., McCarthy, J. D., & Zald, M. N. (Eds). (1996). *Comparative perspectives on social movements.* Cambridge, UK: Cambridge University Press.

McDonald's Corporation. (2005). McDonald's corporate responsibility. Retrieved August 30, 2005, from http://www.mcdonalds.com/corp/values/socialrespons.html

McGraw, P. (2003). *The ultimate weight solution: The 7 keys to weight loss freedom.* New York: Free Press.

McKenzie-Mohr, D., & Smith, W. (1999). *Fostering sustainable behavior: An introduction to community-based social marketing.* New York: New Society.

McLeroy, K. R., Bibeau, D., Steckler, A., & Glanz, K. (1988). An ecological perspective on health promotion programs. *Health Education Quarterly, 15,* 351-377.

McNutt, J. G., & Boland, K. M. (1999). Electronic advocacy by nonprofit organizations in social welfare policy. *Nonprofit and Voluntary Sector Quarterly, 28,* 432-451.

Mercury News Wire Services. (2004, March 10). Fat may soon be No. 1 cause of preventable deaths in U.S.: Government pleads with Americans to change habits. Retrieved August 9, 2004, from http://www.mercurynews.com/mld/mercurynews/ news/8149652.htm

Meyer, R. J., & Kahn, B. E. (1991). Probabilistic models of consumer choice behavior. In T. Robertson & H. Kassarjian (Eds.), *Handbook of consumer behavior* (pp. 85-123). Englewood Cliffs, NJ: Prentice-Hall.

Minkler, M., Frantz, S., & Wechsler, R. (1982-1983). Social support and social action organizing in a "grey ghetto": The Tenderloin experience. *International Quarterly of Community Health Education, 3,* 3-15.

Mitchell, P. (2002). Accidental allies: The American news media and social change. *Social Marketing Quarterly, 8*(2), 36-40.

Mokdad, A. H., Bowman, B. A., Ford, E. S., Vincor, J. S., & Kaplan, J. P. (2001). The continuing epidemics of obesity and diabetes in the United States. *Journal of the American Medical Association, 286*(10), 1195-1200.

Mokdad, A. H., Ford, E. S., Bowman, B. A., Dietz, W. H., Vincor, F., Bales, V. S., et al. (2003). Prevalence of obesity, diabetes, and obesity related health risk factors, 2001. *Journal of the American Medical Association, 289,* 76-79.

Moore, M. H. (2000). Managing for value: Organizational strategy in for-profit, non-profit and governmental organizations. *Nonprofit and Voluntary Sector Quarterly, 29*(1), 183-204.

Moore, M. (Producer/Director). (2002). *Bowling for Columbine* [Motion picture]. United States: Iconolatry Productions.

Mothers Against Drunk Driving. (n.d.). MADD history. Retrieved July 26, 2005, from http://www.madd.org/aboutus/0,1056,1122,00.html

Mutch, R. E. (1988). *Campaigns, Congress, and courts.* Westport, CT: Praeger.

Nader, R. (1965). *Unsafe at any speed: The designed-in dangers of the American automobile.* New York: Grossman.

National Campaign to Prevent Teen Pregnancy. (2002). National Campaign accomplishments. Retrieved August 19, 2005, from http://www.teenpregnancy.org/about/accomplishments.asp

National Cancer Institute. (2003, February 27). *Theory at a glance: A guide for health promotion practice.* Retrieved August 28, 2005, from http://cancer.gov/aboutnci/oc/theory-at-a-glance

National Cancer Institute. (n.d.). The nation's investment in cancer research: A plan and budget proposal for FY 2006. Retrieved August 1, 2005, from http://plan.cancer.gov/prevention.shtml#energy

National Center for Chronic Disease Prevention and Health Promotion. (2004, August 17). Promoting healthy eating and physical activity for a healthier nation. Retrieved August 16, 2005, from the Centers for Disease Control and Prevention Web site: http://www.cdc.gov/nccdphp/promising_practices/promoting_health/burden.htm

National Center for Health Statistics. (2004). *Health, United States, 2004 with chartbook on trends in the health of Americans.* Hyattsville, MD: Centers for Disease Control and Prevention. Retrieved August 31, 2005, from http://www.cdc.gov/nchs/data/hus/hus04trend.pdf#070

National Center for Health Statistics. (2005, February 8). Prevalence of overweight among children and adolescents: United States, 1999-2002. Retrieved August 16, 2005, from the Centers for Disease Control and Prevention Web site: http://www.cdc.gov/nchs/products/pubs/pubd/hestats/overwght99.htm

Nelkin, D. (1987). *Selling science: How the press covers science and technology.* New York: Freeman.

Nestle, M. (2002). *Food politics: How the food industry influences nutrition and health.* Berkeley: University of California Press.

Nestle, M., & Jacobson, M. (2000, January/February). Halting the obesity epidemic: A public health policy approach. *Public Health Reports, 15,* 12-24.

Novelli, W. D. (2004, June). Marketing social change. Speech presented at the 21st Annual Summer Series on Aging, Lexington, KY. Retrieved August 25, 2005, from the AARP Web site: http://www.aarp.org/research/press-center/speeches/a2004-09-07-marketing.html

Obese Chinese now total 90 mln, to hit 200 mln in a decade. (2005, June 18). Retrieved September 1, 2005, from the China View Web site: http://news.xinhuanet.com/english/2005-06/18/content_3101580.htm

Office of the High Commissioner for Human Rights. (2003). *Universal declaration of human rights*. New York: United Nations.

Ofosu, H. B., Lafreniere, K. D., & Senn, S. Y. (1998). Body image perceptions among women of African-American descent: A normative context? *Feminism & Psychology, 8*, 303-323.

Ogden, C. L., Flegal, K. M., Carroll, M. D., & Johnson, C. L. (2002). Prevalence and trends in overweight among US children and adolescents, 1999-2000. *Journal of the American Medical Association, 288*, 1728-1732.

Olson, M. (1965). *The logic of collective action*. Cambridge, MA: Harvard University Press.

O'Malley, M. (2002, April 23). Pope confronts sexual abuse. Retrieved August 29, 2005, from the CBC News Web site: http://www.cbc.ca/news/features/pope_clergy.html

Partnership to Promote Healthy Eating and Active Living. (2001, March). Summit on promoting healthy eating and active living: Developing a framework for progress. *Nutrition Reviews, 59*(3, Part II, special issue).

Partnership to Promote Healthy Eating and Active Living [Home page]. (2004a). Retrieved August 1, 2005, from http://www.ppheal.org

Partnership to Promote Healthy Eating and Active Living [Home page]. (2004b). Summit. Retrieved August 16, 2005, from http://www.ppheal.org/summit.html

Pechmann, C., & Reibling, E. T. (2000, May). Planning an effective anti-smoking mass media campaign targeting adolescents. *Journal of Public Health Management Practice*, (May), 80-94.

Perl, P. (2003, March 30). The incredible shrinking Duyers. *Washington Post Magazine*, pp. 6-12, 17, 23-25.

Perry, C. L., Baranowski, T., & Parcel, G. S. (1990). How individuals, environments, and health behavior interact: Social learning theory. In K. Glanz, F. M. Lewis, & B. K. Rimer (Eds.), *Health behavior and health education* (pp. 161-186). San Francisco: Jossey-Bass.

Perry, C. L., Luepker, R. V., Murray, D. M., Kurth, C., Mullis, R., Crockett, S., et al. (1988, September). Parent involvement with children's health promotion: The Minnesota home team. *American Journal of Public Health, 78*(9), 1156-1160.

Petersen, L. (1990, May 14). Risky business: Marketers make a beeline for schools. *Adweek's Marketing Week*.

Petty, R. E., & Cacioppo, J. T. (1986). *Communication and persuasion: Central and peripheral routes to attitude change*. New York: Springer-Verlag.

Plummer, J. T. (1985, January). How personality makes a difference. *Journal of Advertising Research, 24*, 27-31.

Powell, C. (2003, September 22). Remarks (USUN press release No. 144 [03]). Retrieved August 1, 2005, from the United Nations Web site: http://www.un.int/usa/03print_144.htm

Pringle, H., & Thompson, M. (1999). *Brand spirit*. Chichester, UK: John Wiley.

Prochaska, J. O., & DiClemente, C. C. (1983). Stages and processes of self-change of smoking: Toward an integrative model of change. *Journal of Consulting and Clinical Psychology, 51*, 390-395.

Protess, D. L., Cook, F. L., Doppelt, J. C., Ettema, J. S., Gordon, M. T., Leff, D. R., et al. (1991). *The journalism of outrage*. New York: Guilford Press.

Puska, P., Tuomilehto, J., Nissinen, A., & Vartainen, E. (1995). *The North Kerelia project: 20 years results and experiences.* Helsinki, Finland: National Public Health Institute.

Putnam, R. D. (2000). Bowling alone: The collapse and revival of American community. New York: Simon & Schuster.

Rahman, A. (1999). Micro-credit initiatives for equitable and sustainable development: Who pays? *World Development, 27*(1), 67-82.

Rangan, V. K., Karim, S., & Sandberg, S. K. (1990, May-June). Doing better at doing good. *Harvard Business Review, 63*(3), 42-54.

Revill, J., & Harris, P. (2004, January 18). US sugar barons "block global war on obesity". *The Observer.* Retrieved September 1, 2005, from the Guardian Unlimited Web site: http://observer.guardian.co.uk/international/story/0,6903,1125730,00.html

Ritzer, G. (2004). *The McDonaldization of society: Revised new century edition.* Thousand Oaks, CA: Pine Forge Press.

Roberto, N. (2002). *How to make local governance work: Listening to the citizen's voice and taking action—The final scorecard.* Manila, The Philippines: Asian Institute of Management.

Roberts, R. (2003, June 12). Serious business. *Washington Post,* p. 11.

Rogers, E. M. (1995). *Diffusion of innovations* (4th ed.). New York: Free Press.

Rogers, E. M., Aikat, S., Chang, S., Poppe, P., & Sopory, P. (Eds.). (1989). *Proceedings from the Conference on Entertainment: Education for Social Change.* Los Angeles: Annenberg School of Communications.

Rogers, E. M., Dearing, J., & Chang, S. (1991). AIDS in the 1980s: The agenda-setting process for a public issue. *Journalism Monographs, 126,* 1-47.

Rosenstock, I. M. (1990). The health belief model: Explaining health behavior through expectancies. In K. Glanz, F. M. Lewis, & B. K. Rimer (Eds.), *Health behavior and health education* (pp. 39-62). San Francisco: Jossey-Bass.

Rothschild, M. D. (1999). Carrots, sticks and promises: A conceptual framework for the management of public health and social issue behaviors. *Journal of Marketing, 63*(4), 24-37.

Russert, T. (2004). *Big Russ and me.* New York: Miramax Books.

Sachs, J. (2005). *The end of poverty: Economic possibilities for our times.* New York: Penguin Press.

Sahn, D. E., & Stifel, D. (2003). Progress toward the millennium development goals in Africa. *World Development, 31*(1), 23-52.

Sajna, M. (1996, November 21). Smoking. *University Times, 29*(7). Retrieved September 1, 2005, from the University of Pittsburgh Web site: http://136.142.42.14/utimes/issues/29/112196/09.html

Sandelman & Associates. (2003, Fall). Media driving health concerns. *Tracks,* pp. 1-2. Retrieved September 1, 2005, from http://www.sandelman.com/news/pdf/03 fall.pdf

Sargeant, A. (1999). *Marketing management for nonprofit organizations.* Oxford, England: Oxford University Press.

Satcher, D. (2001, March). Remarks from David Satcher, M. D., Ph.D., Assistant Secretary for Health and Surgeon General, *Nutrition reviews, 59*(3, Part II), S7-S9.

Scearce, D., & Fulton, K. (2004). *What if? The art of scenario thinking for nonprofit organizations.* Emeryville, NY: Global Business Network.

Scholastic Inc. (2005). Community programs, awards and grants. Retrieved August 18, 2005, from http://www.scholastic.com/aboutscholastic/community/index.htm

Schwartz, P. (1996). *The art of the long view: Paths to strategic insight for yourself and your company.* New York: Currency Doubleday.

Segawa, S., & Segal, E. (2000). *Common interest: Common good.* Boston: Harvard Business School Press.

Seiders, K., & Petty, R. (2004). Obesity and the role of food marketing: A policy analysis of issues and remedies. *Journal of Public Policy and Marketing, 23*(2), 153-169.

Sen, S., & Bhattacharya, C. B. (2001). Does doing good always lead to doing better? Consumer reactions to corporate social responsibility. *Journal of Marketing, 38*(1), 225-243.

Senderowitz, J. (1990). Relating to the media. In P. L. Coleman & R. C. Meyer (Eds.), *Proceedings from the Enter-Educate Conference: Education for Social Change* (pp. 16-17). Baltimore, MD: Center for Communications Programs, Johns Hopkins University.

Shore, B. (1995). *Revolution of the heart.* New York: Riverhead Books.

Siegel, M., & Doner, L. (1998). *Marketing public health: Strategies to promote social change.* Gaithersburg, MD: Aspen.

Singhal, A., & Rogers, E. M. (1999). *Entertainment-education: A communication strategy for social change.* Mahwah, NJ: Lawrence Erlbaum.

Smith, A. (1997). Society and self interest. In D. Boaz (Ed.), *The Libertarian reader: Classic and contemporary writing from Lao-tzu to Milton Friedman.* New York: Free Press.

Smith, C. (1994, May-June). The new corporate philanthropy. *Harvard Business Review, 72*(3), 105-116.

Smith, W. (2000). There's a lion in the village: The fight over individual behavior versus social context. *Social Marketing Quarterly, 6*(3), 6-12.

Social Investment Forum [Home page]. (2005). Retrieved August 17, 2005, from http://www.socialinvest.org

Solomon, M., & DeJong, W. (1986, Winter). Recent sexually transmitted disease prevention efforts. *Health Education Quarterly, 13*(4), 301-316.

Soroka, S. N. (2002). *Agenda-setting dynamics in Canada.* Vancouver, BC: University of British Columbia.

Spiro, R. J., Feltovich, P. L., Jacobson, M. J., & Coulson, R. L. (1991). Cognitive flexibility, constructivism, and hypertext: Random access instruction for advance knowledge acquisition in ill-structured domains. *Educational Technology, 31*(5), 24-33.

Stannard, S., & Young, J. (1998). Social marketing as a tool to stop child abuse. *Social Marketing Quarterly, 4*(4), 64-68.

Stein, T. S. (2002). *Workforce transitions from the profit to the nonprofit sector.* New York: Kluwer Academic/Plenum.

Strauss, R. S., & Knight, J. (1999, June). Influence of home environment on the development of obesity in children. *Pediatrics, 103*(6), e85. Retrieved August 28, 2005, from http://pediatrics.aappublications.org/cgi/content/abstract/103/6/e85

Stunkard, A. J., & Wadden, T. A. (Eds.). (1993). *Obesity: Theory and therapy* (2nd ed.). New York: Raven Press.

Subway. (2004, July 14). Findings reveal kids are aware of obesity but not concerned [Press release]. Retrieved August 18, 2005, from http://www.subway.com/Publishing/Pub Relations/PressRelease/pr071404-2.pdf

Thomas, K. (2002, May 27). "Social norming" may be strategy for good behavior. *USA Today.* Retrieved August 28, 2005, from http://www.usatoday.com/news/education/2002-05-28-social-norming.htm

Uhlman, M. (2003, November 12). Schools find a mission in fighting child obesity. *Philadelphia Inquirer,* p. A01.

UK politics: Gummer—why I called beef safe. (1998, December 8). Retrieved August 9, 2005, from the BBC News Web site: http://news.bbc.co.uk/1/hi/uk_politics/229669.stm

United Nations Division for Social Policy and Development. (2001). Report on the world's social situation. Retrieved August 1, 2005, from the United Nations Web site: http://www.un.org/esa/socdev/rwss/overview.html

United Nations General Assembly. (2000). *United Nations millennium declaration* (No. A/RES/55/2). New York: United Nations.

United Nations Global Compact. (2005). Participant information. Retrieved August 17, 2005, from http://www.unglobalcompact.org/Portal/Default.asp?

U.S. Agency for International Development. (2004, October 25). President Bush's emergency plan for AIDS relief to award $100 million to help orphans and vulnerable children [Press release]. Retrieved August 28, 2005, from http://www.usaid.gov/press/releases/2004/pr041025.html

U.S. Census Bureau, Housing and Household Economic Statistics Division. (2004, July 8). Historical income tables—households. Retrieved July 30, 2005, from the U.S. Census Bureau Web site: http://www.census.gov/hhes/income/histinc/h03.html

U.S. Census Bureau, Housing and Household Economic Statistics Division. (2005, May 13). Historical income tables—income equality. Retrieved July 30, 2005, from the U.S. Census Bureau Web site: http://www.census.gov/hhes/www/income/histinc/ie6.html

U.S. Chamber of Commerce. (2003). Chamber study shows obesity lawsuits no diet aid: Problem lies with how much, not where, consumers eat [Press release]. Retrieved September 1, 2005, from http://www.uschamber.com/press/releases/2003/july/03-116.htm

U. S. Department of Health and Human Services. (2001a, December 13). Overweight and obesity threaten U.S. health gains [Press release]. Retrieved September 1, 2005, from http://www.hhs.gov/news/press/2001pres/20011213.html

U.S. Department of Health and Human Services. (2001b). *The surgeon general's call to action to prevent and decrease overweight and obesity 2001.* Rockville, MD: Author. Retrieved August 16, 2005, from http://www.surgeongeneral.gov/topics/obesity/calltoaction/CalltoAction.pdf

U.S. Department of Health and Human Services. (2004). *Health, United States, 2004: With chartbook on trends in the health of Americans.* Hyattsville, MD: Author. Retrieved August 16, 2005, from http://www.cdc.gov/nchs/data/hus/hus04trend.pdf#070

Vigdor, J. L. (2004). Community composition and collective action: Analyzing initial mail response to the 2000 Census. *Review of Economics and Statistics, 86*(1), 303-312.

Viswanath, K., & Finnegan, J. R., Jr. (2002). Reflections on community health campaigns: Secular trends and capacity to affect change. In R. Hornik (Ed.), *Public health communication: Evidence for behavior change* (pp. 289-312). Mahwah, NJ: Lawrence Erlbaum.

Von Eschenbach, A. C. (2004, January 20). Energy balance: The complex interaction of diet, physical activity, and genetics in cancer prevention and control [Director's update]. Retrieved September 1, 2005, from the National Cancer Institute Web site: http://www.nci.nih.gov/directorscorner/directorsupdate-01-20-2004

Wall, W. L. (1994, June 21). Companies change the ways they make charitable contributions. *Wall Street Journal,* pp. 1, 19.

Wallace, N. (2000, November 16). Activists use e-mail to combat torture. *Chronicle of Philanthropy, 13*(3), 33.

Wallack, L. (1990). Media advocacy: Promoting health through mass communication. In K. Glanz, F. M. Lewis, & B. K. Rimer (Eds.), *Health behavior and health education* (pp. 370-386). San Francisco: Jossey-Bass.

Wallack, L., Dorfman, L., Jernigan, D., & Themba, M. (1993). *Media advocacy and public health.* Thousand Oaks, CA: Sage.

Wansink, B., & Huckabee, M. (2005, Summer). De-marketing obesity. *California Management Review, 47*(4), 6-18.

Webb, O. J., & Eves, F. F. (2005). Promoting stair use: Single versus multiple stair-riser messages. *American Journal of Public Health, 95,* 1543-1544.

Wechsler, H., Davenport, A., Dowdall, G., Moeykens, B., & Castillo, S. (1994). Health and behavioral consequences of binge drinking in college: A national survey of students at 140 campuses. *Journal of the American Medical Association, 272,* 1672-1677.

Wechsler, H., & Kuo, M. (2003). Watering down the drinks: The moderating effect of college demographics on alcohol use of high-risk group. *American Journal of Public Health, 93*(11), 1929-1933.

Wechsler, H., Nelson, T. E., & Lee, J. E. (2003). Perception and reality: A national evaluation of social norms marketing interventions to reduce college students' heavy alcohol use. *Journal of Studies on Alcohol, 64*(4), 484-494.

Weeden, C. (1998). *Corporate social investing.* San Francisco: Berrett-Koehler.

Weinreich, N. K. (1999). *Hands-on social marketing: A step-by-step guide.* Thousand Oaks, CA: Sage.

Weinstein, N. D. (1988). The precaution adoption process. *Health Psychology, 7*(4), 355-386.

What campuses are doing. (2003, February 5). Retrieved August 5, 2005, from the Higher Education Center Web site: http://www.edc.org/hec/socialnorms/campuses

White, R., & Cunningham, A. (1991). *Ryan White: My own story.* New York: Dial Books for Children.

Wiebe, G. D. (1951-1952). Merchandising commodities and citizenship on television. *Public Opinion Quarterly, 15,* 679-691.

Wilhelm, I. (2005, May 26). Business group seeks to better aid relief charities. *Chronicle of Philanthropy, 17*(16), 31.

Wish, J. R., & Gamble, S. H. (Eds.). (1971). *Marketing and social issues: An action reader.* New York: John Wiley.

Women's Health Initiative. (n.d.). Retrieved July 29, 2005, from the National Heart, Lung, and Blood Institute Web site: http://www.nhlbi.nih.gov/whi/

World Health Organization. (2002). *Communicable Diseases.* Geneva: Author.

World Health Organization. (2004). *Obesity and overweight.* Retrieved August 28, 2005, from http://www.who.int/dietphysicalactivity/publications/facts/obesity/en/

Yankelovich, D. (1991). *Coming to public judgment: Making democracy work in a complex world.* Syracuse, NY: Syracuse University Press.

Yankelovich, D. (1992, October 5). How public opinion really works. *Fortune, 126*(7), 102-106.

Zapka, J. G., & Dorfman, S. (1982). Consumer participation: Case study of the college health setting. *Journal of American College Health, 30,* 197-203.

Zyman, S. (1999). *The end of marketing as we know it.* New York: Harper Business.

Index

About the Author

Alan R. Andreasen is Professor of Marketing at the McDonough School of Business of Georgetown University and Executive Director of the Social Marketing Institute. He has been a faculty member at the University of California, Los Angeles, the University of Illinois, the University of Connecticut, and the State University of New York at Buffalo. He holds PhD and MS degrees from Columbia University and an Honors BA from the University of Western Ontario in Canada.

A specialist in consumer behavior and a world leader in the application of marketing to nonprofit organizations, social marketing, and the market problems of disadvantaged consumers, he is the author or editor of 16 books and numerous monographs. His most recent books are *Marketing Social Change* (1995); *Strategic Marketing in Nonprofit Organizations* (6th ed.), coauthored with Philip Kotler of Northwestern University (2003); *Marketing Research That Won't Break the Bank* (2003); and *Ethics in Social Marketing* (2001).

He has published more than 110 articles and conference papers on a variety of topics, including strategic planning, marketing decision making, consumer behavior, marketing in nonprofit organizations, consumer satisfaction, marketing regulation, social marketing, and marketing research. He is a member of several academic and professional associations and serves on the boards of reviewers of the *Journal of Consumer Research,* the *Journal of Consumer Policy, Social Marketing Quarterly,* and the *Journal of Public Policy and Marketing.* He is a Past President of the Association for Consumer Research.

An internationally known educator and marketing consultant, he has advised, carried out research, and conducted executive seminars for a widely diverse set of nonprofit and private sector organizations, as well as several government agencies. Among the nonprofit organizations with whom he has worked are the World Bank, the American Cancer Society, AARP, the U.S. Agency for International Development, Centers for Disease Control and Prevention, the American Red Cross, the United Way of America, Boys & Girls Clubs of America, the National Endowment for the Arts, the National Cancer Institute, Habitat for Humanity International, PBS, the American Farmland

Trust, the American Forestry Association, and public health programs in Egypt, Thailand, Colombia, Jamaica, Mexico, Indonesia, and Bangladesh. He has also worked with for-profit organizations, such as KitchenAid, Pepsi-Cola, and the Aspen Highlands Ski Corporation.